CW01239091

Spiritual Philosophers

Also Available at Bloomsbury

Philosophical Mysticism in Plato, Hegel, and the Present, Robert Wallace
Nietzsche and the Antichrist: Religion, Politics, and Culture in Late Modernity, ed. Daniel Conway
Nietzsche and Friendship, Willow Verkerk
Understanding Derrida, Understanding Modernism, ed. Jean-Michel Rabaté
Modernism between Benjamin and Goethe, Matthew Charles

Spiritual Philosophers

From Schopenhauer to Irigaray

Richard White

BLOOMSBURY ACADEMIC
LONDON • NEW YORK • OXFORD • NEW DELHI • SYDNEY

BLOOMSBURY ACADEMIC
Bloomsbury Publishing Plc
50 Bedford Square, London, WC1B 3DP, UK
1385 Broadway, New York, NY 10018, USA

BLOOMSBURY, BLOOMSBURY ACADEMIC and the Diana logo
are trademarks of Bloomsbury Publishing Plc

First published in Great Britain 2020

Copyright © Richard White, 2020

Richard White has asserted his right under the Copyright, Designs and Patents Act, 1988, to be identified as Author of this work.

For legal purposes the Acknowledgments on p. viii constitute an extension of this copyright page.

Cover design by Charlotte Daniels
Cover image: Wassily Kandinsky, *Accent in Pink* (1926)
(© Musee National d'Art Moderne, Centre Pompidou, Paris, France / Bridgeman Images)

All rights reserved. No part of this publication may be reproduced or transmitted in any form or by any means, electronic or mechanical, including photocopying, recording, or any information storage or retrieval system, without prior permission in writing from the publishers.

Bloomsbury Publishing Plc does not have any control over, or responsibility for, any third-party websites referred to or in this book. All internet addresses given in this book were correct at the time of going to press. The author and publisher regret any inconvenience caused if addresses have changed or sites have ceased to exist, but can accept no responsibility for any such changes.

A catalogue record for this book is available from the British Library.

A catalog record for this book is available from the Library of Congress.

ISBN:	HB:	978-1-3501-2911-5
	ePDF:	978-1-3501-2912-2
	eBook:	978-1-3501-2913-9

Typeset by Integra Software Services Pvt. Ltd.
Printed and bound in Great Britain

To find out more about our authors and books visit www.bloomsbury.com and sign up for our newsletters.

For Clarinda

Contents

Acknowledgments — viii

Introduction — 1
1. Schopenhauer on Compassion — 17
2. Nietzsche on Generosity — 37
3. Kandinsky on Art — 55
4. Benjamin on Wisdom — 73
5. Jung on Religion and the Sacred — 91
6. Hillman on Spirit and Soul — 109
7. Foucault on the Care of the Self — 127
8. Derrida on Mourning — 145
9. Irigaray on Love — 163

Conclusion — 181

Notes — 187
Bibliography — 207
Index — 217

Acknowledgments

This book took shape over the course of several years. Many of the ideas discussed in this book first saw the light of day as lectures or presentations given at various venues, and earlier versions of some sections were published in different journals and collections. For a long time, and without really knowing why, I found myself drawn to a variety of recent philosophers and other thinkers. Eventually, I came to realize that what they all shared was a sense of the *spiritual* dimension of life and a willingness to explore important spiritual themes quite apart from any presuppositions about religion or the nature of the sacred. As Pierre Hadot has pointed out, the ancient philosophers saw philosophy as a spiritual practice and as a kind of spiritual medicine that helps the soul to come to terms with all the vicissitudes of life. In this book, the focus is on more recent philosophers—from Schopenhauer to Irigaray—but the goal is to consider spiritual themes in modern thinkers from the same overarching perspective—not spiritual as "non-physical," but spiritual in the sense of living a life that is fully attuned to this world, and the "higher" or "greater" realities that we defer to.

Many thanks to Liza Thompson, Lucy Russell, and Lisa Goodrum, my editors at Bloomsbury, for guiding this work to publication, and thanks to my anonymous referees for seeing some promise in the original book proposal. I am grateful for all their comments which have helped me considerably. Thanks also to my colleagues in the Philosophy Department at Creighton University with whom I have discussed these ideas over the years, in papers and in personal conversations. I am especially grateful to my fellow panelists, Patrick Murray and Jeanne Schuler, with whom I developed my ideas about spiritual philosophy—and the spiritual philosophers—over a number of years at the annual European Studies Conference. I would like to thank the Creighton University College of Arts and Sciences for allowing me a sabbatical that helped me to finish this project. Finally, thanks to all of my students, especially those who took my class on "Ultimate Questions," and who challenged me to think about the "spiritual philosophers" with clarity and depth.

Parts of this book are drawn from articles that I have published previously. I would like to thank the publishers and editors for permission to reprint revised portions of the following:

"Schopenhauer and Indian Philosophy: On the Limits of Comparative Thought." *International Philosophical Quarterly* 50.1 (2010): 57–76.

"Nietzsche on Generosity and the Gift-Giving Virtue." *British Journal for the History of Philosophy* 24.2 (2016): 348–64.

"Walter Benjamin: The Storyteller and the Possibility of Wisdom." *Journal of Aesthetic Education* 51.1 (2017): 1–14.

"Foucault on the Care of the Self as an Ethical Possibility and a Spiritual Goal." *Human Studies* 37.4 (2014): 489–504.

"Spirit, Soul and Self-Overcoming: A Post-Jungian View." *The Philosophy of Spirituality: Analytic, Continental and Multicultural Approaches to a New Field of Philosophy*. Edited by Heather Salazar and Roderick Nicholls. Leiden: Brill, 2018. 293–311.

"Dialectics of Mourning." *Angelaki: Journal of the Theoretical Humanities* 20.4 (2015): 179–92.

"Kandinsky: Thinking about the Spiritual in Art." *Religion and the Arts* 23.1–2 (2019): 26–49.

I am also grateful for permission to reproduce material from:

The Collected Works of St. John of the Cross, translated by Kieran Kavanaugh and Otilio Rodriguez Copyright © 1964, 1979, 1991 by Washington Province of Discalced Carmelites ICS Publications 2131 Lincoln Road, N.E. Washington, DC 20002–1199 USA. www.icspublications.org.

The Upanishads, translated by Eknath Easwaran, founder of the Blue Mountain Center of Meditation, copyright 1987, 2007; reprinted by permission of Nilgiri Press, P. O. Box 256, Tomales, Ca 94971, www.bmcm.org.

Introduction

This book looks at the original task of philosophy in which thinking illuminates the spiritual view of life. Its focus is on the modern Western world, and it includes spiritual thinkers from Schopenhauer in the first half of the nineteenth century to Irigaray in the present time; it also refers to non-Western and premodern accounts of spirituality, as the encounter with such traditions is an important part of the story. The book is not meant to be exhaustive, and I have limited my account to nine thinkers whom I regard as among the most important modern writers on spiritual themes. In a world where spirituality is seriously challenged or ignored because of the increasing dominance of reductive scientific materialism, I think these are the "spiritual philosophers" who can illuminate spiritual possibilities into the future. I use the term *philosopher* in a broad sense to suggest someone who has a profound but critical understanding of important things, and this would include not only Schopenhauer, Nietzsche, and Derrida, but also Kandinsky, Jung, and Hillman. The goal of this book is to look more closely at spirituality and spiritual experience from this philosophical perspective, quite apart from all explanations, religious or otherwise, and not to reject spiritual conclusions that derive from a different set of beliefs than our own. I think this account will be helpful to anyone who affirms a religious standpoint, for religious experience is a special case of spiritual experience, while it should also appeal to a growing number of people who consider themselves to be spiritual but not religious.

For the purposes of this book, we can think of the spiritual philosophers as seekers who are involved in a spiritual quest and who focus on spiritual themes such as compassion, generosity, love, mourning, wisdom, and the soul. The final goal of this quest is enlightenment which is to be achieved through critical reflection and an intuitive apprehension of the way things are. Critical reflection is important because we should not believe everything that we want to believe, and without reason we are drawn to whatever appeals to our own desires. But at the same time, we must remain true to our intuitions and what our emotions disclose to us, and this goes beyond a purely intellectual understanding of the world. Even in the absence of counter-arguments, the deductions of pure reason are not always compelling, while our intuitive or emotional grasp of things can be faulty if we do not refer back to the supporting claims of reason. All of which suggests an interplay between reason and intuition, which brings us closer to the truth. In this way, we may gradually achieve a sense of the big picture, or the greater reality of which our own lives are a much smaller part, and I will argue that it is this sense of belonging to a greater or a higher reality that is a defining feature of spiritual life. This is not just a matter of intellectual concern, however, for our relationship to this greater reality is absolutely important to who we are; and insofar as *philosophy* is an attempt to clarify this relationship, it makes sense to think of it as a spiritual quest that includes intellectual, intuitive, and emotional aspects, which are an essential part of our being in the world.

Of course, some may feel that they need immediate answers to all of the mysteries of life; and if this is the case, then fundamentalism becomes an easy road to follow. Others accept the extreme difficulty of these questions and the possibility that they may never be answered once and for all or with any degree of satisfaction. The ability to live with uncertainty or the absence of final answers to ultimate questions is sometimes referred to as "negative capability." Most immediately, the idea comes from Keats, who uses it to explain the greatness of writers like Shakespeare: "I mean Negative Capability, that is when man is capable of being in uncertainties, mysteries, doubts, without any irritable reaching after fact and reason."[1] In this sense, for example, Socrates sought the truth, and he made spiritual and moral progress toward the Good, but he accepted his own ignorance, and he thought of himself as a *lover* of wisdom, though not as someone who possessed all the answers. Now it seems likely that philosophical conversation will continue, and even though we may reach provisional though uncertain conclusions of our own, negative capability must remain a spiritual and a philosophical virtue because it testifies to the openness of thought and the openness of the world. In the end, there may not be any *final* answers, but there are spiritual pathways which begin a trail of reflection that we can choose to follow or leave to go on our own way. All of this is a philosophical inquiry into the heart of what really matters, and it is a spiritual inquiry in the sense that here philosophy becomes a form of spiritual practice.

Spirituality in philosophy

These ideas can be placed in a broad historical context: It has been argued that the earliest Western philosophers thought of philosophy as a kind of spiritual medicine that could help people to deal with the maladies of the soul. These thinkers viewed philosophy as a way of coming to terms with the fear of death and all the misfortunes that we may encounter in this life, including sickness, the reversal of fortune, and loss; but perhaps more than anything else, they taught people how to live in attunement with nature or the cosmos itself. In this respect, as Pierre Hadot argues in his important work, *Philosophy as a Way of Life*, Socrates, Plato, Pythagoras, the Stoics, and the Epicureans were all focused on the question of how to live a good life, how to achieve happiness, what it means to flourish as a human being, and the spiritual exercises that could lead us to this point. The latter might include meditation on one's own mortality or the death of others; setting intentions for oneself at the beginning of each day and self-examination at the end of the day; and the creative visualization of future possibilities to anticipate or disarm them in advance. As Hadot observes: "Wisdom, then, was a way of life which brought peace of mind (*ataraxia*), inner freedom (*autarkeia*), and a cosmic consciousness. First and foremost, philosophy presented itself as a therapeutic, intended to cure mankind's anguish."[2]

Plato's story of the cave epitomizes the philosophical quest as a kind of spiritual journey: We all begin in the darkness of the cave, which is everyday life, chained down by our prejudices and all the fixed ideas that we have inherited from the society that we belong to. We spend our time preoccupied by shadows or things that are not really important or "real." But one man manages to lose his chains; he is disoriented but he makes his way out of the cave where he is finally able to gaze at the sun which is the equivalent of the Good or the highest reality: "Last of all he will be able to see the sun, and not mere reflections of it in the water, but he will see it in its own proper place, and not in another; and he will contemplate it as it is."[3] Then he returns to the cave, because he wants to help others make the same spiritual journey toward the light and everything that is of highest concern. All of which suggests that there are different levels of reality. Many will stay in the cave and they will remain absorbed by whatever lies immediately in front of them, whether this is money, prestige, or power. But it is possible to make spiritual progress by moving toward the light and perhaps to escape from the cave altogether. And when we achieve enlightenment, we must return to the cave because we feel compelled to help others make the same spiritual journey. In this respect, the spiritual quest is not a selfish pursuit, and those who are spiritually accomplished—including Socrates—must be teachers because they want others to share the same spiritual freedom.

We can say that philosophy in this most basic sense is a kind of spiritual wisdom that teaches us how to live, and the earliest Asian thinkers would certainly be in agreement with this view, for the core of Buddhism, Daoism, Confucianism, and Vedanta philosophies involves the same ideal of spiritual cultivation which leads to progress toward the enlightenment goal. Hadot argues that in the West we lost this spiritual version of philosophy once the Church came to dominate every aspect of intellectual life.[4] Thomas Aquinas famously said that philosophy is "the handmaiden of theology," and for the longest time, philosophy was used to rationalize and justify religious claims about the existence of God, the nature of God, and other aspects of the divine. For at least a millennium, the Church promulgated the meaning of the good life, while philosophy became an important but secondary project—for even if philosophy could apprehend the truths of this world, it could not justify the revealed truths of religion.

With the decline of the established church, and the rise of modern science, there was once again an opportunity for philosophy to return to its roots. For some time, however, since at least Descartes and the other early modern philosophers, philosophy has sought to define itself as a scientific enterprise with its own methodology and its own systematic investigation into basic foundations and principles. This tradition still remains strong, but it confines philosophy as an intellectual enterprise; while the spiritual question—how shall I live?—becomes a more subjective consideration that can never be settled by reasonable argument since it is held to be just a matter of personal opinion. So now there is a gap between contemporary Western philosophy and non-Western thought, which to a much greater extent retains the original sense of philosophy as a kind of spiritual wisdom. Indeed, non-Western philosophy remains popular precisely because it appeals to us as human beings who face the most fundamental questions about how to live—and this includes attention to the spiritual aspects of life, which are not dismissed as subjective, but accepted here as *real*.

But this is still not the whole story. At some point in the nineteenth century, probably starting with Schopenhauer, and the retrieval of ancient Vedanta and Buddhist philosophies, we begin to see Western philosophers and other systematic thinkers returning to spiritual questions that had previously been ignored or left to the pronouncements of religion. These philosophers and other writers, from Schopenhauer to Nietzsche and beyond, take spiritual matters seriously. And they discuss spiritual themes because they are important for their own sake, and not just as a way of supporting the religious standpoint or defending the existence of God. Schopenhauer inspires Nietzsche who proclaims the death of god or the demise of traditional ideas about religion and the sacred. Nietzsche himself influences numerous others, including Jung, Foucault, and Derrida, who develop their own ideas about spirituality and the sacred in a more contemporary context, and all of these thinkers continue to be influential. In this way, then, we can perhaps discern a hidden genealogy of spiritual philosophy—one that we can return to whenever we need a spiritual compass. And this spiritual undercurrent in modern philosophy—broadly conceived—is the real subject of this book.

In today's world, advances in modern science and social progress have called established religion into question. It appears that there is no limit to the possibility of scientific explanation, and by comparison, religious beliefs—like miracles—can seem absurd if taken literally. Likewise, religious authority is often associated with reactionary social positions, and because of this, and enduring religious rivalries, religion is often viewed as a source of discord and conflict. At the same time, however, a purely secular worldview seems impoverished, for it is not able to offer us anything much greater than our own existence here and now. And so, like the prisoners in Plato's cave we begin to experience the spiritual emptiness of our lives. For in spite of our consumer culture, and all of our technological achievements—or perhaps because of these things—we feel the absence of the spiritual and what some have called the "disenchantment" of modern life. Despair and addiction of every kind become a common response to the oblivion that we feel. We may come to realize that there has to be more to life than just wealth, popularity, or personal success, but secularism cannot affirm transcendent values, and it views spirituality as just a "life choice" which is neither more nor less valid than any other life choice that does not interfere with others. And so we reach the situation where traditional versions of religion are increasingly challenged while the purely secular position is also viewed as inadequate. In fact, we have become "post-secular" because traditional religion and traditional atheism have both been found to be wanting. But this can finally lead to the recovery of spirituality, and a return to the "spiritual philosophers," who can offer us some guidance.

The meaning of the spiritual

So what is spirituality? This is a difficult question to answer because everyone seems to use the word differently, and there are no objective measures of spiritual achievement. But it does not mean that everything about spirituality is subjective or emotional, and here we consider some ideas that can bring it into focus. Now admittedly, this discussion may not be definitive, but it offers a guiding thread for the chapters on the nine thinkers that follow this Introduction, and it suggests some ways in which they can be viewed as "spiritual philosophers."

First, it is helpful to note that the word "spiritual" is derived from the Latin *spirare*, meaning to breathe. This implies the very basic character of spirituality, as fundamental as breathing, and that to be truly alive is to be living in a spiritual way. Irigaray points out that breathing is the first autonomous action, which involves taking charge of one's own life. In this respect, however, it is both "physical" and "spiritual" in nature, and, as Irigaray observes, some people have always understood this:

> In the East it is more common to remember that living is equivalent to breathing. And the Sages there care about acquiring a proper life through practicing a conscious breathing. This breathing brings them little by little to a second birth, a birth assumed by oneself, willed by oneself and not only by our parents, and a physiology that dictates its laws to us.[5]

If she is right, then the "spiritual" is not unworldly in character but an accomplishment of this life, here and now.

Going further, it would be helpful to separate spirituality from "spiritualism"—the latter includes ghosts, poltergeists, and astral projection, and this is not what we are interested in here. In fact, it might be better to say that spirituality is about living fully in the present, and it is only distantly related to supernaturalism which can be a kind of escapism. In certain religions there is a sense that the "sacred" belongs to heaven, and this world, by comparison, is a realm of sin and suffering that is meant to test us. This implies that the physical and the spiritual are opposites, and the body is purely *carnal* while the spiritual world is beyond us. But for the thinkers who are described in this book, the spiritual reality of this world is present here and now, and it is entirely possible to have meaningful spiritual experiences in this life, in the absence of any religious framework whatsoever.[6]

For some modern writers, a spiritual life is said to involve cultivating our relationship to the sacred or, as both Rudolf Otto and Carl Jung call it, the "numinous," which suggests more exalted possibilities of experience in this world.[7] According to Otto, the experience of the sacred is the experience of the *mysterium tremendum*, and this makes spirituality into a peak experience which involves a kind of self-overcoming. I think we must admit that life is full of such moments—including the experience of the sublime in nature, the transformative power of a work of art, or the intense experience of love—which make us feel completely alive. But it does not really help to define spirituality in terms of the *sacred*, for then we are just exchanging one undecidable term for another. Even so, the sacred can offer a powerful evocation of spiritual life, while the absence of the sacred can make everything feel empty. In his autobiography, Jung claims that life is inherently mysterious, and this suggests that even the most profound spiritual account must always fall short of the reality that it seeks to describe:

> It is important to have a secret, a premonition of things unknown. It fills life with something impersonal, a *numinosum*. A man who has never experienced that has missed something important. He must sense that he lives in a world which in some respects is mysterious; that things happen and can be experienced which remain inexplicable; that not everything which happens can be anticipated. The unexpected and the incredible belong in this world. Only then is life whole. For me the world has from the beginning been infinite and ungraspable.[8]

By contrast, when the world is reduced to whatever can be described and measured, it becomes impoverished, and it loses what Nietzsche calls its "rich ambiguity." In this respect, the idea of the sacred as a profound mystery is basic and unavoidable. But we still need another way of apprehending the spiritual dimension of life.

More positively then, and as a guiding definition that would allow for other perspectives, I will argue that spirituality—like religion—involves a sense of being connected to a greater power or meaning, and the need to affirm that connection, because it seems to inspire the highest part of who we are.[9] From this it follows that it is possible to feel a strong connection to nature, humankind, the cosmos, or even "truth" itself (as in the case of Socrates or Gandhi). We may have reverence for all of these higher things, and through them we can also experience a sense of the "sacred." For example, if we are upset or alienated from ourselves or from others, we may find solace in visiting a mountain or a river, spending time in a forest that is still unspoiled or watching a flock of cranes as they make their annual migration. This is because it is possible to experience our connection to the greater reality of nature which is inspiring and restores us to ourselves. Likewise, when nature is threatened by pollution, pipelines, overdevelopment, etc., there are people who will protest and do whatever they can to turn the tide. For in this respect, they are devoted to nature, and the environmental movement that they belong to is so powerful precisely because it is a *spiritual* movement, as well as an ethical concern. The same point could be made about Socrates who sacrificed everything for the sake of philosophy and the truth, which he affirmed as more important than his own safety or his life. Today, hundreds of journalists around the world are imprisoned or at risk of being killed because they dare to speak truth to power and, like Socrates, they would also be willing to sacrifice themselves for the truth as a spiritual value.

Now to continue on this path of thinking, there are certain attitudes and responses that seem to affirm spiritual life, because they indicate a desire to move beyond the purely selfish concerns of the ego. As we have seen, spirituality involves self-overcoming, which means putting one's own interests to one side in order to affirm a higher or a greater reality. And in this respect, compassion, forgiveness, mindfulness, wonder, generosity, and reverence are all spiritual responses, and *spiritual virtues*, even if in other contexts they are primarily ethical themes. But there is an important difference between the ethical and the spiritual, and the two do not always go together. To give just one example: Many people would deny that we have an ethical duty to forgive someone who has murdered a friend or a family member, and in such a situation it would certainly be wrong to press someone to forgive if they really were not ready to do so. But as Derrida observes, it is still possible to "forgive the unforgiveable" when someone forgives the perpetrator of a terrible atrocity which has devastated their life. And such an extreme act of generosity would be a *spiritual* accomplishment, if it is not done primarily for one's own sake (to relieve anger or to get on with one's life) but for the sake of the other person, the needs of the community, or to bring peace into the world.[10] Similarly, compassion is not always a moral requirement, and reverence, wonder, and love are only indirectly ethical (when they help us to do the right thing). But these responses—reverence, wonder, forgiveness, generosity, love, etc.—can express our connection to a higher or a greater reality, especially when they exceed whatever is morally required of us, and in this respect they are spiritual virtues.

Next, in order to strengthen the connection with this greater reality—whether this is nature, humankind, truth, the divine, or a combination of these things—certain *spiritual practices* are enjoined, including meditation, prayer, the setting of individual intentions, self-cultivation, or communal devotion. And as we will see, *philosophy* can also be a kind of spiritual practice, especially when it clarifies spiritual themes—for understanding the nature of compassion will make us more compassionate, and grasping the real nature of love will enable us to love others in a more accomplished way. Finally, in addition to spiritual virtues and spiritual practices, there are also *spiritual points of focus*, including art, religion, the soul, and the sacred, which are among the most basic objects of spiritual inquiry, and they can serve as starting points for spiritual reflection, even if we go beyond traditional views concerning these ideas. In this book, we will examine spiritual virtues, including compassion, generosity, and wisdom; spiritual practices, including love, mourning, and the care of the self; and spiritual points of focus, including art, religion, and the soul. Spirituality in this sense is something that can be separated from religion and considered by itself.

All of which brings us to the idea that the spiritual and the religious do not entirely coincide with each other, and just as we can be spiritual but not religious it is also possible to be religious without being spiritual—especially if one has fallen into a thoughtless religious routine, or if one chooses religious hatred instead of compassion. In particular, there is a difference in emphasis between spirituality and religion, for religion is typically associated with fixed beliefs about God and the afterlife which adherents are required to affirm. By contrast, spirituality emphasizes the personal quest for spiritual truth as a process of self-transformation, but it seems to cultivate more agnostic views on fundamental beliefs and the nature of "the absolute." In the end the spiritual goal is to live a genuine life which resonates with ultimate value and meaning, and this requires the cultivation of spiritual virtues and practices such as mindfulness, compassion, the love of wisdom, and good intentions. But from this standpoint, our actual faith beliefs are not so important.

Even so, it may be argued that religion is still necessary insofar as it provides a community of worship that strengthens individuals in their resolve to tie themselves back [*re-ligere*] to the sacred or the holy. But while this may be true to some extent, it is not true by definition, and there are many communities of *spiritual* seekers.[11] There are also many religious communities that *discourage* spiritual striving, which they regard as a threat to an established religious authority. Throughout history, people have been punished for their beliefs when these were at odds with the views of the religious establishment. So while the support of others is something that may encourage us to follow a spiritual path, it is also the case that the requirements of dogma, and deference to traditional authorities, can undermine spiritual autonomy and the possibility of an authentic spiritual quest. In this respect, it may be that whether we are talking about spirituality or religion, the spiritual journey of the individual is the most important thing. And we could also say that a religious experience just *is* a spiritual experience that is mediated by religious beliefs. As William James observes at the beginning of *The Varieties of Religious Experience*:

> I am willing to accept almost any name for the personal religion of which I propose to treat. Call it conscience or morality, if you yourselves prefer, and not religion—under either name it will be equally worthy of our study. As for

myself, I think it will prove to contain some elements which morality pure and simple does not contain, and these elements I shall soon seek to point out … I will myself continue to apply the word 'religion' to it; and in the last lecture of all, I will bring in the theologies and the ecclesiasticisms, and say something of its relationship to them.[12]

In this context, the "personal religion" that James regards as fundamental is ultimately equivalent to what we are calling the *spiritual*. And this implies that spirituality is to be found at the very heart of religion.

Today, the things that we call "spiritual" exist on a wide spectrum from traditional forms of monastic life and spiritual formation to non-Western wisdom, including Daoism and the teachings of the Dalai Lama, and the mindfulness work of Thich Nhat Hanh, all of which originate from a completely different cultural context. But there are many other spiritual practices, including yoga, ritual chanting, astrology, and the divinatory use of the Tarot. Clearly, spirituality in the contemporary context is diverse and wide ranging, and this suggests that there is a real need for different spiritual forms which has not been addressed by traditional religion.

Of course, it can be argued that some forms of contemporary spirituality reflect narcissism and self-involvement, for they enhance the ego instead of the soul. And going further, some commentators, including Slavoj Žižek, have argued that the growth of New Age spirituality is just a function of late capitalism which puts spiritual consumers in the spiritual marketplace.[13] It seems that capitalism commodifies everything, including spiritual life! This is a reasonable criticism, and it must be taken seriously, since spirituality is a big business. But it would be unfair to reject spirituality as such just because some spiritual forms have been appropriated by commercial society. My own view is that compassion, generosity, forgiveness, mindfulness, wonder, and other spiritual attitudes reflect a basic spiritual understanding that can be affirmed even in the absence of an explicitly religious foundation. Spiritual themes such as these form the core of spiritual life. They are essential to human flourishing, and so they should be explored by philosophy and other forms of inquiry.

It is common to say that we now live in a secular society, and the ascendancy of science calls religious explanations into question. Organized religion is no longer as influential as it once was, and there is evidence that a growing number of people are pursuing their own spiritual quest which may or may not be connected to any traditional religion. But all of *this* suggests that a truly secular society in which everything is explained and organized in terms of reason may not be inherently satisfying either. For in spite of our material progress and increasing consumerism we often come to realize that something is missing in our lives, and we remain unfulfilled for as long as spirituality and the spiritual dimension have fallen into oblivion. The defenders of secularism assume that reason is a sufficient guide to life, but they are mistaken, because our lives are not completely rational and we can experience a sense of connection to a greater or higher reality that we must defer to. We call this "spiritual life" and we find ourselves drawn to cultivate our own relation to it.

On the spiritual philosophers

This book focuses on the work of nine different thinkers in the modern Western tradition. Most, though not all, of them are traditional philosophers, but without exception they are all rigorous thinkers and seekers who have come to grips with some important aspects of spirituality, as I have described it above. They may or may not refer to themselves as "spiritual" thinkers, and in some cases—Nietzsche, Schopenhauer, and Benjamin perhaps—they are ambivalent about anything that smacks of idealism. What they all have in common, however, is a strong sense of spiritual possibility which is both critical and inspiring. Since the end of classical antiquity, spirituality in the Western world has usually been regarded as a part of religion and a way of becoming more worthy and devout. But at some point, not too long ago, spirituality began to separate from religion, and spiritual cultivation became an end in itself. Each of the nine thinkers that I have chosen to discuss in this book inaugurates a new path of thinking about spiritual matters. I will not provide a comprehensive account of every spiritual thinker that I discuss, but instead I will focus on a single spiritual theme—or the intersection of two themes—which that thinker clarifies in a critical but thoughtful way, for example, Schopenhauer on compassion, Nietzsche on generosity, and Irigaray on love. In this way, it will be possible to begin a conversation on compassion, generosity, art, wisdom, death, the soul, the self, the sacred, love, etc., which are among the most important aspects of spiritual life. Notice, however, that none of these themes are "otherworldly" or entirely ethical in scope, but they are spiritual themes in the sense that I have outlined above. Finally, the elaboration of spirituality is itself a spiritual activity, and philosophy—which includes both critical and creative thinking—becomes a spiritual aspect of the world when it clarifies spiritual themes and our spiritual life.

I will begin with Schopenhauer, because Schopenhauer is perhaps the first modern thinker to take non-Western philosophy seriously. Early Indian and

Buddhist texts were first translated into European languages toward the end of the eighteenth century, and Schopenhauer made these works an important part of his own philosophical project. In particular, he saw that in many of these ancient texts, compassion was esteemed as the most important ethical and spiritual value, and this resonated with Schopenhauer's own view of things. In this way, especially in his work on ethics and aesthetics, he recovers the spiritual dimension of philosophy, and the sense in which philosophy is itself a spiritual practice. I have argued elsewhere that compassion is the beginning of spiritual life.[14] Schopenhauer is pessimistic, and he does not seem to cherish this life, but he is one of the only thinkers in the Western tradition who affirms the value of compassion, instead of disdaining it, like the Stoics or Nietzsche and other Western thinkers.

After Schopenhauer, the chapter on Nietzsche focuses on his ideas concerning generosity or what he calls "the gift-giving virtue." Nietzsche clarifies *spiritual* generosity, and he shows how it goes beyond the ethical virtue of generosity in Aristotle and other moral philosophers. Even though he was an atheist who proclaimed the death of god, Nietzsche was himself an extremely spiritual thinker, and he hated established religions, like Christianity, for taking the sacred out of this world and projecting it on to an otherworldly realm. In his major works, and with various stratagems, including Dionysus versus Apollo, the overman, and the eternal recurrence, Nietzsche's goal is to inspire the spiritual dimension of life, among other things. And in his most important book, *Thus Spoke Zarathustra*, he celebrates the complete generosity of life as something that we can respond to by embodying it in our own existence in the way that we live our lives.

Kandinsky, the subject of the third chapter, is most well known as the father of modern abstract painting. But he was also the author of an artistic manifesto, *Concerning the Spiritual in Art*. In this book, Kandinsky describes the spiritual relevance of art, and he argues that in an age of complete materialism, which deadens life, the only remedy is to recover the spiritual dimension of art, which lies, for him, on the path of abstraction. Kandinsky is unusual because he was both a brilliant artist and a systematic thinker whose account of art remains inspiring and relevant. We may not agree with his attempt to work out the spiritual language of form and color, but he is one of the first to pose the most important questions concerning art and spirituality. In this chapter, I will argue that Kandinsky's views about the artist as a kind of prophet or a spiritual seer remain compelling.

Next, Walter Benjamin is a brilliant essayist, a philosopher, and a literary theorist, although in the end his work is probably unclassifiable. Today,

Benjamin is perhaps most well known for his essay on "The Work of Art in the Age of Mechanical Reproduction," in which he argues that in contemporary mass society the artwork has lost its aura and its unique power to transform us, although this is not an unwelcome development. But in the same year (1936), he wrote another essay on "The Storyteller" in which he laments the passing of a more traditional kind of spiritual wisdom in the information age we still belong to. In this chapter, I focus my attention on the very idea of wisdom, and whether wisdom is still possible in a society, like ours, which seems to value quantity over quality. Wisdom is a spiritual virtue because it allows us to grasp our relation to the whole; it promotes a thoughtful, critical life; and as a gift we have received, it must be passed on to others. But do we still believe in the value of wisdom? Or at this point, is it held to be anything more than knowledge or information?

Jung is an important thinker for this book. As a psychologist he recovers the spiritual dimension of life that Freud had suppressed, and he writes about the experience of the numinous that gives us access to the sacred. Jung laments the rejection of nature and her archaic powers, and he sees no good in the modern society that disdains myth and anything that cannot be measured. In this chapter, I focus on his account of religion and, in particular, his brilliant work in theology, *Answer to Job*. In his book, Jung deals with the problem of evil, the incarnation of God in Jesus Christ, and the apocalypse, among other things. He argues that religion cannot survive if it refuses to change or adapt itself to different times. Besides, a fixed religion is not a living religion, and in this work he describes some of the inconsistencies and paradoxes associated with establishment Christianity. Jung also describes the spiritual goal of *individuation*, and in this way he tries to effect a significant change in our spiritual lives.

James Hillman is an important follower of Jung who writes about basic spiritual ideas such as spirit, soul, and self-overcoming. In *Beyond Good and Evil*, Nietzsche had challenged thinkers to come up with "new versions of the soul hypothesis," and this is exactly what Hillman does in his own work.[15] He reimagines the relationship between the spirit and the soul as this has traditionally been understood. He shows how the spiritual involves transcendence, self-overcoming, and a peak experience; while the soul is supposed to be deep, rather than high, it is the unique aspect of our being, and it tends toward suffering. But why is the soul neglected? And why do we think of self-overcoming (or the oblivion of the self or soul) as the key to enlightenment? Here, I will focus on an important essay by Hillman in which he describes the history of the spirit and soul concepts. For Hillman, traditional spirituality can be a form of escapism or even self-abandonment. By contrast, the soul is the key to who we are, and it can be grasped through the imagination which affirms the re-enchantment of this world.

Next, the chapter on Foucault looks at his important ideas concerning the care of the self, which he describes as a kind of *spiritual* activity. After writing several important books on power and the different forms of domination and control, in his later work, Foucault became interested in the subject as a point of resistance to all these effects of power, and he sought to explore the practice of self-cultivation, or the care of the self, as a way of becoming free. Foucault looks at other cultures: the ancient Greeks, the Romans, and the early Christians, and he dwells on sexual life as one of the most intense areas of our own becoming. Indirectly, his work connects with the discourse of self-help and self-improvement, while it offers a gloss on Nietzsche's idea of "living one's life as a work of art" and "how one becomes what one is." Foucault's discussion is engaging and inspiring as a spiritual response to the prison house of modern society which dominates the individual life.

The next chapter considers the work of Jacques Derrida and the possibility of mourning which is a crucial theme in his writings. In this respect, Derrida is related to both Freud and Roland Barthes, each of whom dwells on the importance of mourning, though in different ways. Freud himself is not usually viewed as a spiritual thinker, especially with his reductive account of libido; but his work on mourning is important, and it provides an essential backdrop for Barthes and especially Derrida, who elevates mourning as a fundamental aspect of spiritual life—for it is one of the most selfless forms of love. Barthes writes about photography and its relation to death. Derrida writes about several of the friends that he has lost, and he thinks through many of the spiritual difficulties associated with mourning. He shows that mourning is a spiritual possibility insofar as it affirms our connection to the living and the dead. But as he notes, hanging on and letting go are both a kind of betrayal. So how should we mourn or respond to the death of the other?

Finally, in the last chapter I examine the work of Luce Irigaray. Irigaray argues that the sexual difference between women and men is the great "unthought" of philosophy, but it also promises the greatest spiritual rewards for those who would think seriously about it. Beginning from this insight, Irigaray describes the "wisdom of love" between two people who care for each other and who are inspired by each other. Such a relationship would be physical, emotional, intellectual, and spiritual, and it would be the fulfillment of love as a spiritual project. In her work, Irigaray elaborates the ways in which the loving relationship enhances individual autonomy and the spiritual dimension of life, and this makes her the contemporary heir of Diotima in Plato's *Symposium*. Irigaray is also important insofar as she explores the spiritual dimension of teaching, which is another kind of loving relationship, but one that gets neglected, especially when education is reduced to training or just passing on knowledge to others.

Of course, there are many others who could appear in this book, especially if it is viewed as a history of modern spirituality or as a complete record of all the "spiritual philosophers" from Schopenhauer to the present day. But this is not an exhaustive account. My list of nine thinkers is eclectic though not arbitrary, and taken as a whole it helps to clarify the possibility of a hidden spiritual tradition in the modern Western world which is not religious or unworldly, but *philosophical* in nature. Each chapter is a self-standing essay which can be read separately, but the effect of the whole book will be to illuminate the spiritual dimension of modern philosophy and modern life in a more complete and sustained way. The point of this book is to re-inspire thinking about spiritual themes which are among the deepest truths of the world that we belong to; for even if they are "invisible," and they cannot be measured in any straightforward way, they are real, and we may neglect the deepest part of ourselves if we choose to ignore them.

1

Schopenhauer on Compassion

On the face of it, Schopenhauer would seem to be one of the *least* spiritual of all philosophers. He argues for the complete pointlessness of human life, and in passages like the following he appears to taunt the reader with the total absurdity of all of our goals and ambitions: "No satisfaction, however, is lasting; on the contrary, it is always merely the starting point of a fresh striving. We see striving everywhere impeded in many ways, everywhere struggling and fighting, and hence always as suffering. Thus that there is no ultimate aim of striving means that there is no measure or end of suffering."[1] Schopenhauer claims that human existence moves continually between the two poles of dissatisfaction and boredom, and he denies that our lives could ever be meaningful or worth living. Likewise, he describes ultimate reality in terms of the one primordial will, which strives relentlessly for nothing in particular. The will wills through us, but it is not moving toward any final goal. All of this seems to confirm our impossible situation, which we can grasp if we have the strength to look beyond all the illusory goals of our individual existence. Indeed, for Schopenhauer, individual existence itself—the *principium individuationis*—is just another illusion.

And yet, in spite of all of Schopenhauer's pessimism and nihilism, there is a strong counter-current in Schopenhauer's philosophy; and for different reasons, I think it is appropriate to begin the recent history of spiritual philosophy with Schopenhauer's thought. As I have already mentioned, Schopenhauer was among the first to take non-Western philosophy seriously, and he celebrates the Vedanta philosophy of India and Buddhism as wisdom traditions that are just as important—if not more important—than those of Christianity and Judaism. Schopenhauer's grasp of the wisdom traditions of Asia is certainly filtered through his own pessimistic lens, and he does not always have an accurate grasp of key doctrines. But he is a spiritual pioneer, and he opens up the possibility of different ways of apprehending ultimate reality and meaning. In particular, Schopenhauer saw how once we admit the illusory character of individual existence, and the reality of the one primordial will that underlies the whole of nature, we must also come to experience our identity with others and the fact that we are all basically the same. In this way, compassion will emerge as the fundamental relationship between human beings and all other creatures.

According to Schopenhauer, compassion—and not reason—is the only real basis of morality. For apart from compassion there is nothing that can inspire us to care for others if it is not in our own interest to do so. In the West, since at least the time of the Stoics, compassion has been regarded with some suspicion as a kind of weakness that takes us away from our own project of self-determination, although it must be said that here the attitude of the philosophers only reflects the prejudices of everyday life. In Buddhism and other Asian traditions, compassion is regarded as one of the highest virtues—if not the highest—and a form of strength rather than weakness because it involves openness toward the other person and the willingness to be available to them. Perhaps our first impulse is one of flight and the desire not to get involved, but compassion overcomes selfishness and gives priority to the other. Schopenhauer is perhaps the first Western philosopher to grasp the absolute value of compassion in this respect, because he sees it as the necessary consequence of self-overcoming and the illusory nature of the individual self, and his discussion of compassion was only deepened by his study of Asian philosophical traditions, including Buddhism.

Now compassion is certainly an ethical principle, but in this chapter I want to claim that it is also a spiritual principle—in fact, it can be viewed as the beginning of spiritual life. Without compassion we are self-absorbed and self-contained, and we are unable to connect with others or with the higher or greater reality of which we are a part. It is a fairly widespread view among different religious and philosophical traditions that spiritual life begins with the death of the ego, and our need to hold on to a separate self-centered existence. In Christianity and Islam, we are taught to subordinate our own will to the will of God; in Stoicism we are taught to think of our reason as a fragment of the divine Logos, and we should accept whatever happens as the will of the cosmos itself; in Daoism we are taught to reject self-assertion and to follow the way of the Dao. With Buddhism, the achievement of true compassion can also be viewed along these lines as a kind of ego death, for it involves self-overcoming for the sake of others; and since we experience their wellbeing as a part of our own, we can say compassion is a spiritual impulse that speaks to our connection to a higher or greater reality that transcends our own selfish lives.

In the following discussion of Schopenhauer, I focus on his account of the illusory nature of individual existence, and I show how he makes use of the ancient Vedanta perspective. In this respect, one special point of interest would be his philosophy of music. Next, I look at Schopenhauer's view of compassion in relation to Buddhism and the priority of compassion in spiritual life. Schopenhauer is by no means a consistent scholar of ancient Indian philosophy, but he was a pioneer and his work has been profoundly influential. He is without doubt a pessimist, and it is hard to reconcile his life-denying comments with the spiritual standpoint that is typically life affirming. But Schopenhauer saw that the newly available Eastern wisdom was an essential corrective to modern individualism and the blind faith in progress that characterized much of nineteenth-century thought. His scathing and polemical style is meant to transform the individual reader by shaking her deepest convictions; and in this respect, his philosophy was profoundly transformative of the Western spiritual tradition.

Indian philosophy and the illusion of the self

Schopenhauer was one of the first Western thinkers to recognize the value of Asian philosophy. He was profoundly impressed by the *Oupnek'hat*, a translation of the *Upanishads* that he received a few years before the publication of *The World as Will and Representation* (1818), and he described this text as "the most profitable and sublime reading that is possible in the world; it has been the consolation of my life, and will be that of my death."[2] For the rest of his life, Schopenhauer made an extensive study of Indian philosophy (including Buddhism) which appeared to anticipate his own philosophical views. Like other scholars at the beginning of the nineteenth century, Schopenhauer believed that the recovery of ancient Indian wisdom would bring about a new Renaissance in Europe.[3] He also held that the essential truth of Christianity could be understood in relation to its more original expression in Indian thought: For "the innermost kernel and spirit of Christianity is identical with that of Brahmanism and Buddhism ... they all teach a heavy guilt of the human race through its existence itself, only Christianity does not proceed in this respect directly and openly, like those more ancient religions."[4] Now we can certainly admire Schopenhauer's attempt to understand Indian philosophy and to integrate it into the horizon of Western thought. While others, like Hegel, were more dismissive, or simply oblivious, Schopenhauer sought to use Indian philosophy to rethink the Western tradition.[5] Even so, his appropriation of Indian philosophical works, such as the *Upanishads*, the *Bhagavad Gita*, or the *Prajna Paramita*, can also be viewed as a *misappropriation* of Indian thought insofar as he uses these texts to confirm his own philosophical views. For at this point, Indian philosophy is drawn into Schopenhauer's orbit of pessimism, the celebration of nothingness, and denial of the will to live, and the dangerous temptation is to read Indian philosophy retroactively in the light of these modern nihilistic themes.

Among the most essential features of Schopenhauer's philosophy is his claim that the world of empirical reality is nothing more than a dream, or a merely phenomenal occurrence that derives from the will, the underlying reality that is the thing-in-itself. According to Schopenhauer, everything in space and time is a secondary manifestation whose existence depends on the will that sustains it: "As the will is the thing-in-itself, the inner content, the essence of the world, but life, the visible world, the phenomenon, is only the mirror of the will, this world will accompany the will as inseparably as a body is accompanied by its shadow; and if will exists, then life, the world, will exist."[6] From this it follows that individual existence is truly insignificant. As individuals, we move from one desire to another, trying vainly to escape the pain of dissatisfaction or boredom. But since whatever we desire is just the expression of the will that wills through us, we can never know satisfaction since the will is unquenchable and blind. Schopenhauer also argues that nature—the objectification of the will—cares only for the species and not for the individual. Indeed, in some passages he goes out of his way to stress that nature is not just indifferent, but actually cruel in her dealings with human beings. As "Nature" personified is made to declare in *The World as Will and Representation*,

> the individual is nothing and less than nothing. I destroy millions of individuals every day for sport and pastime; I abandon their fate to chance, to the most capricious and wanton of my children, who harasses them at his pleasure. Every day I produce millions of new individuals without any diminution of my productive power; just as little as the power of a mirror is exhausted by the number of the sun's images that it casts one after another on the wall. The individual is nothing.[7]

Schopenhauer argues that once we realize the illusory character of human existence and the unsatisfactory character of all of our individual goals, we can gain release from this wheel of suffering by refusing to affirm the will to live, with ascetic practices, including poverty, chastity, and mortification of the will through the torment of the body: "By the expression *asceticism*," he notes, "I understand in the narrower sense this deliberate breaking of the will by refusing the agreeable and looking for the disagreeable, the voluntarily chosen way of life of penance and self-chastisement, for the constant mortification of the will."[8]

Initially, Schopenhauer claims that all of our actions are determined by the law of cause and effect, and in this respect he is adamant that everything in the phenomenal world happens according to strict necessity. By the end of *The World as Will and Representation*, however, he says that the will can be annulled through self-mortification, and hence, *through an act of will*, we may be released from the sufferings of life. Schopenhauer can only describe this paradoxical doctrine in mystical terms as the effect of "grace." From the perspective of his own philosophy, however, it seems contradictory to claim both that: (1) everything in the phenomenal realm is "absolutely necessary" including human actions since we are "the determined phenomenon" of the will and (2) freedom from the will *can* be achieved through ascetic self-denial: for ascetic self-denial is also an expression of will and it is unclear how the will could ever undermine itself by *willing*. This may be one case where calling something a "mystery" implies an unwillingness to think more critically about it. But Schopenhauer frequently refers to the work of Christian and Indian mystics to support his basic position.

On the face of it, Schopenhauer's account of the individual's relationship to the underlying will bears a close resemblance to Indian philosophical perspectives in the *Upanishads* and the *Bhagavad Gita* which suggest a similar dichotomy between the empirical individual and the absolute reality that underlies us. Of course, each of the *Upanishads* has a different focus, and there are points of tension or philosophical disagreements within the whole collection. But overall, the *Upanishads* seem to offer a unified philosophical account of the nature of reality (which is by no means the same thing as a systematic philosophy). Earlier Vedic texts, such as the *Rg Veda*, are based on the theme of ritual sacrifice to the gods, who are viewed as separate beings. Sometimes there is a single god, like Brahma, who replaces the lesser deities as a universal being and the creator of the world, but he is still considered separate from us. The *Upanishads* go beyond this perspective insofar as it affirms the reality of Brahman as both the ruler of the universe and the inner principle that lies behind all of our sensible, intellectual, and spiritual life. In fact, the *Upanishads* propose a form of "spiritual idealism," according to which, this world cannot be understood in merely physical terms, but neither is it just a mental projection or subjective idealism. The point is that ultimate reality is spiritual in character, and if we are prepared to sacrifice our individual desires and perspectives, we may recover this absolute unconditioned level of consciousness and experience unending bliss. According to this doctrine, the inmost self (or Atman) is identical to the highest reality, and everything else that we consider real is just a derivation from it.

In a passage from the *Katha Upanishad*, there is a description of the individual ego and its relation to the deeper self or Atman:

> There are two selves, the separate ego
> And the indivisible Atman. When
> One rises above I and me and mine,
> The Atman is revealed as one's real Self.
> When all desires that search in the heart
> Are renounced, the mortal becomes immortal.
> When all the knots that strangle the heart
> Are loosened, the mortal becomes immortal.
> This sums up the teaching of the scriptures.[9]

Before we achieve enlightenment, we believe that the separate world of individual beings is the only real world, and so we passionately pursue our individual desires, although we never gain any lasting happiness. Likewise, when we identify with our own individual ego, we treat others as totally separate and different from us and so our alienation persists. But according to the *Upanishads*, through meditation and the will to spiritual progress we can experience the deeper reality of the self as pure consciousness, or Atman, which is the undifferentiated ground of our personal being.

Another of the most basic claims of the *Upanishads* is that Atman itself is Brahman, or ultimate reality, for in the end there is nothing to distinguish the undifferentiated self from the unconditional principle of reality itself. In the *Chandogya Upanishad*, this insight is expressed in the famous slogan, *tat tvam asi* ("you are that!"), which Uddalaka repeats to his son as the basic truth of Vedanta wisdom. But once again, it is a truth that must be *experienced* since it goes beyond intellectual understanding, and it is not given through the testimony of the senses:

> As the rivers flowing east and west
> Merge in the sea and become one with it,
> Forgetting they were ever separate rivers,
> So do all creatures lose their separateness
> When they merge at last into pure Being.
> There is nothing that does not come from him.
> Of everything he is the inmost Self.
> He is the truth; he is the Self supreme.
> You are that, Shvetaketu, you are that.[10]

What is the nature of this underlying reality? The *Upanishads* do not provide a precise account of these things, and especially since ultimate reality is literally beyond words, it tends to remain silent about such issues. But one recurrent image suggests a point of comparison: For just as a lump of salt loses its form when thrown into water, so whoever comes to *this* reality must lose herself in it, and then everything she calls her own must vanish, but what remains is an enduring transcendent joy.[11]

At this point, some clear differences have emerged between Indian philosophy, as expressed in the *Upanishads*, and Schopenhauer's thought. First, in Schopenhauer's philosophy, individuals become pessimistic and world-weary as they become more enlightened; they are suffering from life, and the remedy of asceticism reflects a desire for oblivion. In the *Upanishads*, those who seek the ultimate are driven by an absolute desire for truth; like Nachiketa, the young seeker in the *Katha Upanishad*, they want to grasp the significance of existence and not to escape from it, and they are ready to sacrifice everything else for the sake of eternal bliss. Thus, while Schopenhauer calls for self-abandonment in an absolute sense, the goal of the *Upanishads* is actually self-realization: Ascetic practices are enjoined but only to focus the mind on enlightenment which is the key to escaping from the wheel of rebirth and the path to salvation.

In the *Upanishads*, the most complete reality is found at the level of Brahman and individual lives are viewed as secondary by comparison; this seems to mirror Schopenhauer's own distinction between the will and the individual lives which are its phenomenal manifestations. Thus in the *Brihadaranyaka Upanishad*, Yajnavalka decides he must renounce his life as a householder to find immortality through enlightenment, and he reminds his wife that individuals are not important in themselves but only because they belong to the self that underlies them:

> A wife loves her husband not for his own
> sake, dear, but because the Self lives in him.
> A husband loves his wife not for her own
> sake, dear, but because the Self lives in her ...
> Everything is loved not for its own sake, but
> because the Self lives in it.[12]

But whereas in Schopenhauer this distinction leads to a contempt for individual existence and a reasoned desire not to prolong it, in the *Upanishads* individuals belong to Brahman, and so they must also be viewed as sacred. The face of the divine is everywhere in these works, and there is no sense in which the *Upanishads* could be seen as indifferent to individual existence, let alone regard it with contempt as Schopenhauer suggests. All of this suggests a strong metaphysical basis for compassion, which we will examine in the next part of this chapter. For once we realize that we all belong to the same

Brahman that supports us, then in a real sense we are bound to see the other as another *self*, another fragment of the divine that belongs to the basic unity of being. Sometimes the *Upanishads* are criticized for being too self-involved and apparently unconcerned with our duties to society in general. But against this, the goal of all the *Upanishads* is personal enlightenment, and the spiritual and ethical dimension is present in revering the divine principle in others and following the example of sages, like Uddalaka and Yajnavalkya, who offer a guiding example on how we should live.

Thus it may be correct to say that Schopenhauer's philosophy and Indian philosophy share a similar structure in which empirical reality is regarded as secondary, in relation to the primary principle, which is will or Brahman. Likewise, Schopenhauer's reading of Indian philosophy helped to shape his own philosophical views, as is evident from his frequent use of Vedic concepts like "the veil of Maya," which forms the boundary between the true realm of being and the phenomenal world around us. But once we grant this apparent similarity, the two philosophies offer very different judgments on the value of existence. In the *Upanishads*, Brahman is unconditioned, promising bliss and eternity for all who can apprehend it. In Schopenhauer, the will is characterized by restless striving toward nothing in particular: Eternally dissatisfied, it only brings suffering to those who are in its thrall. The goal of the *Upanishads* and the *Bhagavad Gita* is *moksha*—liberation and peace—which is also characterized as true freedom or freedom from the trivial concerns of the self. For Schopenhauer, the will is the principle of our enslavement, and the only way to break free of it is by extreme asceticism or self-cruelty which undermines the will to live. But this does not lead to the eternal bliss that Krishna promises his devotees. Indian philosophy makes use of ascetic practices, including meditation, to cultivate the self toward its final liberation. But Schopenhauer has little, if anything, to say about meditation and other practices that involve spiritual cultivation (of body and mind). It is significant, however, that he focuses on the most sensational or fanatical aspects of Hindu devotion which are by no means the norm:

> the throwing away of all property; the forsaking of every dwelling-place and of all kinsfolk; deep unbroken solitude spent in silent contemplation with voluntary penance and terrible slow self-torture for the complete mortification of the will, ultimately going as far as voluntary death by starvation, or facing crocodiles, or jumping over the consecrated precipice in the Himalaya, or being buried alive, or flinging oneself under the wheels of the huge car that drives round with the images of the gods amid the singing, shouting, and dancing of bayaderes.[13]

In the end, Schopenhauer's own nihilism—by which I mean his rejection of this world as a meaningless phenomenon—informs his reading of Indian philosophy. But this is not something that the original philosophers of the *Upanishads* or the *Bhagavad Gita* would share with him.

As I have already suggested, however, Schopenhauer is not entirely consistent here. As we have seen, he preaches asceticism and self-denial as the only remedy to life, and he advises us to "kill the will" in order to achieve liberation and salvation: "Thus he resorts to fasting, and even to self-castigation and self-torture, in order that, by constant privation and suffering, he may more and more break down and kill the will that he recognizes and abhors as the source of his own suffering existence and of the world's."[14] But this means that for Schopenhauer, there is also a reality which is *beyond* willing. It may help to think about this in the context of Buddhism. In Buddhist philosophy, the first noble truth says that life is suffering, or at least unsatisfying, and the second noble truth says that suffering is caused by our craving and our attachment to the things of this world, including ourselves. So far, this seems to correspond to Schopenhauer's view that willing is the ultimate reality and that this leads to endless dissatisfaction and distress. The third noble truth calls for the cultivation of nonattachment—which corresponds to Schopenhauer's willing not to will, or even killing the will—and this can be achieved by following the eightfold path (which is the fourth noble truth). The problem is that according to the Buddhist view, all of our attachment and all of our willing actually follow from ignorance or a failure to understand. But if we could achieve nonattachment, we would experience the true reality of the world as something that is completely interdependent and impermanent, which is nothing other than nirvana itself. For the "authentic" Buddhist, the priority of the will is not a given but a false belief based on ignorance, while the cultivation of compassion and nonattachment is a profound expression of wisdom, since it reflects the way things are.

Similarly, for the Vedanta philosopher, everyday reality is ultimately viewed as an illusion, and this leads to the blissful experience of Brahman as a cosmic unity which exists beyond the pain of separation and individuation. More examples could be given. But the basic point here is that ultimate reality is experienced blissfully as the absolute oneness that supports and sustains all separate beings. And this suggests that the overcoming of the individual will—which Schopenhauer advocates through asceticism and self-denial—must eventually bring us to a new understanding of ultimate reality as the underlying truth of the world that can only be experienced with joy.

Spirituality and music

Now I will argue that Schopenhauer comes close to this view with his discussion of art and particularly his account of music. In fact, he celebrates the metaphysical character of music and its ability to reveal the inner nature of the world to us. He claims that through the experience of music we are able to experience ultimate reality and meaning, and he makes this point with a memorable formulation: "Music is an unconscious exercise in metaphysics in which the mind does not know it is philosophizing."[15] Perhaps the truth of this claim can only be validated by personal experience: Schopenhauer believes that great music draws us in because it reveals the truth of the world to us, and so it breaks through the realm of appearances. "Therefore, from our standpoint, where the aesthetic effect is the thing we have in mind, we must attribute to music a far more serious and profound significance that refers to the innermost being of the world and of our own self."[16] Many others have had a similar insight concerning music, and they have tried to put this into words, although this is difficult. For instance, in one of his own discussions of music, Roger Scruton seems to be making a similar point about "the innermost being of the world" when he explains:

> In some way it [a great musical work] is setting an example of the higher life, inviting you to live and feel in a purer way, to free yourself from everyday pretenses. That is why it seems to speak with such authority: it is inviting you into another and higher world, a world in which life finds its fulfillment and its goal.[17]

And at the end of this discussion, he notes: "We single out great works of art generally, and great works of music in particular, because they make a difference to our lives. They grant us an intimation of the depth and worthwhileness of things. Great works of art are the remedy for our metaphysical loneliness."[18] I think these comments are very much in line with Schopenhauer's own views on music and especially with the sense that music discloses a higher realm of being or a "metaphysical" order that is usually hidden from us.

According to Schopenhauer, music is the greatest of all the arts, for it "stands quite apart from all the others. In it we do not recognize the copy, the repetition, of any Idea of the inner nature of the world. Yet it is such a great and exceedingly fine art, its effect on man's innermost nature is so powerful."[19] First, music sensitizes us. In particular, it stimulates and evokes our emotional life without harming us, and it allows us to experience the immensity of our own inner world. In this way our lives are enriched, and we can experience the real depth of our inner life which is increasingly difficult to know in the mass society that we belong to. Music stimulates the soul, and in this way it helps us to resist the homogenization of modern consumer culture. Second, music reflects to us the continual movement and striving of life, and it allows us to follow this striving—through every degree of satisfaction and dissatisfaction, and across the whole range of emotions—but without requiring our own personal involvement. And in this respect, music cultivates an attitude of nonattachment and disengagement from the world while it presents all the drama of the world to us. Finally, in a way that Schopenhauer admits it is difficult to articulate, music allows us to *experience* ultimate reality or the unity that is beyond our own separate existence, and this is why music can be so profoundly affecting and moving. To lose oneself in music is akin to the blissful experience of oneness that many have described. This is an experience that the earliest Indian philosophers wrote about and which poets and mystics have often tried to evoke. For them it was an experience that partakes of the deepest bliss—as in the joyful Vedanta claim, "That art thou!"—for it implies the ultimate continuity of all things, and it restores us to a state of unity with the world. Schopenhauer thought of ultimate reality in terms of willing and the will, but he was mistaken on this point, and he himself seemed to realize that the emphasis on life as willing does *not* survive the achievement of enlightenment. Great music is inspiring, and it discloses the spiritual depth of the world to us. In opposition to traditional metaphysics (which is based on reason), it involves an *experience* of spiritual illumination and fulfillment. And for Schopenhauer, only this can explain the profound satisfaction that music can bring.

Buddhism and compassion

The comparison between Schopenhauer and Buddhism is most apparent when we turn to ethics and the foundational role of compassion which both of them espouse. Schopenhauer argues that morality rests upon the fact that we are all manifestations of the one primordial will. Once again, he uses the formula of the *Upanishads* to elucidate his claim:

> The will is the in-itself of every phenomenon, but itself as such is free from the forms of that phenomenon, and so from plurality. In reference to conduct, I do not know how this truth can be more worthily expressed than by the formula of the Veda already quoted: Tat tvam asi ("This art thou!"). Whoever is able to declare this to himself with clear knowledge and firm inward conviction about

every creature with whom he comes in contact, is certain of all virtue and bliss, and is on the direct path to salvation.[20]

Here, Schopenhauer argues that since the will or the in-itself is unconditioned and hence undivided, our own separate existence must itself be an illusion; this means that we are all one, and someone else's distress is ultimately my own. From this it follows that compassion—feeling *with* or feeling *for* another person—is the basis of our ethical life.

Schopenhauer's discussion of compassion is most sustained in his essay *On the Basis of Morality*. In this work, he argues that reason alone could never be an incentive for moral action and only the subjective feeling of compassion can serve as the basis of moral life. In this respect, Schopenhauer's position is quite different from the mainstream philosophical tradition which tends to view compassion as an irrelevant emotion, or even a form of weakness, insofar as it tempts one away from the requirements of justice and the need to be oneself. Schopenhauer affirms compassion, and this is a point of connection with Buddhist and Indian philosophies, for in Buddhism, compassion is the most important of all the virtues. The Buddha himself is known as the compassionate one, and the Dalai Lama, the most well known of all Buddhist leaders, has described the ideal of "the great compassion"—unlimited and unconditional compassion for all sentient beings—as the goal that we should strive for.[21] Thus on the face of it, there is a strong affinity between Schopenhauer's ethics and that of Buddhism, and this is something that can be further examined.

In his essay, Schopenhauer distinguishes three basic motivations: egoism, the most common, derives from short-term or long-term self-interest and assumes the primary reality of individual existence and the illusion of the veil of Maya. Egoism involves calculation in order to achieve one's goals, and this would include living in accordance with justice as the best way to minimize damage to one's own wellbeing. The second motivation is malice which involves delight in the sufferings of others—for if we are used to making comparisons between our own self and others, the misery of another person could actually promote a sense of our own wellbeing since *we* are not the ones who are suffering. Finally, compassion is the third motivation which Schopenhauer describes as the opposite of cruelty. For just as cruelty involves delight in the suffering of someone else, compassion involves being distressed by the suffering of another person and wanting to help her. Schopenhauer argues that compassion comes from a very different standpoint than egoism or malice because it involves a more or less conscious realization that the difference between self and other is illusory, so someone else's suffering is, at some level, also my own: As he writes: "Although it is given to me merely as something external, merely by means of external intuitive perception or knowledge, I nevertheless *feel it with him, feel it as my own*, and yet not *within me*, but *in another person*."[22] So when I feel compassion, I am not just empathizing with another person's misery, or imaginatively identifying what it must be like for her. According to Schopenhauer, I actually feel *her* pain. But can one really feel another person's pain in this direct and nonmetaphorical way? Even though it seems counterintuitive to understand compassion like this, it *is* unclear how we can respond to someone else's misery so strongly when, on the face of it, we feel for them precisely because *they* are the ones who are suffering and not ourselves! According to Schopenhauer, it is a mystery that appears to offer some evidence for the ultimate unreality of our separate, individual lives; since it suggests that *I* can only feel another's pain in this nonmetaphorical way, if *we* are ultimately the same. And hence,

> I no longer look at him as if he were something given to me by empirical intuitive perception, as something strange and foreign, as a matter of indifference, as something entirely different from me. On the contrary, I share the suffering *in him*, in spite of the fact that his skin does not enclose my bones. Only in this way can *his* woe, *his* distress, become a motive *for me*; otherwise it can be absolutely only my own. I repeat that this *occurrence is mysterious*, for it is something our faculty of reason can give no direct account of, and its grounds cannot be discovered on the path of experience. And yet it happens every day.[23]

In this way, as David Cartwright points out, compassion receives a metaphysical explanation rather than a psychological one.[24] But this is not altogether a good thing, for presumably there are psychological explanations of compassion which do not require such a metaphysical leap. Here, Schopenhauer is really struggling with the reality of compassion against the pull of Western individualism. He is the first to question the latter, but it still has its hold on him.

We can consider some of the affinities between Schopenhauer's account of compassion and the Buddhist point of view: Both of them assert the priority of compassion. For Schopenhauer, compassion is the basis of morality. Likewise, in Buddhism, compassion (or *karuna*) is one of the four supreme virtues; in the Mahayana tradition it is probably the most important virtue of all, for the Mahayana ideal of the bodhisattva is the saint who out of compassion refuses Nirvana until everyone else has been enlightened. For Schopenhauer, compassion is also a kind of wisdom. It seems that whoever experiences compassion must know either consciously or unconsciously that the strong sense of the individual as a separate self-contained being is an illusion, for whatever hurts another can also be distressing to us. Schopenhauer affirms this position:

> Individuation is mere phenomenon or appearance and originates through space and time. These are nothing but the forms of all of the objects of my cerebral cognitive faculty and are conditioned by them. And so even plurality and diversity of individuals are mere phenomenon, that is, exist only in *my representation*. My true inner being exists in every living thing as directly as it makes itself known in my self-consciousness only to me.[25]

In Buddhism, compassion is also recognized as a form of wisdom and the two—wisdom and compassion—are taken together as different aspects of the same essential insight: that we are not isolated individuals, separate and unrelated to each other. The bodhisattva ideal is the expression of an embodied wisdom that can only be achieved through compassion, and this is expressed in the traditional vow of the bodhisattva, according to which:

> I take upon myself ... the deeds of all beings, even of those in the hell ... I take their suffering upon me ... I think not of my own salvation, but strive to bestow on all beings the royalty of supreme wisdom. So I take upon myself all the sorrows of all beings ... Truly I will not abandon them. For I have resolved to gain supreme wisdom for the sake of all that lives, to save the world.[26]

Likewise, the Buddhist doctrine of dependent origination suggests that everything is interdependent and affected by other factors in order to be what it is. In the phenomenal realm, at least, there is no separate or self-contained existence—everything is *sunyatta* or emptiness, understood as the absence of independent being. But to recognize this is to break down the fixed separation between self and others and to become less selfish and more compassionate in becoming wise. Schopenhauer is moving toward this position. He certainly recognizes that compassion is a form of wisdom as well as an ethical impulse. And I would add that he recognizes the *spiritual* aspect of compassion insofar as it involves a sense of connection to a greater or a higher reality.

Another significant affinity between Schopenhauer and Buddhism is Schopenhauer's claim that compassion must be extended to all sentient beings, including animals, which are often ignored or treated as mere objects in the Judeo-Christian tradition. As Schopenhauer complains: "The morality of Christianity has no consideration for animals, a defect that is better admitted than perpetuated. This is the more surprising since, in other respects, that morality shows the closest agreement with that of Brahmanism and Buddhism, being merely less strongly expressed, and not carried through to its very end."[27] Once again, he is probably right about this fundamental difference between the two traditions. In Buddhism especially, the suffering of all creatures is regarded as a great evil. "Do no harm!" applies to animals just as much as to people. Against this, Martha Nussbaum points out that Aristotle's views are representative of the Western tradition.[28] The latter argues in the *Rhetoric* that compassion must be limited to humans and he even says that it would be a mistake to feel compassion for an animal or for someone who was bad.[29] In this way, the world gets divided into two sets of creatures, those whose suffering matters and those whose suffering is irrelevant. According to Schopenhauer and the Buddhist philosophy, *all* creatures are worthy of compassion and are to be viewed accordingly as the members of a single community. As Schopenhauer correctly observes: "With the Hindus and Buddhists ... the *Mahavakya* (the great word) '*tat tvam asi*' (this art thou) applies and is always to be expressed over every animal in order that we may have before us, as a guide to our conduct, the identity of his inner nature and ours."[30]

In spite of such similarities, however, there are some apparent differences between these two perspectives on the nature of compassion. For example, Schopenhauer believes in the unchanging nature of the individual character. What we do is just an expression of who we are and the circumstances in which we find ourselves; and as John Atwell argues, Schopenhauer seems to believe that nothing can happen except what actually does happen because everything is subject to the unvarying laws of nature.[31] "[T]he difference of characters is innate and ineradicable," Schopenhauer writes, "The wicked man is born with his wickedness as much as the serpent is with its poisonous fangs and glands; and he is as little able to change his character as the serpent its fangs."[32]

With Buddhism, however, there is a strong sense that one can transform one's outlook through meditation and other reflective practices. In his *Ethics for the New Millennium*, the Dalai Lama asks his readers to cultivate compassion by reflecting on the suffering of others and not to resist compassion as if it were a form of weakness:

> When we enhance our sensitivity toward others' suffering through deliberately opening ourselves up to it, it is believed that we can gradually extend our compassion to the point where the individual feels so moved by even the subtlest suffering of others that they come to have an overwhelming sense of responsibility towards those others. This causes the one who is compassionate to dedicate themselves entirely to helping others overcome both their suffering and the cause of their suffering. In Tibetan, this level of attainment is called *nying je chenmo*, literally "great compassion.[33]

Various spiritual exercises such as *Tonglen* are also meant to increase our ability to experience compassion, so that we can become more mindful of others.[34] Historically, this has always been an important part of Buddhism.

Now Schopenhauer's position on the fixity of human character seems dogmatically opposed to such a possibility. And yet, Schopenhauer does argue that we can change our lives in the light of knowledge concerning our situation: once we realize that fulfilling worldly ambitions and goals will never make us completely happy we may decide to turn away from the world to achieve happiness—or at least the end of misery—through ascetic denial. But would this represent a basic change in character, or just another way of achieving the same selfish ends? My sense is that Schopenhauer can be interpreted in both ways, especially given his view that the individual will can will *not* to will itself any more.

This leads to another important point: I think that Schopenhauer correctly describes the phenomenology of compassion, even down to the strangeness of this experience, which seems to involve feeling another's pain. At the outset, our collective identity with others in the will inspires compassion: I feel your pain because there is no boundary between us. But for Schopenhauer, the more we understand about the human situation, the more we come to realize that compassion is inadequate, for only extreme asceticism and denial of the will can help us to achieve the final liberation. Schopenhauer puts it this way:

> The man who sees through the *principium individuationis*, and recognizes the true nature of things-in-themselves, and thus the whole, is no longer susceptible of such consolation; he sees himself in all places simultaneously, and withdraws. His will turns about; it no longer affirms its own inner nature, mirrored in the phenomenon, but denies it. The phenomenon by which this becomes manifest is the transition from virtue to *asceticism*. In other words, it is no longer enough for him to love others like himself, and to do as much for them as for himself, but there arises in him a strong aversion to the inner nature whose expression is his own phenomenon, to the will-to-live, the kernel and essence of that world recognized as misery. He therefore renounces precisely this inner nature, which appears in him and is expressed already by his body.[35]

A few pages later he continues on the same theme:

> As he himself denies the will that appears in his own person, he will not resist when another does the same thing, in other words, inflicts wrongs on him. Therefore, every suffering that comes to him from outside through chance or the wickedness of others is welcome to him ... He therefore endures such ignominy and suffering with inexhaustible patience and gentleness, returns good for all evil without ostentation.[36]

In these passages, someone who is finally enlightened seeks to destroy the will as it manifests itself in his or her own existence. But now that this person knows that it is the *same* will in all individuals, why should he or she respond positively to others, by returning "good for all evil"? For in caring for others—being good to them in any way—he is only cultivating another manifestation of the will to live, which he has already abandoned. It could be said that the ascetic accepts the abuse of others because he no longer cares about himself; their cruelty is just another kind of abuse that will help to undermine his will to live. But then, why does he still return good for evil? Why does he even care about other people, their feelings, or their rights? At the high point of asceticism, surely every manifestation of the will to live (including that of other people) should be viewed with scorn. There is no longer any reason to keep following moral rules or care about others for exactly the same reason that there is no reason to care about oneself. So the paradox here is that Schopenhauer maintains the value of compassion even when it seems from his own metaphysical view that there is no good reason to do so. He seems drawn by the spiritual attraction of compassion, although the logic of his position is basically against it.

One final point that suggests a difference between Schopenhauer and Buddhist views on compassion is this: Schopenhauer argues in *The World as Will and Representation* that once an individual has seen through the *principium individuationis*, he or she will be more willing to care for others and even die for them. For it would seem that from the ultimate perspective of the will there really is no reason to prefer my own individuality over that of any other— from the perspective of the will, individuals as such are merely phenomenal manifestations; they are not completely real and neither is the separate and distinct self that I take myself to be. And he adds: "Yet the great number of the other individuals whose whole well-being or life is in danger can outweigh the regard for one's own particular well-being. In such a case, the character that has reached the highest goodness and perfect magnanimity will sacrifice its well-being and its life completely for the well-being of many others."[37] This passage suggests that once we have seen through the veil of Maya, to the reality of the will and the illusory character of individual existence, we would still make decisions and *calculations* about whether it is worth saving others—a position which should have been transcended. For this is to think of compassion and sacrifice for others along the lines of a policy where only *reasonable* sacrifices are to be made! Against this, the myths and legends of early Buddhism are full of incredible sacrifices, such as the story of Mahasattva who sacrifices himself for a hungry tigress.[38] The point is that at the level where separate selves are not supposed to exist, one can hardly calculate between self and other; one can only respond to need and distress, and this could involve an excessive, uncalculating response, like that of the bodhisattva who sacrifices himself without reservation. By emphasizing policy and calculation, Schopenhauer seems to betray his underlying individualism, which he fails to transcend even in compassion and the radical denial of the will.

Thus, while both give compassion priority, there are some good reasons for distinguishing Schopenhauer's account from that of Buddhism. Paradoxically, what lies behind some of these differences may be Schopenhauer's implicit belief in the fixity of the individual self (or ego)—the self whose character cannot change; the self who continues to make calculations involving self and others even at the highest level of insight; and the self who still acknowledges the other person when it has abandoned its own self. Buddhism, of course, does not accept the account of the self as a fixed and substantial being. The doctrine of "dependent origination" implies interdependence and the absence of separate identities, and the Buddhist account of "the five aggregates" also undermines the very idea of a fixed and enduring self. This reflects a very different version of compassion which may be subject to other problems, but it avoids the difficulties of Schopenhauer's account. The latter is drawn to compassion *and* to the value of "personal salvation," but these are in conflict with each other.

As Roger-Pol Droit observes, in the nineteenth century Buddhism was misunderstood and feared by many of its European critics as a "cult of nothingness," which involved the worship of oblivion by millions who, it was said, sought nothing more fervently than their own nonbeing.[39] This was a misrepresentation of true Buddhism, but many intellectuals, including sympathetic thinkers such as Schopenhauer and Nietzsche, were seduced by this view. Against this, it must be said that nonattachment is not at all the same thing as indifference or a total lack of concern. And as Schopenhauer must have known, Buddhism is inspired by compassion for others and such compassion is not a means to the end of nonbeing, but the highest task, which the bodhisattva refuses to abandon until all sentient beings have been delivered from suffering. Once again, this can be seen quite clearly in the case of contemporary Buddhism and some of its leading exponents, including the Dalai Lama, Thich Nat Hanh, and others who promulgate an "engaged Buddhism" with detailed policies of social involvement and concern.[40] These Buddhist leaders have shown in their own lives that the doctrine of nonattachment does not lead to indifference or quietism. They have a strong sense of the value of life, and they regard this world as a realm of significance and beauty.

Schopenhauer is a spiritual philosopher because he was profoundly concerned with what we might call meaning of life questions, and he made use of different wisdom traditions to achieve a deeper understanding. In particular, he argued against the priority of the individual self or ego, and he was among the first in Western philosophy to argue for the absolute importance of compassion as the foundation of ethics and, by implication, the origin of spiritual life insofar as it requires self-overcoming. There are some problems in Schopenhauer's interpretation of Asian philosophy, and these derive from his attempt to appropriate Eastern wisdom for a Western cultural view. But in the end, his work is profoundly important, and at times it is inspiring. He is, perhaps in spite of himself, a spiritual philosopher who provokes spiritual questions that would otherwise be ignored.

2

Nietzsche on Generosity

Nietzsche proclaims the death of God. And he argues that traditional religion is objectionable because it deprives this world of its sacred character by projecting the highest values onto another realm, which is heaven or the hereafter. In Nietzsche's famous proclamation, the madman says that God is dead, but he also says that "*we have killed him*," and "All of us are his murderers," and now we must become worthy of this deed.[1] This is a difficult teaching, presented in a strange parabolic form. On the one hand, to say that we have killed God is to suggest that we have made God into a completely shallow being—the divine ruler—and now the scientific hypothesis rejects such a being on the basis of the same will to truth that we have been taught to value. At the same time, however, Nietzsche's parable begins with the madman crying out, "I seek god! I seek god!" The people in the marketplace ridicule him—"did he get lost, or emigrate?" they ask—for they have long abandoned their own religious beliefs. So this is old news to everyone, including the madman; and yet, the madman still *seeks* God. And this implies that in spite of everything, he is still looking for the sacred or the spiritual aspect of life which has withdrawn in the modern Western world.[2]

Clearly, this is a very different kind of atheism than the one associated with David Hume or contemporary writers such as Richard Dawkins or Christopher Hitchens, who rely upon the scientific view.[3] For even though he rejects traditional theism, Nietzsche remains a spiritual thinker with a strong sense of the sacred character of this life, which needs to be affirmed. Nietzsche's masterpiece, *Thus Spoke Zarathustra*, is a phantasmagorical work consisting of stories, dreams, parables, visions, and riddles. And at various points Zarathustra celebrates the sacred character of existence here and now, in poetry and in prophecy, and against scientific reductionism which impoverishes the world.

There are many spiritual themes in Nietzsche's work: the eternal recurrence measures our spiritual attunement to the world; the goal of self-overcoming is crucial; and in *The Birth of Tragedy*, Nietzsche is insistent on the importance of myth as an essential horizon that binds society together. The Greeks had Apollo and Dionysus to inspire and enhance their lives, especially in tragedy, but Socrates spoiled everything with his optimism and his belief that life itself must be completely reasonable. According to Nietzsche, we are the heirs of Socrates, and it is his "reason" which has finally disenchanted the world.[4] This plays out with the death of God, and the urgent challenge that now arises, to "become worthy of this deed." What exactly did Nietzsche envisage here? On the one hand, there is the doctrine of the "overman," but this has no explicit content, and it is more exhortatory than anything else. But perhaps he also had in mind the creation of great art and poetry, the contemplation of nature, and the deepening of human relationships as some of the ways in which we could make ourselves more worthy, and so rekindle our connection to the sacred powers of life. The point is that Nietzsche is spiritual but not religious, whereas thinkers like David Hume and the new atheists are neither spiritual nor religious, and perhaps their thought is not so attractive or compelling because it disdains the need for meaning and a sense of belonging that characterizes spiritual life.

In this chapter, I focus on the idea of generosity as a spiritual theme in Nietzsche's philosophy. Aristotle says that generosity is an ethical virtue and it can be understood as a mean between extravagance and meanness; and typically, we think that generosity involves giving money or property to others. But in Nietzsche, there is a strong sense of spiritual generosity which is ultimately a reflection of the complete generosity of life. Like compassion, generosity is both a moral and a spiritual virtue, and as "the gift-giving virtue" it involves the gift of oneself or the gift of (spiritual) life. It is the generosity of abundance that wants to give, like the sun that bestows its rays on the world. In what follows, I argue that it is this sense of spiritual generosity which goes beyond the separation of the "giver" and the "receiver." It is also the key to some of Nietzsche's most important ideas, including the overman, the eternal recurrence, and even the will to power. My discussion will focus on one short section of *Thus Spoke Zarathustra*, which offers the most powerful but condensed expression of these ideas.

On the gift-giving virtue

Generosity and gift-giving are important themes in Nietzsche's philosophy. In *Thus Spoke Zarathustra*, the overman is praised as the one who squanders himself and gives himself away, while the eternal recurrence evokes the complete abundance of life which ultimately leads to joy. This chapter focuses on

Nietzsche's account of the gift-giving virtue which comes at the end of part one of *Thus Spoke Zarathustra*. "On the Gift-Giving Virtue" [*von der schenkenden Tugend*] is an important section, but it has not received much scholarly attention, and this is surprising, since it is a key to Nietzsche's writing on the meaning of the gift.[5] I begin with a brief discussion of this section. Then I contrast my own reading with some other interpretations, and I show how there are important comparisons to be made between Nietzsche's account of generosity and the traditional viewpoint. Specifically, I argue that the "gift-giving virtue" may be understood in terms of spiritual generosity, which leads to "sovereignty" as an outcome. By "sovereignty" I mean the complete disposal over all of one's powers and openness to the inspiring possibilities of life. On this reading, the promotion of sovereignty is an essential aspect of Nietzsche's thought.[6]

At the start of *Thus Spoke Zarathustra*, Zarathustra tires of his solitude in the mountains and goes down to impart his wisdom to others: "I bring men a gift," he tells the hermit, and so he goes under. To begin with, his present is clearly the overman, for the latter is the focus of all his teachings and an inspirational ideal which is meant to advance humankind. As Zarathustra proclaims: "I love him whose soul squanders itself, who wants no thanks and returns none: for he always gives away and does not want to preserve himself."[7] For the most part, however, the overman is negatively defined. He is someone who goes beyond humanity as it has been hitherto, but there is no precise formula or blueprint for what an overman should be like. The gift-giving virtue is also somewhat ambivalent and a principle of exhortation rather than a specific description. But there is some continuity between the two ideas insofar as the gift-giving virtue expresses the spirit of the overman, and gift-giving remains a relevant virtue, even though the overman is eventually surpassed by the eternal recurrence as Zarathustra's deepest thought. The eternal recurrence is overwhelming because it involves the return of everything, including the small man, or "the last man," that the overman was supposed to overcome. But in the end, there is no final goal or progress, and there is only the pure abundance of life which we can embrace once we are able to affirm the eternal recurrence of all things.

Now there is clearly a deep connection between the gift-giving virtue and the traditional virtue of generosity, although this is never directly addressed. Zarathustra also describes the gift-giving virtue as a kind of *selfishness* in wanting to give, when we might have thought that it would be inspired by a concern for others. And when he addresses the sun—"You great star, what would your happiness be had you not those for whom you shine?" Zarathustra implies that the one who gives is also dependent on the one who receives.[8] All of which suggests that the gift-giving virtue is by no means a straightforward ideal, and we must come to grips with it as a dominant thought that will be difficult to define. Coming at the very end of part one of *Thus Spoke Zarathustra*, "On the Gift-Giving Virtue" provides a parabolic commentary on all of these important themes. Zarathustra comments in this section that "all names of good and evil are parables: they do not define, they merely hint. A fool is he who wants knowledge of them!"[9] But "On the Gift-Giving Virtue" is *itself* a parable concerning the nature of virtue, and so any attempt to define exactly what Nietzsche meant would be problematic on Nietzsche's own terms. As with any parable, then, we shall try for a creative reading that we can incorporate into the context of our lives. Needless to say, this reading must also be in accordance with the spirit of Nietzsche's philosophy.

I will begin with a summary and a preliminary analysis of Nietzsche's text: In the first part of "On the Gift-Giving Virtue," the disciples give Zarathustra a staff with a golden handle on which a serpent is coiled around the sun. Zarathustra is delighted with this gift, and he uses it for his parting address. Holding the staff before him, Zarathustra describes the gift-giving virtue as the highest virtue. He doesn't say what the gift-giving virtue is, but he does say that gold has attained the highest value because it is *like* the gift-giving virtue: "because it is uncommon and useless and gleaming and gentle in its splendor; it always gives itself."[10] Next, Zarathustra praises his disciples for their own gift-giving virtue, although it is far from clear whether they have actually achieved this: "Verily, I have found you out, my disciples: you strive, as I do for the gift-giving virtue … because your virtue is insatiable in wanting to give."[11] At the end of this passage, he comments that such a virtue is a form of selfishness, but the selfishness of the gift-giving virtue is something "whole and holy" and derives from plenitude rather than lack. Finally, Zarathustra offers some exhortatory verses which recall the original praise of the overman: Presumably, the point here is not to communicate information, but to attune the listener to the overman who represents the highest possibilities of life. And he concludes, "Power is she, this new virtue, a dominant thought is she, and around her a wise soul: a golden sun, and around it the serpent of knowledge."[12] So far, then, we have these fragments of parabolic wisdom that must be more carefully understood before we can really grasp what the gift-giving virtue is: the gift-giving virtue is useless; the gift-giving virtue is a kind of selfishness; and the gift-giving virtue is power. The successful interpretation of this opening section should make sense of these puzzling claims.

The second section of "On the Gift-Giving Virtue" focuses more directly on the gift-giving virtue as a pure celebration of life and affirms this earth here and now as a sacred domain. Zarathustra asks his disciples to remain faithful to the earth, and he talks of virtue that has flown away from the earth and attached itself to otherworldly hopes and meanings. The effect of all this has been to devalue and diminish the world we live in; we are no longer capable of cherishing the earth because of our longing for the hereafter—or oblivion—and have incorporated these mistaken valuations at the deepest level of the body itself, repudiating our physical nature as something which is hostile to all spiritual possibilities. In this section, the emphasis is on world-historical themes: Our values and our beliefs are all symptoms of the body's ultimate health, and the attachment to false realities is itself a form of degeneration that gets passed down from one generation to the next. Zarathustra seeks to impose his will on the future by promoting those values and ideas that would inspire and enhance human existence. In a later part of *Zarathustra*, "On the Three Evils," he is quite explicit about this when he re-describes the gift-giving virtue as "the lust to rule."[13] Presumably, this is because from one point of view, the gift-giving virtue involves imposing one's will on others, by raising them up and making them worthy of the future ideal. This is an expression of the will to power, and it conforms to other passages in which Nietzsche describes his own task as the legislation of the future.[14] But the future depends on the present, and the first thing is to orient individuals toward the empowering possibilities of life. In his commentary on this part of *Thus Spoke Zarathustra*, Laurence Lampert writes that the disciples "are not to avoid falling into temptation but to try the tempting paths not yet taken."[15] In short, the disciples must risk themselves by taking new paths and hazarding their own lives as an experiment, which may or may not be successful. In this way, they will create a new goal: "You that are lonely today, you that are withdrawing, you shall one day be the people; out of you, who have chosen yourselves, there shall grow a chosen people—and out of them, the overman."[16] Here, then, the ultimate end of the gift-giving virtue is still the overman, but this now seems like a more remote outcome and not the absolute goal of all human life. All of which implies some distance from the original teaching of the overman in the earlier sections of *Thus Spoke Zarathustra*, where Zarathustra exhorts the people to affirm the overman *now*.

In the third part of "On the Gift-Giving Virtue," Zarathustra sends away his disciples. He tells them that they should leave him to follow their own path, and so he exhorts them to take command of their lives: "You are my believers—but what matter all believers? You had not yet sought yourselves: and you found me. Thus do all believers: therefore all faith amounts to so little. Now I bid you lose me and find yourselves; and only when you have all denied me will I return to you"[17] And this makes sense, for the one who teaches the overman cannot be happy with followers who obey heteronomous commands. In this way, the intended goal of Zarathustra's teaching and the gift-giving virtue itself becomes the *sovereignty* of the individual, and when this is achieved, we can say that we are on a path that may eventually lead to the overman: "And that is the great noon when man stands in the middle of his way between beast and overman and celebrates his way to the evening as his highest hope: for it is the way to a new morning."[18] Notice, however, that now we have moved from the "world-historical" register to the life of the individual as the most immediate point of concern. At this point, the goal of the gift-giving virtue becomes explicitly associated with the ideal of self-appropriation, or what Nietzsche later describes in *Ecce Homo* as "how one becomes what one is." From which it can be inferred that the gift-giving virtue is all about inspiring others to become themselves, and the greatest gift is to open the path to sovereignty.

So much for this brief summation of "On the Gift-Giving Virtue," but what must also be emphasized here is the progress in Zarathustra's own self-understanding, which is reflected by his change in mood between each part. In the first section of "On the Gift-Giving Virtue," the gift-giving virtue is described as a principle of pure generosity: it gives itself; and like the sun, it illuminates everything with its own light. Likewise, Zarathustra praises his disciples for wanting to become "sacrifices and gifts," but the emphasis here is on giving without any consideration of how the gift is to be received. As Stanley Rosen comments, "The virtue of giving is that of strength, not generosity or disinterested philanthropy."[19] But we usually think that gift-giving must be other-directed: I give you what you need and what I give must be of value to both of us, or I cannot be considered generous. According to Zarathustra, the gift-giving virtue follows from the correct attunement to life: "When your heart flows broad and full like a river, a blessing and a danger to those living near: there is the origin of your virtue."[20] In this respect, the gift-giving virtue is "selfish" because it expresses the sheer exuberance of life in its highest examples, like the overman or Zarathustra, and this is inspiring to others, such as the disciples, who benefit from such a "gift." The gift-giving virtue is "power," for it is the complete affirmation of life which is capable of embracing existence while it resists every negative or life-denying ideal. The gift-giving virtue is "useless" because it cannot be measured in the ordinary terms of social utility, and it is not the means to any further values. And it is the "highest" virtue, because it is an expression of the most complete affirmation of life, and there is nothing *beyond* life that could lead to a higher transcendence.

In the second section of "On the Gift-Giving Virtue," the gift-giving virtue becomes the celebration of the earth; this leads to the overman at some point in the future, but the latter is now regarded as a more distant goal. What is *more* important is to "give the earth a meaning, a *human* meaning." Lawrence Lampert explains Zarathustra's goal at this point in terms of his commitment to the future and the judgment of posterity. Indeed, "his appeals to live and die for a future a long way off present themselves as a pure love of posterity, of mankind in the form of the superman, aided by contempt for the present."[21] I would argue that Zarathustra is less concerned with posterity, for in the course of three sections of "On the Gift-Giving Virtue," the future-oriented goal of the overman is gradually replaced by the need to inspire the individual who confronts him in the present—and this could be the disciple or even the reader herself.

Hence, in the final section of "On the Gift-Giving Virtue," Zarathustra is focused on his followers, and he is concerned that they should find their own way. For "one repays a teacher badly if one always remains nothing but a pupil."[22] Here Zarathustra realizes that giving and receiving are actually inseparable from each other, and the gift-giving virtue becomes giving in such a way that the recipient is able to receive the gift well. Later, in "The Night Song," Zarathustra describes the same disjunction between giving and receiving as a point of real unease: "Oh, wretchedness of all givers! Oh, darkening of my sun! Oh, craving to crave! Oh, ravenous hunger in satiation! They receive from me but do I touch their souls? There is a cleft between giving and receiving; and the narrowest cleft is the last to be bridged."[23] Following Emerson, Gary Shapiro notes that gift-giving is a risky business:

> In giving a gift one undertakes the hermeneutical project of discovering what is appropriate to the true character of the recipient. If I fail to interpret him properly, he will feel that some violence or degradation has been done; but if the donor succeeds in reading the heart of the donee the latter may feel that his private space has been invaded and his very joy at the gift will confirm the donor in his interpretation of the man behind the mask.[24]

Zarathustra has given himself by coming down from the mountain to teach people about the overman, but now he realizes that people need to *receive* something else: not a set of teachings about the overman, but the possibility of their own sovereignty as "unique and incomparable human beings" (to use the most striking formulation from *The Gay Science* 335). In this respect, the gift-giving virtue—and Nietzsche's philosophy itself—is all about giving, or restoring people to *themselves*, through the awareness of their own unique existence which had previously been obscured: "You say you believe in Zarathustra? But what matters Zarathustra? You are my believers—but what matter all believers? You had not sought yourselves: and you found me ... Now I bid you lose me and find yourselves; and only when you have all denied me will I return to you."[25] Clearly, there has been a shift in Zarathustra's teaching from the more self-regarding portrait of the overman that he celebrated in the prologue. We can go on to consider some of the ways in which this change in Zarathustra's self-understanding helps us to grasp Nietzsche's mature account of generosity and the real meaning of the gift-giving virtue.

On the generosity of life

Gift-giving is an important thread that runs through the first part of *Thus Spoke Zarathustra*, but it continues through the rest of the book, and I think we must say that it is an essential aspect of Nietzsche's philosophy as a whole. It would be a mistake, however, to think of this kind of generosity in purely ethical terms along the lines of Aristotle and other moral thinkers. Generosity is an important moral virtue, but as Aristotle points out, there are some limits to generosity because people can be too generous or extravagant, or they can give to the wrong people or at the wrong time. In *Thus Spoke Zarathustra*, however, the context for generosity is not simply ethical, and there is a parallel between the relentless striving of the overman and the "unexhausted procreative will of life."[26] Life is a principle of generosity; it squanders itself and holds nothing back, while the overman is one who reflects this generosity of life in his own existence. Both are described in terms of excess and *overflow*.[27] And because the generosity of the overman seems to involve a relationship to life itself, rather than the individual's own flourishing, we can say that it is a spiritual virtue rather than an ethical one.[28]

From most philosophical perspectives, claims about life or the generosity of life are spurious because they cannot be proved or because they seem to presuppose "life" as some kind of a subject. And with few exceptions, even those with religious beliefs have ignored the generosity of life as a theme for philosophical reflection. At the same time, however, life—the universe, everything—is abundant, and showing gratitude for what we have been given is a fundamental spiritual attitude, regardless of one's religious beliefs or lack of them. At the start of the book, Zarathustra exhorts people to remain faithful to the earth and not to believe in otherworldly hopes. He also proclaims the overman as the meaning of the earth, and he tells people they must let their will say that the overman *shall be* the meaning of the earth. In this respect, the overman is one of the keys to life itself. In pointed contrast, Zarathustra also describes "the last men" who live lives of "wretched contentment."[29] They are self-absorbed and they no longer strive for anything beyond themselves, and they feel no pain because they shield themselves from all the vicissitudes of life. The overman does not cling to himself and he opens himself up to all the chances and the possibilities of fate. And this is what we may call a *spiritual* attitude because it trusts in the value of this life, while it also affirms the sacred character of existence which is given to us here and now.

Elsewhere, Nietzsche announces the death of god, but he affirms the value of this life against traditional religion which has frequently undermined it. He denies that the suffering of life is an objection to the world's existence or its goodness. And through his prophet Zarathustra, Dionysus, eternal recurrence, and other devices, he proclaims that this world is sacred. This is the meaning of Zarathustra's roundelay which appears near the end of the book:

> The world is deep,
> And deeper than day can know.
> Deep is its woe –
> Yet joy is deeper than heartache:
> Woe says go!
> But all joy wants eternity –
> Wants deep, deep eternity![30]

Here, Nietzsche celebrates the sacred as something that can be found at every moment in this life. And this is the point at which life seems to justify itself. At the outset, Zarathustra tries to think through this ideal possibility in terms of the overman, but he is also drawn to the thought of eternal recurrence, which includes all of the problems of life that must be affirmed as a part of the whole.

Zarathustra announces that he must go down because he has become too full of wisdom: "like a bee that has gathered too much honey; I need hands outstretched to receive it."[31] Likewise, he implies that while his "generosity" will move and inspire others, it is not based on any need to be with others in order to fulfill himself—hence it is a "whole and holy" selfishness. The problem is that all of this implies a delight in his own power, where the benefit to others is merely coincidental. The greatness of the giver seems to be more important than the benefit of those who receive his gifts. But is this right? We usually think about generosity and gift-giving in terms of giving something to *others*. And as

Aristotle argues in book four of the *Nicomachean Ethics*, just as someone can be mean by giving nothing or too little, it is also possible to give too much, and the person who lavishes presents on others, even when they are undeserving, should not be considered generous but foolish or wasteful.

Nietzsche seems to be arguing, through Zarathustra, that the gift-giving virtue involves giving oneself away rather than money or things—for the gift-giving virtue is like gold, which "always gives itself." And unlike Aristotle's account of generosity, the gift-giving virtue doesn't seem to involve any sort of calculation. It is a gift-giving virtue precisely because whatever is given is given freely and without the expectation of any kind of return. But can we call it "generosity" if it derives more from an inner necessity—the need to give—than from the needs of other people? And should we not say that the generosity of gift-giving is only a virtue insofar as it is other-directed? To give well, or to be accomplished at the gift-giving virtue, the giver must know what the other person needs as well as what she doesn't need; she cannot give too much—or too little—for she would shame the other person if her gift is excessive, or inappropriate, and this would not be virtuous. She must know when to give and how to give her present—but all of these things depend upon knowing and esteeming the person who is to receive the gift. Giving without reference to the recipient cannot be considered true generosity, and this seems to undermine Zarathustra's assertion that the gift-giving virtue is a higher form of selfishness.

Now I have argued that Zarathustra comes to realize this much in the course of his discourse on the gift-giving virtue. As we have seen, *Thus Spoke Zarathustra* is explicitly concerned with the forms of gift-giving and the disjunction between giving and receiving; but in the end, the discussion of the gift-giving virtue becomes focused on the issue of personal sovereignty. Sovereignty is a difficult concept to specify, but we have already suggested that it is "the complete disposal over all of one's powers, and openness to the inspiring possibilities of life." Bringing all of these themes together, we may now argue that the gift-giving virtue is the generosity of spirit that fosters another person and inspires her to "become what she is." Such generosity of spirit can be viewed in a variety of different ways, and it will be possible to articulate some of its basic aspects. But first, I want to look briefly at three alternative interpretations to the one that I am developing here. Nicolai Hartmann offers a significant discussion of the gift-giving virtue in his *Ethics* of 1926; Joseph Kupfer gives an account of the gift-giving virtue at the end of his essay "Generosity of Spirit"; and John Coker offers a nuanced account of the *bestowing* virtue in his essay "On the Bestowing Virtue (*von der Schenkenden Tugend*) a Reading." These are by no means the only possible interpretations of Nietzsche's text, but with each of these examples, the consideration of a different kind of interpretation may help to clarify my own.

Some interpretations of the gift-giving virtue

According to Hartmann, the gift-giving virtue, or "radiant virtue" in the English translation, is a vast overflowing, and the individual who possesses this virtue seems to glow like the sun with spiritual gifts. People who are in the presence of such a virtuous individual will be profoundly affected by her; they will feel blessed with gifts, and yet they will not be able to articulate exactly *how* they have been ennobled and enriched: "The imparter of spiritual values … simply overflows—out of the fullness of his life. Thereby he obeys the basic law of spiritual Being, putting himself at its service as a faithful steward. He yields in his personality to this high law. For this he lives. And in so doing he lives pre-eminently for those who receive his gifts."[32] Or again, "He is lavish of himself; like the sun, he shines on the just and the unjust. His tendency is to dispense to all—and yet to none."[33] Presumably there are people like this, but according to Hartmann their virtue is largely unconscious and their effect on others is just a function of who they are. In this respect, Hartmann's account of the gift-giving virtue avoids the dialectic of the giver and the receiver that is at the heart of Nietzsche's presentation in *Thus Spoke Zarathustra*. At first, as we have seen, the gift-giving virtue can be grasped as a pure and unselfconscious generosity of spirit or a "radiant" virtue of pure bestowal. But by the end of the third section of "On the Gift-Giving Virtue," the gift-giving virtue involves an attunement to others, rather than a random scattering of spiritual bounty. The gift-giving virtue becomes other-directed in the course of Zarathustra's presentation; and by the fourth part of *Thus Spoke Zarathustra*, Zarathustra talks to the higher men, one at a time, in a manner that is appropriate to each of them. Hartmann's radiant virtue remains self-absorbed, although he does write that "he [the bestower] goes forth in yearning to him who will receive his gifts," and "he misses the fellowship of a mind that receives."[34] Hence, as Hartmann himself admits, the "radiant virtue must first awaken a need for its gift, and must therefore plead for itself."[35] But he does not seem to think this requires realigning the virtue toward the receiver. For this reason, I do not think that Hartmann's chapter offers an adequate interpretation of the gift-giving virtue. Indeed, sometimes, as he describes it, it does not seem like a virtue at all, only the expression of a powerful but harmonious personality.

Another difficulty with Hartmann's account is that he never clearly specifies the content of the "radiant" virtue. Hartmann's description is inspiring but vague:

> Radiant virtue ... dispenses gifts which stand in no universal relation to other values, which are not serviceable for other ends, having worth only in their own content, in their own structures, which as means are worthless but as ends in themselves are autonomous; they are imponderables which hover above the weighty and positive values of life. Of this kind is everything aesthetically of value, such as the artist bestows; but not less of this kind is mere admission to participation in the fullness of the real, the opening of eyes to hidden riches everywhere; also, all making of others sensitive to the imponderables, all disclosure of meanings even within the sphere of common everyday life.[36]

In this passage, Hartmann focuses on the point that the radiant or gift-giving virtue involves the transmission or triggering of spiritual goods. This much seems right, but he does not explain the nature of these spiritual goods or, consequently, the content of the gift-giving virtue itself.

Kupfer argues, as I do, that the gift-giving virtue is a form of generosity of spirit. He comments, "Instead of seeking material goods for the sake of giving, Nietzsche's most completely generous individuals seek greatness of character. They want to become rich in virtue so that they may give of their moral bounty ... The self is freely lavished because it is overfull."[37] Now Kupfer suggests that in the gift-giving virtue, it is a virtue itself that is communicated, or given, by one person to another. And hence, the gift-giving virtue, "entails helping other individuals develop the virtue we possess."[38] For example, a courageous person could inspire others with her own courage in a situation of duress, while someone who has generosity of heart could explain to others how to practice forgiveness: "By explaining the forgiveness process, including how to meet obstacles along its way, we show other individuals how to develop forgiveness," and hence, "we can be generous with our generous-heartedness in a direct, edifying way."[39] This is a provocative reading and it hazards a very precise interpretation of the gift-giving virtue. But while there may be people who have these gifts, I do not think we should settle for this interpretation. For one thing, it is too narrow: It reduces the gift-giving virtue to a species of moral instruction, and this would be at odds with Nietzsche's vision of the gift-giving virtue as something which truly affects the individual with the inspiring possibilities of life. According to Zarathustra, the gift-giving virtue is the highest virtue of all; it is not narrow or limited by the virtues associated with it, and so it would be a mistake to view it as just the ability to communicate one's ethical powers. Likewise, I think that Hartmann is right to emphasize that the gift-giving virtue is more of a spiritual virtue than an ethical virtue since it involves the triggering of spiritual possibilities and the possibility of an authentic spiritual life. My own interpretation will emphasize Nietzsche's broader task, which is to determine "how one becomes what one is." Nietzsche thought of himself as an educator, but the goal of his teaching is not limited to the cultivation of particular virtues. It involves the provocation of sovereignty itself, and this presupposes a true generosity of spirit which directs his maieutic art.

Finally, Coker elaborates on the rhetorical complexity of the "bestowing" virtue: On the one hand, it is a determinate virtue which is closely related to generosity or even magnificence in the Aristotelian sense. On the other hand, it is also "a meta-level discourse about discourse about value and virtue (including the bestowing virtue itself)."[40] Coker is right to emphasize that the bestowing or gift-giving virtue is in some sense a discourse about the nature of virtue itself. Along with Shapiro, he takes his cue from two of Zarathustra's pronouncements: "Upward flies our sense: thus it is a metaphor of our body, a metaphor of elevation. Metaphors of such elevations are the names of the virtues";[41] and "Watch for every hour, my brothers, in which your spirit wants to speak in metaphors: there lies the origin of your virtue. There your body is elevated and resurrected; with its rapture it delights the spirit so that it turns creator and esteemer and lover and benefactor of all things."[42] From this, Coker argues that the virtues, including the gift-giving virtue, must be viewed as forms of self-affirmation in which we celebrate the earth by sublimating our own bodily powers as fundamental virtues. As he puts it: "Zarathustra encourages us to turn our gifts, our natural or bodily endowments or 'gifts', into presents, our virtues; in this way we make peace between moon and sun."[43] In this way we also give meaning to the body and to the earth itself.

Coker's interpretation highlights the different levels of reflection that run through the text, giving us an account of the gift-giving virtue as something that is ultimately ambiguous and even "undecidable." His reading serves as a warning to anyone who ignores metaphorical or dramatic elements of the text. On the other hand, what he has to say about the gift-giving virtue as a specific virtue is less convincing. He comments: "Bestowers [gift-givers] are 'driven', 'consumed with desire', and have a 'consuming passion' for their ideal, so much so that they 'consume themselves' in and with it: 'Then (on the great noon) will he who goes under bless himself for being one who goes over and beyond.'"[44] This reduces the gift-giving virtue to a single theme, the dominant thought or passion of the superior person who expends himself in communicating this vision to others. But such a need to give or to make one's mark upon the world is ultimately self-serving, and it is characterized by a *need for others* who are to receive this gift and act accordingly. I have argued that Zarathustra comes to realize this much in the course of his discourse, "On the Gift-Giving Virtue," and this leads him to a less self-involved account of what the gift-giving virtue is. By the end of this section, his goal is not to communicate his own vision but to enable the sovereignty of others.

The three interpretations that I have discussed help to illuminate Nietzsche's difficult ideal, although they all fall short of it. In what follows, I suggest an alternative reading that brings out the spiritual generosity of the gift-giving virtue and its relation to the sovereignty of the individual as an empowering goal. Sovereignty is something like autonomy, not in the narrow ethical sense, but in the sense of *acting in one's own name.* This not only includes self-determination, but also involves a fundamental attunement to spiritual possibilities or the inspiring powers of life.

Spiritual generosity

I have suggested that the goal of the gift-giving virtue is the sovereignty of the other person and that *der schenkenden Tugend* involves knowing what, knowing how, and knowing when to give to the other person in order to provoke or inspire sovereignty—where the latter is understood as an unfolding process rather than a final accomplishment of being. But how does the gift-giving virtue inspire sovereignty in the other? To answer this question, we can now consider some of the different things we can give to another to allow her to become what she is, and these are all different aspects of spiritual generosity.

First, letting the other one be. You cannot just impose your own will on others. And there are times when it is better to stand back and withdraw in order to accept the other person and allow her to be herself. This is what Zarathustra comes to realize when he leaves his disciples so they will not remain mere followers but begin to seek for themselves. Of course, this can be difficult, because our initial impulse is usually to impose our ideas on the other, and to shape her accordingly, especially if we really care for her wellbeing. But there is no greater gift than to enhance the freedom of another human being. And the intentional self-withdrawal that lets the other one be is not anything passive, since it involves the activity of self-overcoming that puts our own desires out of play. As a writer, Nietzsche challenges established views, but at the same time he never seeks to overwhelm the reader with his own ideas since that would be to undermine sovereignty, and so he cultivates an ironic perspective. For example, he rejects idealism, but the gross materialism that he expounds cannot be taken completely seriously: In *Ecce Homo* he argues that philosophers should say more about diet and the weather, and elsewhere, when he writes about Schopenhauer, he claims that pessimism is ultimately the product of bad digestion. In this way, then, he seems to step aside to allow the reader freedom to come to grips with his ideas.

Second: Letting someone be must also be accompanied by attention and the willingness to be available to another person—not just in the sense of responding to her needs, but proactively anticipating problems and difficulties before they arise. In the prologue to *Thus Spoke Zarathustra*, Zarathustra teaches the doctrine of the overman to the assembled multitude. Later, he focuses on what his small band of followers really need, and he sends his disciples away so they will not remain under his spell. In the fourth part of *Thus Spoke Zarathustra*, it is important to note that Zarathustra speaks personally to each of the higher men, and he gives them the appropriate message that each of them needs to hear. Once again, this is exactly what Nietzsche intends with his own writings, which are calculated to hook the interested reader by opening up the deepest spiritual possibilities within the soul that had previously lain dormant. In *Beyond Good and Evil* section 295, he writes about "the genius of the heart" that knows how to inspire and provoke others:

> The genius of the heart who silences all that is loud and self-satisfied, teaching it to listen; who smooths rough souls and lets them taste a new desire—to lie still as a mirror, that the deep sky may mirror itself in them—the genius of the heart who teaches the doltish and rash hand to hesitate and reach out more delicately; who guesses the concealed and forgotten treasure, the drop of graciousness and sweet spirituality under dim and thick ice, and is a divining rod for every grain of gold that has long lain buried in the dungeon of much mud and sand; the genius of the heart from whose touch everyone goes away richer, not favored and surprised, not as if blessed and oppressed with the goods of others, but richer in himself, newer to himself than before, broken open, blown open and sounded out by a thawing wind.[45]

It is not a stretch to think that here Nietzsche is actually describing himself. In Plato's *Symposium*, Alcibiades says something very similar about the effect of Socrates on his own sense of self and the renewal of possibilities that Socrates inspires. For this is how Socrates practices his craft as a spiritual midwife—not propounding his own set of theories or forcing ideas on others, but knowing how to inspire each individual soul that he encounters, and revealing to him, or her, profound spiritual possibilities that were previously only hinted at. Both Nietzsche and Socrates are educators of the soul who inspire the reader/interlocutor to go beyond the cave of everyday life. But such teachers can only appeal to us by paying very close attention to who we are and what is most likely to interest or inspire us. And this is a skill which depends upon a patient concern and availability which is oriented toward the spiritual situation of others.

Third: Compassion. Besides allowing the other to be and being available and attentive to them, there is another impulse which is something like compassion. This is the ability to see into the life of another person, to understand where they are coming from and all the difficulties they may have endured to shape them as they are. Such identification involves compassion or pity [*Mitleid*] and it is the very opposite of the judgmental stance. Now on the face of it, this is problematic: One of the main reasons that Nietzsche condemned *Mitleid* was because he did not view it as a form of spiritual generosity. On the contrary, he rejects pity as demeaning both to the one who pities and to the one who is pitied: "Having seen the sufferer suffer, I was ashamed for the sake of his shame; and when I helped him, I transgressed grievously against his pride ... 'Be reserved in accepting! Distinguish by accepting!' Thus I advise those who have nothing to give. But I am a giver of gifts: I like to give, as a friend to friends."[46] As Bernard Reginster points out, however, Nietzsche's position on pity is by no means a straightforward one, and he argues that Nietzsche "clearly advocates certain forms of compassion and benevolence."[47] In *Beyond Good and Evil*, for example, Nietzsche says: "A man who is by nature a *master*—when such a man has compassion, well *this* compassion has value!"[48] For Nietzsche, compassion (or pity) usually implies condescension or losing oneself in another's distress. But at the same time, *Nietzschean* compassion is not directed toward suffering but to "missed opportunities" which involve the failure to achieve sovereignty.[49] Thus, for example, there is an interesting note included in *The Will to Power*, lodged between several attacks on pity, in which Nietzsche seems to admit that something *like* pity—or compassion—could also be an aspect of the gift-giving virtue. And this passage seems to confirm the idea that Nietzsche is most of all concerned with the challenge to individual sovereignty or "how one becomes what one is":

> My kind of "pity."—This is a feeling for which I find no name adequate: I sense it when I see precious capabilities squandered ... Or when I see anyone halted, as a result of some stupid accident, at something less than he might have become. Or especially at the idea of the lot of mankind, as when I observe with anguish and contempt the politics of present-day Europe, which is, under all circumstances,

also working at the web of the future of *all* men. Yes, what could not become of man, if—! This is a kind of "compassion" although there is really no "passion" I share.[50]

Nietzsche seems to give us something here and then he takes it back again; but taken as a whole, the passage confirms the concern for others which underlies the gift-giving virtue. It also explains why he wrote all his books and praised "the genius of the heart" as one of the most precious gifts of all.

Now there are other aspects of spiritual and emotional generosity that are discussed in Nietzsche's writings, especially in his reflections on friendship, education, the nature of true nobility, and philosophy. This is a neglected feature of Nietzsche's work which is especially appealing, and it stands in stark contrast to all of the polemical comments that he is more well known for. In *Thus Spoke Zarathustra*, the sovereignty or autonomy of the individual is Zarathustra's (and Nietzsche's) focus of concern, and the gift-giving virtue is suggestive of some of the ways in which this sovereignty can be fostered. The wisdom of the gift-giving virtue is oracular in tone, but it lends itself to an interpretation that emphasizes spiritual generosity: Self-withdrawal and letting the other person be herself, availability and (Nietzschean) compassion are forms of spiritual generosity that focus on the spiritual wellbeing of the other person. Their overall tendency is to promote the sovereignty of the individual, which involves taking charge of one's own existence—or self-appropriation—*and* being open or attuned to the spiritual fullness of life. But this is not just a personal achievement which derives from extreme self-discipline or restraint. It is the gift of life itself and the ultimate outcome of the gift-giving virtue.

Generosity and gift-giving are significant ethical virtues, but in this chapter I have argued that the gift-giving virtue is a spiritual virtue that reflects the generosity of life itself. The relevance of this ideal goes far beyond the interpretation of Nietzsche's philosophy, for there are many examples of personal sacrifice and other remarkable acts that cannot be comprehended in terms of the moral calculus of credit and debit. For example, for someone to sacrifice their life for someone else is an example of pure generosity that goes beyond whatever duties people have to each other. Likewise, in the case of a great loss or personal injury an act of forgiveness can be astonishing, because it goes beyond whatever is required or expected of us. As Derrida puts it, it is sometimes possible to "forgive the unforgiveable."[51] Once again, this implies that such an act cannot belong to the ethical sphere of life—even if we call it "supererogatory." But it is an act which expresses the complete generosity of life, which at this point acts through us. And it is a spiritual virtue which inspires and enhances the life of the one who forgives and the one who is forgiven. In this chapter, I have argued that Nietzsche's gift-giving virtue belongs to the generosity of life since it involves the free promotion of another's sovereignty as an end in itself.

Nietzsche calls the gift-giving virtue a form of noble selfishness. I have argued that it cannot be selfishness in any ordinary sense because it is directed toward others—it involves knowing them and valuing who they are—and in the preliminary analysis of different kinds of spiritual generosity, I have considered some relevant aspects which Nietzsche—and Zarathustra—would certainly affirm. The gift-giving virtue involves a profound sense of the spiritual possibilities of the other person, and it guides her toward the fulfillment of such possibilities without *imposing* fixed ideas upon her. On the other hand, the gift-giving virtue is also a sign of power and strength insofar as it disdains the typical limitations of self-concern. In *Ecce Homo*, Nietzsche describes *Thus Spoke Zarathustra* as "the greatest present" ever made to humankind, and he adds, "This work stands altogether apart … perhaps nothing has ever been done from an equal excess of strength."[52] Clearly, Nietzsche regarded his own work as an expression of the gift-giving virtue. And we can say that he has a powerful sense of the *sacred* character of existence which cannot be reduced to the ordinary perspectives of utility and exchange. So finally, his account of the gift-giving virtue illuminates the sacred as that which is excessive and always unexpected, for it is nothing other than the pure generosity of life.[53]

3

Kandinsky on Art

What is the relationship between art and spirituality? How does a work of art express spiritual ideas and themes? And would it be helpful to think of the artist as a kind of visionary or a spiritual seer? These are the guiding questions behind this chapter, and it seems appropriate to focus this discussion on Kandinsky who was both an artist and a spiritual philosopher.

To begin with, art has often been linked to a sense of the sacred and the transfiguration of life. In some of the earliest cave paintings, including those at Lascaux, animals like horses, deer, and bison are lovingly portrayed, and they project a powerful aura as sacred beings that should be honored. Likewise, for many centuries and at least until the Renaissance, art was subordinate to religion. In the West, religious paintings were used to illustrate religious stories, but these paintings also inspired meditation on spiritual themes such as suffering, sacrifice, love, and devotion to the deeper values in life. Significantly, even those religions that forbid direct representations of the divine use decorative designs to embellish places of worship and sacred texts.

More recently, and with the growing secularization of modern life, art has sometimes been seen as a new religion.[1] As Nietzsche writes in *Human, All Too Human*: "Art raises its head where the religions relax their hold. It takes over a host of moods and feelings engendered by religion, lays them to its heart, and itself grows more profound and soulful, so that it is now capable of communicating exaltation and enthusiasm as it formerly could not."[2] In a similar sense, Matthew Arnold predicts that "most of what now passes with us for religion and philosophy will be replaced by poetry."[3] By the end of the nineteenth century, the artist was viewed by many—including Ruskin, Nietzsche, Matthew Arnold, and Oscar Wilde—as a spiritual visionary of the most authentic spiritual life. Wassily Kandinsky belongs to this current of ideas: Although he was a devout Christian and sympathetic to theosophy, he saw art as one of the most direct ways of achieving spiritual enlightenment, and he thought of his artistic life as a spiritual path that he had been called to.

Kandinsky is remembered as the father of abstract art in the first part of the twentieth century, and he is one of the greatest artists of his time. But he is also a profoundly spiritual thinker who published *Concerning the Spiritual in Art* in 1912. This book is an artistic manifesto and a sustained meditation on the relationship between art and spirituality. Kandinsky felt great despair at the rise of materialism in the nineteenth century, and he lamented the oblivion of the spiritual dimension of life which this entailed. He also reflected on his artistic goals, and in his book he was able to articulate his own account of art and what it means to be an artist. According to Kandinsky, art is a spiritual power that can inspire us with the spiritual possibilities of life: "One way or another true art inevitably acts on the soul. The soul vibrates and 'grows'. That is the exclusive aim of the artist, whether he himself is fully aware of it or not."[4] Only art can save us because only art can overcome the soulless materialism of everyday life; and in this respect, the artist has great responsibilities because he or she is a spiritual leader who has been entrusted with a great gift.

Today, Kandinsky's position may seem to be just a reflection of the historical age that he belonged to. But in this chapter, I argue that in some important ways Kandinsky was right: At this point, religion is increasingly challenged by scientific reductionism and philosophy has become a more peripheral concern. But art—as painting, literature, music and film, etc.—remains a very powerful force that can restore our sense of being connected to the deepest issues of life and meaning. Kandinsky has his own account of the relationship between art and spirituality, and his work offers a series of insights concerning this issue. Of course, we may not be persuaded by his theories of form and color; but more than any other thinker, he begins a significant conversation on the relationship between art and spirituality that we can continue—especially if we share his conviction that art inspires the spiritual aspects of life, and it calls to us at the deepest level to become ourselves.

Kandinsky's philosophy of art

Along with Malevich, Klee, and Mondrian, Kandinsky was one of the early pioneers of modern abstract painting, but unlike some of the later abstract expressionists, his paintings have an explicitly spiritual purpose which he affirms in his intellectual masterpiece. *Concerning the Spiritual in Art* remains influential, even more than a hundred years after it was written; and according to John Golding, it is "possibly the most influential single statement to have been produced by any twentieth-century artist."[5] It would be a mistake to think of Kandinsky's manifesto as a rigorously argued work of aesthetics. It is a polemic that rejects nineteenth-century materialism with scorn, and it is heavily influenced by theosophy, spiritualism, and other popular movements that flourished at that time. But it also offers a series of compelling insights which illuminate the spiritual aspects of art and of painting in particular. Kandinsky always believed that art had the power to transform humanity, and both his paintings and his writings are inspired by a revolutionary impulse to recover the spiritual truth of the world.

Kandinsky, Franz Marc, and other artists formed the Blue Rider group, and they published *The Blaue Reiter Almanac* in 1912. They had the sense that art was about to undergo a tremendous spiritual revolution, and this was something which they wanted to hasten. The same theme dominates the beginning of *Concerning the Spiritual in Art*, where shortly before the cataclysm of the First World War Kandinsky describes the "nightmare" of materialism which seemed to characterize modern life:

> Our minds, which are even now only just awakening after years of materialism, are infected with the despair of unbelief, or the lack of purpose and ideal. The nightmare of materialism, which has turned the life of the universe into an evil, useless game, is not yet past; it holds the awakening soul still in its grip. Only a feeble light glimmers like a tiny star in a vast gulf of darkness. This feeble light is but a presentiment, and the soul when it sees it, trembles in doubt whether the light is not a dream, and the gulf of darkness reality.[6]

For Kandinsky, art is the antidote to materialism, because art rejects the complete reduction of life to economic considerations and "the demand that everything should have a use and practical value."[7] In his book, Kandinsky offers some evidence that materialism is finally in decline: With the rise of modern science and the discovery of subatomic particles, and other challenges to popular materialist thinking; and with the emergence of "art for art's sake" which explicitly counters the attempt to bring art into the framework of "practical" materialist concerns. Kandinsky rejects "art for art's sake" because he strongly believed that the *content* of art is important and that art is much more than decoration. But he also saw that "art for art's sake" was born out of despair with the modern world, and he thought that the best way of combating materialism was by restoring the connection between art and spirituality, which means focusing on the *spiritual* content of the artwork.

In this regard, Donald Kuspit is right to emphasize the strong polemical tone of Kandinsky's book, for it challenges us to become aware of the absolute necessity of art in the context of spiritual oblivion. As Kuspit remarks:

> I have always been struck by the sheer force of will animating *On the Spiritual in Art*. The spiritual is a force to be reckoned with. For Kandinsky, the spiritual attitude exists in and through its opposition to the materialistic attitude—that is, exists dialectically—with which it is at war, just as the internal necessity that informs, indeed, drives the spiritual attitude exists in and through its opposition to the external necessity that motivates the materialistic attitude. Spirituality comes into its own—becomes deeply meaningful and transformative of art and life—only as resistance to and transcendence of materialism. Such resistance and transcendence are clearly "religious" in character.[8]

All of this speaks very clearly and well to the overall character of Kandinsky's text, with the call for a spiritual revolution in art as the prelude to a spiritual revolution in life. It also underlines the fact that Kandinsky himself was one of the most self-conscious artists who thought deeply about everything that he did. His book *Concerning the Spiritual in Art* contains important insights which repay a close examination of the text. Here, I will consider three themes which are key to understanding his artistic theory: (1) the overarching concept of spiritual evolution and associated ideas like "inner necessity" and "spiritual vibration"; (2) the language of form and color which is said to correlate art with spiritual reality; and (3) the ideal of the artist as a spiritual leader, which includes Kandinsky's own project of abstract or "non-objective" painting as part of a spiritual revolution in art.

To begin with, Kandinsky believes in the necessity of spiritual evolution which he describes metaphorically in his chapter "The Movement of the Triangle." This is a strange conceit. According to Kandinsky, the historical life of the spirit is equivalent to "a large acute-angled triangle divided horizontally into unequal parts with the narrowest segment uppermost."[9] The whole triangle is moving slowly, both forward and upward, and in every segment of the triangle are artists. Some can see beyond the limits of their segment and so they help to advance things. While others, who are lower, are acclaimed for their views, but even though they appeal to popular taste they retard the movement of the whole. At the apex of the triangle there often stands "one man and only one" who is misunderstood by all of those beneath him. Thus, even Beethoven was ridiculed as a madman by those who did not understand his music. Kandinsky says that in those periods when art is without its "champion," the "true spiritual food is wanting" and these are times of spiritual distress—artists contend for notoriety; they produce all their work without any great enthusiasm; and art loses its soul.[10]

In spite of this apparent decline, however, Kandinsky affirms that "the spiritual triangle, slowly but surely, with irresistible strength, moves onwards and upwards."[11] Kandinsky writes, poetically, that in such dark times—which include his own and presumably ours too—the "invisible Moses" descends from the mountain, with fresh stores of wisdom. The artist is the first to hear him, and "almost unknowingly" he follows the call. And from this point on, the artist yearns to find a material expression for the spiritual form or "the new value" that lies within her soul. As Kandinsky comments in an essay in *The Blaue Reiter Almanac*:

> At a certain time what is inevitable ripens, i.e., the creative *spirit* (which could be called the abstract spirit) makes contact with the soul, later with other souls, and awakens a yearning, an inner urge. When the conditions necessary for the maturation of a certain form are met, the yearning, the inner urge, the force is strengthened so that it can create a new value in the human spirit that consciously or unconsciously begins to live in man. Consciously or unconsciously man tries, from this moment on, to find a material form for the spiritual form, for the new value that lives within him.[12]

This is an account of spiritual evolution which seems to mirror the *physical* evolution of humankind, and it suggests a dialectical movement of history, which swings from materialism to its spiritual antithesis. Perhaps Kandinsky intended this as a self-fulfilling prophecy. For in the very act of proclaiming it he would be moving things along this path. But what exactly is the "spiritual form" that inspires and informs the soul of the artist? His response is ambiguous, but this is what he says:

> After the period of materialist effort, which held the soul in check until it was shaken off as evil, the soul is emerging, purged by trials and sufferings. Shapeless emotions such as fear, joy, grief, etc., which belonged to this time of effort, will no longer greatly attract the artist. He will endeavour to awake subtler emotions, as yet unnamed. Living himself a complicated and comparatively subtle life, his work will give to those observers capable of feeling them lofty emotions beyond the reach of words.[13]

Presumably these "subtle" or "lofty" emotions are *spiritual* emotions and reflections of the spiritual world which they correspond to. The suggestion here is that art awakens and enhances our inner life.

In fact, this is one of the basic ideas behind Michel Henry's discussion of Kandinsky in his book *Seeing the Invisible*. Henry argues that Kandinsky's abstract paintings convey the invisible essence and intensity of life itself. Or as he puts it, in a remarkable passage:

> Ever since a walk in the countryside around Munich where the violence of a colour perceived in the undergrowth gave rise to an intense emotion and he

decided to paint what surrounded this colour—the view of this woods—*in order to represent his emotion*, he knew with a knowledge that is constituted by this emotion itself, that he wanted to paint this emotion and this emotion was the only thing that he would paint thereafter. This was the content of all possible paintings: the profusion of life in himself, its intensification and exaltation.[14]

I am not entirely convinced by this formulation because I think that *all* art can intensify the experience of the inner life, and so there is no compelling need to turn to abstraction. Likewise, the "spiritual" may be an orientation toward life, but it is by no means the same thing as "life" itself; and in Kandinsky the physical and the spiritual aspects of life are kept separate from each other. For Kandinsky, there is the physical world which exists in front of us, but there is also a spiritual world which is invisible, although it shapes and informs all of our experiences and our sensibilities. And *this* is what Kandinsky wanted to paint. He says that artists should remain open to this aspect of life and cultivate their sensitivity to spiritual energies and possibilities. And they must learn to listen to the spiritual vibration that permeates everything in the world. As Kandinsky puts it, "The world sounds. It is a cosmos of spiritually active beings. Even dead matter is living spirit."[15] But he also says that we have no words to describe our spiritual enlightenment because this is an exceptional experience that transcends the framework of our everyday lives. The fact is, Kandinsky never defines the spiritual except negatively, and much of what he says is suggestive at best. But we can review his intuitions later to determine whether they are in accordance with our own experience of such things.

Kandinsky says that the spirit vibrates in the artist's soul. Then, he or she responds by creating an artwork that reproduces the same spiritual vibration. But at this point, the artist must not be a slave to convention, and he or she should follow spiritual necessity or "the inner need":

> The artist must be blind to distinctions between "recognized" or "unrecognized" conventions of form, deaf to the transitory teaching and demands of his particular age. He must watch only the trend of the inner need, and hearken to its words alone. Then he will with safety employ means both sanctioned and forbidden by his contemporaries. All means are sacred which are called for by the inner need. All means are sinful which obscure that inner need.[16]

After this, the spectator encounters the artwork, and once again, if the spectator is refined enough to recognize the spiritual aspect of great art, then he or she will experience the same inner vibration—or the inner sound—that originally inspired the artist. All of this implies a view of art as the communication of inspiration such as we find in Plato's *Ion*, in which artistic inspiration moves through a magnetic chain, from the divine realm to the artist and then to the artwork, to the rhapsode (or interpreter) and all the way down to the spectator.[17] At each level, one is inspired by the contagious enthusiasm of artistic genius, and this means it is possible for the artwork to communicate the highest spiritual refinement to the individual viewer. This account explains why great artists like Beethoven, Picasso, Stravinsky, or Schoenberg were not immediately recognized in their own lifetime, for they were at the apex of the spiritual triangle, and it takes time for others to reach the same level because their spiritual sensibilities must be refined and sensitized to these new possibilities. But now it seems impossible to understand how anyone could fail to appreciate such genius!

For Kandinsky, another sign of this spiritual evolution was how the various arts were drawing together and learning from each other. Kandinsky gives several examples, but he says that they are finding "the best teacher" in music, because music avoids the representation of nature, which limits painting, literature, and most of the other arts. Music offers a direct expression of the artist's soul in musical sound, and so it is the *freest* of all the arts. Kandinsky even describes the painter's "envy" of the musician, for according to one popular view—affirmed by Schopenhauer and others—music is a direct revelation of ultimate reality; while painting has to follow the mediation of physical representation:

> A painter who finds no satisfaction in mere representation, however artistic, in his longing to express his inner life, cannot but envy the ease with which music, the most non-material of the arts today, achieves this end. He naturally seeks to apply the methods of music to his own art. And from this results that modern desire for rhythm in painting, for mathematical, abstract construction, for repeated notes of colour, for setting colour in motion.[18]

Kandinsky always rejected the idea that he was just painting music. But here he follows the lead of music and especially the new experimental music which sought to escape the traditional limitations of musical form. He was impressed by Scriabin and especially Schoenberg: "His music leads us into a realm where musical experience is a matter not of the ear but of the soul alone—and from this point begins the music of the future."[19] But this is also the opening that painting needs to transcend the everyday world, for the latter is an obstacle to spiritual achievement, especially in an age of materialism when spiritual themes have withdrawn from view. In this way, Kandinsky describes and justifies what is soon to become abstract painting or "non-objective" art. This is not to say that he repudiates every other kind of painting or places his own art above all others. In several passages, he returns to the idea of "inner necessity," and he describes his work in these terms, but he always leaves open the possibility that other artists may require the *traditional* forms of representation to express their own spiritual truth and the spiritual forms which they apprehend.[20]

At this point, then, we can move to the second part of Kandinsky's book, called "About Painting," which considers the possibility of an underlying grammar of colors and forms which could express spiritual energies and feelings. The ideas here are based on Kandinsky's own artistic intuitions and experiments, and they remain somewhat tentative. But they are an important aspect of his spiritual quest and are driven by a sense of inner necessity. In a remarkable passage from his autobiographical essay, Kandinsky describes the first set of oil paints that he bought when he was still a child. For Kandinsky, the individual colors expressed different spiritual forms and values, and he gives a very powerful account of them as "magical" beings, each of which seemed to possess a different personality of its own:

> The feeling I had at the time—or better: the experience of the color coming out the tube—is with me to this day. A pressure of the fingers and jubilant, joyous, thoughtful, dreamy, self-absorbed, with deep seriousness, with bubbling roguishness, with the sigh of liberation, with the profound resonance of sorrow, with defiant power and resistance, with yielding softness and devotion, with stubborn self-control, with sensitive unstableness of balance came one after another these unique beings we call colors—each alive in and for itself, independent, endowed with all necessary qualities for further independent life and ready and willing at every moment to submit to new combinations, to mix among themselves and create endless series of new worlds ... It sometimes seemed to me that the brush, which with unyielding will tore pieces from this living color creation, evoked a musical sound in this tearing process. Sometimes I heard a hissing of the colors as they were blending. It was like an experience that one could hear in the secret kitchen at the alchemist, cloaked in mystery.[21]

The passage shows Kandinsky's fascination with color which began at an early age. But what is just as intriguing, in his book, is his very methodical and systematic attempt to show how art and spiritual life may be more finely correlated with each other. I will briefly summarize some of the claims that he makes.

According to Kandinsky, the colors on the painter's palette provoke a double effect. At first, there is a physical effect, in which the eye is charmed by the beauty of colors and responds with pleasure on a purely physical level. But the effect can also go much deeper, causing a vibration of the soul, or a spiritual response, in which the color touches the deepest part of our being. Kandinsky describes the properties that we see when we look at an isolated color and allow it to act by itself: the warmth or coldness of the color tone, and then its clarity or obscurity. He says that warmth involves a tendency toward yellow and coldness is a tendency toward blue. So yellow and blue form the first great dynamic contrast. He notes that the yellow square also has an *eccentric* movement insofar as it seems to move closer to us, while the blue surface is *concentric* because it seems to move away. Yellow is a terrestrial color whose violence can be very aggressive, whereas blue is a celestial color that tends to evoke great calm. Green expresses earthly contentment and tranquility because it absorbs the conflicting momentum between yellow and blue.

Going on, Kandinsky explains clarity as a tendency toward white and obscurity as a tendency toward black. He describes white as a profound silence, full of possibility, whereas black is nothingness without possibility which corresponds to death. Mixing black and white together creates gray, which tends toward despair and the absence of hope. Red is a warm color, lively and agitated. Red and green form the third great contrast, and orange and violet form the fourth. Kandinsky goes on to discuss the influence of form and color, and he asserts: "A yellow triangle, a blue circle, a green square, or a green triangle, the yellow circle, a blue square—all these are different and have different spiritual values."[22] Now Kandinsky recognized that it would be a superhuman task to elaborate the spiritual values of every form and color, especially since each is affected by associated forms on the same canvas which can alter their spiritual effect. But all of this is just a preliminary attempt to describe things from his own painterly perspective. "These statements have no scientific basis," he admits, "but are founded on spiritual experience."[23] Elsewhere, he comments more decisively that: "the sound of colours is so definite that it would be hard to find anyone who would try to express bright yellow in the bass notes, or dark lake in the treble."[24] This sounds plausible, but how much of this is idiosyncratic, and how much of this is culturally determined?

For Kandinsky, color is perhaps the most powerful way in which an artist can affect the human soul. He was certainly articulating his own associations here, for as Peter Selz points out in a comment that as far as I know is still true: "Specific reactions to specific colors have never been proved experimentally."[25] Selz offers some examples in support of his claim: "Yellow ... signified the earth for Leonardo, had gay, happy characteristics for Goethe, meant friendliness to Kant and heavenly splendor to Van Gogh, suggested the night to Gauguin and aggressiveness to Kandinsky. We might add that it symbolizes jealousy in German usage, an emotion which is associated with green in English idiom."[26] And yet, it can hardly be denied that Kandinsky *knew* color, and the effect that certain colors and shapes have on each other within the total context of the artwork. This is like the composer who "knows" the principles of musical harmony even if she is unable to explain all of the musical choices that she makes:

> Neither the quality of the inner need, nor its subjective form, can be measured or weighed. Such a grammar of painting can only be temporarily guessed at, and should it ever be achieved, it will be not so much according to physical rules (which have so often been tried and which today the Cubists are trying) but according to the rules of the inner need, which are of the soul.[27]

In the end, perhaps all we really know is that a painting stirs the soul of the viewer in the same way that music stirs the soul of the listener, and the good artist or the good musician has a basic understanding of how to bring this about. At the very least, then, Kandinsky is describing his own apprehension of colors and the different energies between them, but he also understands that a good artist is not just painting for himself, but communicating spiritual truth to others, and this involves a sense of how these things can be expressed successfully in the painting.

Finally, there remains the issue of the artist as spiritual leader: Kandinsky seems to think of himself as the dedicated artist or the "spiritual visionary" who will introduce a new revolution in art. Toward the end of his book, he offers an ascetic account of art that he followed in his own life, noting that:

> The artist is not born to a life of pleasure. He must not live idle; he has a hard work to perform, and one which often proves a cross to be borne. He must realize that his every deed, feeling and thought are raw but sure material from which his work is to arise, that he is free in art but not in life.[28]

Then he specifies the duties of the artist vis-à-vis those who don't possess artistic talents: "1) He must repay the talent which he has; 2) his deeds, feelings, and thoughts, as those of every man, create a spiritual atmosphere which is either pure or poisonous. 3) These deeds and thoughts are materials for his creations, which themselves exercise influence on the spiritual atmosphere."[29] In short, the artist has not only great power, but also great responsibilities. For Kandinsky, art is in some respects a new religion which will allow us to apprehend the higher spiritual truths. And so it makes sense to think of artists as spiritual leaders who devote themselves to the creation of art as an ethical imperative or as a religious obligation: "Whither is this lifetime tending?," he asks, "What is the message of the competent artist?" And he responds by quoting Schumann: "To send light into the darkness of men's hearts—such is the duty of the artist."[30]

For Kandinsky, the artist is the harbinger of spiritual renewal. These are the general lines of Kandinsky's philosophy of art, and now I will look at some of the spiritual implications of his position.

The challenge of the spiritual

In his book, Kandinsky provides reproductions of four of his own paintings, including one called *Composition 2*. According to Kandinsky, the "Compositions," as opposed to the "Sketches" and the "Improvisations," were among his most sustained and accomplished works which began with an inner feeling and came to fruition only after a long period of maturation. Kandinsky painted ten "Compositions" in his lifetime, and they are among his most important works. Significantly, the first three Compositions were seized by the Nazis from galleries in Germany. They were exhibited at the infamous Exhibition of Degenerate Art in 1937, and it is likely that they were destroyed along with works by Franz Marc, Paul Klee, and other artists. Clearly, the spiritual possibilities that Kandinsky championed were completely at odds with the *political* appropriation of art, and it is hardly surprising that his own work was rejected by the Third Reich.[31] But in the 1930s, Kandinsky's work was criticized by other writers for its apparent withdrawal from the real world, and he was accused of painting "cosmic swirls" instead of documenting life.[32] These are troubling accusations, but they are exactly the same kinds of criticisms that people routinely make against spirituality in general. It is said that spiritual life is self-involved or that spirituality is just a form of escapism from the real issues and problems that we face. How do we respond to these charges? And how are we to make sense of "spirituality" which is on the face of it an inherently vague concept? We must begin by asking how Kandinsky understood spirituality from his own artistic standpoint.

Kandinsky was a devout Christian, and by all accounts he was a profoundly "spiritual" person. I will give one example from several that he relates: In his autobiographical essay, *Reminiscences*, Kandinsky tells how as a child in Russia he spent many hours playing with a favorite toy horse that had distinctive yellow markings on its body and its mane.[33] Later, as a young man of 30, he was offered a prestigious position as a university professor of law. He agonized over whether to take this job, but eventually he decided to devote his life to art. For a long time he did not know if he had made the right decision. Then, sometime after he moved to Munich to study painting, he was walking near his house when he saw a real horse that looked exactly like his childhood toy with the same identical markings; and for years afterward, he would encounter this horse on the street. He came to think of it as an "immortal" because it never seemed to change; and by connecting Munich to his early life in Russia, it seemed to give him back his childhood. So was he right to devote his life to painting instead of teaching law? The appearance of the horse settled his mind completely on that point! And in telling this story, Kandinsky shows his appreciation for the *magical* dimension of life and all the everyday miracles that inspire a sense of wonder and a spiritual response. He simply refused to see this as "just a coincidence" as many people would. Likewise, in his book *Concerning the Spiritual in Art*, he comments that the *refusal* of miracle and mystery is one of the defining features of modernity which confirms the oblivion of spiritual life, for: "it is the conviction that nothing mysterious can ever happen in our everyday life that has destroyed the joy of abstract thought. Practical considerations have ousted all else."[34]

I think this is a powerful story, and it shows Kandinsky's attunement to spiritual possibilities and themes. But even though he lived a very serious spiritual life, he never really gives a clear definition of what spirituality is. For the most part, he seems to think of the spiritual as the negative possibility of the material, although this suggests a kind of dualism where the "spiritual" has no purchase in the physical world:

> Is everything material? Or is everything spiritual? Can the distinctions we make between matter and spirit be nothing but relative modifications of the one or the other? Thought which, although a product of the spirit, can be defined with positive science, is matter, but of fine and not coarse substance. Is whatever cannot be touched with the hand, spiritual? The discussion lies beyond the scope of this little book; all that matters here is that the boundaries drawn should not be too definite.[35]

I think we must take Kandinsky at his word here, and we must avoid any attempt to look at his theory of spirituality in art as if it were something more precise and complete. At the same time, however, we can try to grasp his underlying sense of what "spirituality" is.

To begin with, it will be helpful to distinguish Kandinsky's account of spirituality from his views on *spiritualism* and other related themes. Spiritualism involves an interest in the occult and invisible realms beyond this one, whereas spirituality is more concerned with living mindfully and authentically with others here and now, as opposed to an afterworldly "heaven." In Kandinsky there is some overlap between the two ideas, for he was a devotee of theosophy and he endorsed Madame Blavatsky's ideas of spiritual evolution which were popular at that time.[36] However, if we focus on the question of *spirituality*, then the following points are most important: First, it seems obvious that for Kandinsky, spirituality must be understood in opposition to materialism. Kandinsky longed for a revolution in art because he thought that only a new kind of art could challenge the stranglehold of materialism on contemporary life. We are preoccupied with money and business and we only seem to care about what is immediately in front of us. Only whatever can be measured is considered real. And our inner life, or the life of the spirit, is neglected as something secondary or it is said to be "purely subjective." In this sense, spirituality must be viewed as the dialectical reversal of materialism and the recovery of the deeper truth that has been rejected or ignored. For Kandinsky, there is no question of compromise, and especially after the First World War, the complete rejection of materialism seemed to entail the necessity of *abstract* art, which is the pure expression of spiritual truth.

Drawing from this, the next point is that for Kandinsky, the idea of *inner necessity* is the origin of an authentic spiritual life. True artists have an absolute need to create, and they must discover the forms which are the most suitable ways of expressing their own artistic vision. Kandinsky himself used many different artistic techniques before settling on abstraction as the form that was most authentically his own. There are several passages that could be cited here, including his claim that: "the artist is not only justified in using, but it is his duty to use only those forms which fulfill his own need. Absolute freedom, whether from anatomy or anything of the kind, must be given the artist in his choice of material."[37] This inner necessity is a creative drive that must be satisfied in order to experience spiritual and artistic fulfillment. And this is to emphasize the priority of self-expression over the formal requirements of conventional beauty. We could talk about inner necessity in terms of the *quest* for a deeper truth, which we are bound to undergo if we want to live a truly spiritual existence. For Kandinsky himself it was the path to abstraction that was absolutely necessary, but he recognized that other paths are possible for other people and may also lead to the spiritual truth of the world.

Kandinsky describes the spiritual goal of art toward the end of his book, when he notes that: "painting is an art, and art is not vague production, transitory and isolated, but a power which must be directed to the improvement and refinement of the human soul—to, in fact, the raising of the spiritual triangle."[38] In another essay which appeared at around the same time, he explains: "A distinctive complex of vibrations is the goal of a work. The refinement of the soul through the accumulation of distinctive complexes—this is the goal of art."[39] These are condensed ideas, which are not always supported by complete arguments; but it is clear that for Kandinsky the idea of inner necessity refers to the artist's sense of a spiritual or creative destiny which is then transferred to the artwork and experienced by others to inspire and enhance their own spiritual growth.

The last point is this: For Kandinsky, spirituality is not just an emotional or a subjective state of mind. A spiritual life is connected to ultimate reality and truth—and this is the spiritual life, as opposed to the material reality that we are typically aware of. And the spiritual truth of the great work of art is something that is available to everyone. It is not culturally limited, although we may have to learn to understand and appreciate the work of art if we don't know how to respond to it at first. Spiritual life is just as real as physical life, but it is more important because it belongs to a higher reality and truth. And in this respect, art uncovers the higher truth about the world by triggering spiritual possibilities that we would not otherwise be aware of. For Kandinsky, the ultimate spiritual reality can be achieved through the language of painting. For Schoenberg and Scriabin it comes through the spiritual values of music. In certain Asian traditions, the mantra or the mandala is a way of focusing the mind which leads to openness and spiritual enlightenment. But these are all different means to the same final goal, which is the revelation of a spiritual world, not as an unworldly place but as a deeper reality that surrounds and contains us, which we can experience through art, religion, and love, among other things. In brief, Kandinsky understood spirituality primarily in opposition to materialism as the sense of inner necessity that typifies the subjective, creative life and as the revelation of ultimate reality and truth which the artwork discloses. Kandinsky doesn't tie down basic concepts in the way that we might want him to. Even so, he offers an insightful account of art and spirituality, and this is something that can be built on.

Responses to the three questions

At the beginning of this chapter, I raised three basic questions on the relationship between art and spirituality, and I have used these questions to reflect on Kandinsky's important work, *Concerning the Spiritual in Art*. The questions were: (1) What is the relationship between spirituality and art? (2) How does a given work of art express spiritual themes or ideas? (3) Is the artist a visionary or a spiritual seer? Now we can return to these questions and at the same time we can reconsider the relevance of Kandinsky's response, more than a century after *Concerning the Spiritual in Art* was originally published.

First, on the relationship between art and spirituality: If we look at the entire history of art, it is clear that in the Western tradition at least, art has usually illustrated the *spiritual* truths offered by religion: Brueghel's Crucifixion, Leonardo's Last Supper, Michelangelo's painting of the creation of Adam which adorns the ceiling of the Sistine Chapel, and numerous other works. In many passages Kandinsky seems to identify art with its spiritual purpose. In a later essay, he says quite straightforwardly: "My book *Concerning the Spiritual in Art* and also *The Blue Rider* had as their main purpose to awaken this capacity, absolutely necessary in the future, for infinite experiences of the spiritual in material and abstract things."[40] For Kandinsky, art is inherently spiritual in its orientation since it is a form of spiritual life.

In recent years, however, very few creative artists have devoted themselves to presenting explicitly religious ideas in their work, although many artists explore spiritual themes that are manifest in the world. Witness the example of Anselm Kiefer or Barnett Newman, Mark Rothko and even Francis Bacon, to name but some among many.[41] Such artists offer us paintings that try to say something about our experience of the sacred or spiritual questions like the meaning of life, even when rational discussion falls short. Thus, a painting like Picasso's *Guernica* shows the terrible reality of war, while at the same time it points us toward the sacred reality of life as another perspective that is pointedly absent.[42]

The next question is: How does a work of art convey spiritual themes? It seems clear that traditional paintings along with literature, drama, and other arts can convey spiritual meaning and truth. For example, many paintings seem to look for the spiritual in nature, in the sense that they cherish the particular and inspire us with a love of the world. Contemporary artists also deal with important spiritual themes such as love, compassion, suffering, and death, and in most cases, the artist uses representation to convey these spiritual values and ideas. Kandinsky himself believed that abstract painting was a more direct way of expressing these ideas through the language of color and form. He argues: "The more obvious is the separation from nature, the more likely is the inner meaning to be pure and unhampered."[43] For him, abstract painting is supposed to be like music—a nonrepresentational form that appeals directly to our spiritual being— and I would say that to a great extent, Kandinsky's own paintings work in the way that he describes. We can see this, for example, in some of his later works which are so fascinating and unearthly. The painting titled "Several Circles" (1926) features a dark blue circle partially overlaid by another black circle to create a kind of solar eclipse alongside radiant worlds and moons drifting through deep space. It is a powerful picture which seems to show the origin of the cosmos itself. Another painting, "Accent in Pink" (1926), shows new worlds emerging from a central space, and as Roger Lipsey argues, it suggests something like the derivation of the many from the One: "One might describe it as an icon of cosmic renewal: new worlds pour from a central opening and float out into deep space to become a universe. Close to the center, a little version of the overlapped circles motif suggests the biological division of cells, as if the worlds in this canvas split off from an original unity."[44] Both of these works seem to illustrate Kandinsky's idea that the creation of a work of art is the creation of a new world and new vibrations that enhance the reality of spiritual life.[45]

Kandinsky's own paintings inspire new possibilities within the soul. They are like mantras or yantras which are intended for meditation, and they are meant to focus the mind or put it in harmony with a pattern of spiritual vibrations. Of course, they require work, but not in the sense that we need to learn Kandinsky's iconography and all the received ideas about different colors and shapes. The task is rather one of focused meditation and reflection on the pure presence of these artworks which demand our individual attention. As Kandinsky explains:

> I consider it just as logical, however, that the painting of an object in art makes very great demands on the inner experience of the pure painterly form, that therefore an evolution of the observer in this direction is absolutely necessary and can in no way be avoided. Thus are created the conditions for a new atmosphere. In this atmosphere will be created much, much later the *pure art* which hovers before us in our fleeting dreams of today with an indescribable attraction.[46]

Even though Kandinsky's own art is very different from traditional paintings, I think this account remains helpful in the sense that the understanding of art often inspires us with spiritual possibilities that appeal to the deepest part of who we are—and we must stay open for this.

Finally, would it be helpful to think of the artist as a spiritual seer? In many ways, the meaning of art is tied to spiritual ideas and values, and Kandinsky was right to emphasize the importance of the artist in bringing about this spiritual renewal. For some time now, critics have appeared to agree with Hegel that art is "dead" or that art has somehow lost its ability to express the fundamental truth of any given age.[47] But such a conclusion can be challenged and rethought. Today, philosophy seems to be a fringe activity; religion is still popular but it abounds in fixed ideas and dogmas about this life and the next, and it is not always capable of inspiring subjective thought. But art remains a very powerful force in the sense that it continues to stir the soul in significant ways—with great paintings, but also with music, films, operas, novels, poetry, and architecture. In this respect, the artist remains a kind of spiritual seer and possibly the one figure who escapes the received ideas of everyday life. Robert Wuthnow has noted this in his discussion of contemporary artists:

> It is only a slight exaggeration to say that artists have increasingly become the spiritual leaders of our time. Many of us, whether we are aware of it or not, look to visual artists, writers, and musicians for spiritual guidance, insight and inspiration. Artists are sometimes among the few who take time to reflect on the deeper meaning of life and to search for ways to express both the turmoil of their search and the tentative insights they have gained.[48]

Perhaps we don't expect artists to be moral saints in the way that Kandinsky did, but artists have a kind of radical authenticity, insofar as they remain true to themselves and to their art. And from this there usually follows a very real engagement with spiritual issues and matters of ultimate concern.

Today, critics are basically agreed on Kandinsky's importance as an artist, but there is some disagreement on the relevance of his writings concerning spirituality and art. For example, Charles Pickstone is disdainful, for while he enjoys Kandinsky's paintings, he seems to view the spiritual writings as a kind of youthful mistake. As he notes, "It all seems a little unnecessary. His works can simply be enjoyed as painted marks on canvas, as pure opticality. Demythologizing them probably improves them, much as one enjoys Faust without having to believe in an implausible Devil ... the work is perfectly comprehensible without the spiritual arcana."[49] As we have seen, Kandinsky was an artist with a real sense of mission, but for Pickstone this driving purpose is basically irrelevant. I would disagree with this reading, and speaking personally, I would have to say that being aware of Kandinsky's spiritual manifesto and the explicitly spiritual purpose of his art has helped me to understand his paintings, as well as the overall context of their emergence. It is also the case that *Concerning the Spiritual in Art* raises important questions about art and spirituality that allow us to think much further about these issues.

It is sometimes held that in recent years, art has fallen victim to business and the evils of commodification.[50] Now, more than ever before, it is said that art belongs to the marketplace, and its value is primarily its commercial value which is measured by the price paid for it at auction. By contrast, Kandinsky's emphasis on the spiritual value of art helps us to think more clearly and more thoughtfully about the significance of the artwork. The spiritual value of art is by no means its only value, but it helps to underline the fact that great works of art are often so powerful because they affect us at a profoundly spiritual level. The great work of art recalls us to ourselves; it makes us more aware of the spiritual world that we belong to, and it inspires reflection on important spiritual themes. This is what art does more directly and more effectively than anything else. In different ways, Kandinsky's writings and paintings help to illuminate the spiritual dimension of art, although this is ignored by those who reject the spiritual dimension of *life*. Perhaps, in the future, we can look forward to a more "robust" account of the relationship between art and spirituality, and such an account would consider music, literature, dance, and the other performing arts, as well as painting. In this chapter I have argued that Kandinsky's pioneering work, *Concerning the Spiritual in Art*, remains an important starting point for reflections on this theme.

4

Benjamin on Wisdom

Walter Benjamin is hard to classify: He is not strictly a philosopher, a literary theorist, a sociologist, or a theologian, but he made a profound contribution to all of these different fields. As a scholar and a lover of literature, Benjamin wrote about the German tragic drama, and he has some extraordinary essays on surrealism, Proust, Baudelaire, and Kafka. But at the same time, he sought to come to grips with the nature of modern experience, and this preoccupation led to some of his most powerful writings on the reality of life in the modern city—Paris, Moscow, Naples, etc.—and his reflections on how the urban experience can be transformative of human beings and human nature itself. Benjamin was profoundly interested in the new information age, which we still belong to, and he wrote extensively about the new technologies, including photography, and especially film with its potential for creating solidarity in an age of ideological conflict. He was very much aware of the political and historical context in which he was writing, and like other writers of that time, he had a strong sense of living at a decisive moment in world history, where democracy seemed to be on the way out, and a choice had to be made between socialism and fascism. This explains the ideological perspective of his work. But there is also a real soulfulness in some of his writings, including the account of his childhood in *Berlin Chronicle*; autobiographical essays such as "Unpacking My Library" or "One Way Street," which is a series of aphorisms and observations concerning modern life and structured in terms of our lived experience of the city.

In many ways, Walter Benjamin is one of the most original thinkers of the twentieth century. In this chapter, I focus on the idea of wisdom, which is an underlying theme, and a guiding thread that connects a number of his concerns. Benjamin was certainly critical of the information age, and even though in some respects he remained optimistic about the future possibilities of mass society, he also had a strong sense that in the modern world human experience has been flattened and something important has been lost. Here, I argue that what has been lost is the possibility of *wisdom* or something which is more than just information. Wisdom is the true depth of understanding, which is not to be associated with technical expertise, but with a strong sense of what is important and what is not important; a feeling for how our individual lives relate to the big picture; a critical perspective on the world; and a sense of human community and the importance of others. This kind of wisdom is a *spiritual* virtue because it involves the experience of connection to that which is higher or greater than ourselves. And without this kind of wisdom, we must live in the cave of ignorance, where, according to Plato, we are preoccupied by "shadows" and things which are not really important at all. Benjamin emphasizes that wisdom is also an embodied virtue, and it is *practical* as opposed to being merely theoretical. It is difficult to articulate the true nature of wisdom, but as much as anything else, it includes a sense of attunement to the higher possibilities of life which are worthy of reverence and respect.

Benjamin remains a significant thinker, because the spiritual situation that he describes in the first part of the twentieth century, with the emergence of new technologies and the information age, reflects something of our own situation with the internet and the new electronic culture that has profoundly affected all of our lives. In some ways its effects have been beneficial, for the transmission of knowledge has never been so efficient or effective. But in other ways, the electronic age has diminished human experience by reducing everything to a uniform framework of truth, and it has undermined community. It would be interesting to know what Benjamin would have thought about the internet, and this is a question that I will ask in this chapter. In what follows, I begin by gathering some of the main strands of Walter Benjamin's essay "The Storyteller," which deals with the significance of storytelling and what its decline entails. Then I look at three significant themes—*understanding, community,* and *embodiment*—which demonstrate Benjamin's continued relevance in the modern electronic age. Finally, I focus on the very possibility of *wisdom* which is Benjamin's goal as well as the storyteller's.

Reading "The Storyteller"

Walter Benjamin published two important essays in 1936. The first and certainly the most well known is "The Work of Art in the Age of Mechanical Reproduction," which considers the place of art in contemporary mass society.[1] In this essay, Benjamin offers an account of art that emphasizes its origin in religion and ritual.

We may think of the magnificent cave paintings that were discovered in Lascaux, the frescoes that filled churches in Renaissance Italy, and the correlative sense of art as an aspect of the sacred. Indeed, Benjamin argues that until quite recently, the individual artwork has always possessed an "aura" insofar as it is unique and commands the viewer with its own aesthetic authority or standing. Anyone who has ever lined up at the Louvre for a chance to see the Mona Lisa behind its protective Plexiglas shield will understand this idea of the aura which is typically associated with great works of art. Benjamin insists, however, that in the age of mechanical reproduction, the individual artwork is losing its uniqueness—and its aura—as art becomes available for mass consumption. And according to Benjamin this is actually a good thing, because it restores aesthetic experience to the more everyday context that it belongs to. As he puts it:

> The technique of reproduction detaches the reproduced object from the domain of tradition. By making many reproductions it substitutes a plurality of copies for a unique existence. And in permitting the reproduction to meet the beholder or listener in his own particular situation, it reactivates the object reproduced. These two processes lead to a tremendous shattering of tradition which is the obverse of the contemporary crisis and renewal of mankind.[2]

"The Work of Art in the Age of Mechanical Reproduction" is a brilliant essay, filled with insight and provocative in the extreme, but it remains frustrating and even off-putting because it seems to challenge the spiritual significance of art itself. For Benjamin, art has revolutionary possibilities, but in this essay he wants to free us from everything that emphasizes autonomy, uniqueness, and distance as a threat to social transformation. Of course, much of this is polemical. The essay was written at a critical point in history when fascism was in the ascendant, and so it is not surprising that it begins with Marx's idea of the superstructure and it ends with the need to politicize art. His actual words are significant, and they reveal the strategic intention of his essay: "This is the situation of politics which Fascism is rendering aesthetic. Communism responds by politicizing art."[3] In "The Work of Art in the Age of Mechanical Reproduction," Benjamin rejects the aura and everything that seems to confer "authentic" distinction on the artwork, as part of a quasi-theological perspective that must be overcome. Perhaps we should think of this essay as an example of *speculative* thinking in the best sense. It is not the main focus of concern in this chapter, but it does provide us with an important counterpoint to what we are about to discuss.

By contrast, the second major essay that Benjamin published in 1936—"The Storyteller"— speaks of the decline of storytelling and the possibility of shared experience, with a real sense of loss.⁴ Benjamin is quick to say that the decline of storytelling is not "a symptom of decay," and he adds: "It is, rather, only a concomitant symptom of the secular productive forces of history, a concomitant that has quite gradually removed narrative from the realm of living speech and at the same time is making it possible to see a new beauty in what is vanishing."⁵ In this respect, "The Storyteller" looks more to the present than to the past or to the future, and it avoids the polemical perspective that characterizes the essay on the work of art. I suggest that the essay focuses on the lost art of storytelling not in order to turn the clock back, but to establish the real possibility of *wisdom* which modern life increasingly ignores and consigns to oblivion. What is wisdom, we ask, and can it be taught? But there can be no answer, if, as Benjamin claims, all of our knowledge has now become so much *information*. In "The Storyteller," Benjamin describes the information age which is the nucleus of our own experience of the internet and other electronic media. In this respect, "The Storyteller" may actually be the most relevant and important essay for helping us to understand some of the underlying features of our own contemporary life.

On the face of it, "The Storyteller" purports to be a reflection on the works of Nikolai Leskov, a nineteenth-century Russian author who is celebrated as a man of the people and the most Russian of all writers. The essay discusses other authors, including Hebel, who offer written versions of popular stories, but its focus is on the art of storytelling and the reasons for its decline in modern times. At the beginning of the essay, Benjamin notes that after the profound dislocation of the First World War, men returned from the battlefield completely unable to communicate their experiences. They were shell-shocked, and as Benjamin comments movingly: "A generation that had gone to school on a horse-drawn streetcar now stood under the open sky in a countryside in which nothing remained unchanged but the clouds, and beneath these clouds, in a field of force of destructive torrents and explosions, was the tiny, fragile human body."⁶ War, industrialization, the growth of the city, and other rapid changes associated with modernity have undermined reflective understanding, and the inability to communicate significant experience has now become a feature of modern life.

By contrast, Benjamin speculates, perhaps romantically, that in earlier times both the master craftsman and the traveling journeyman shared the same workshop, and between them they knew all the stories associated with "local tales and traditions" as well as those from places much further afield. They told these stories in the workshop to pass the time and to make their work more interesting and productive. Thus storytelling takes place in a collective context, and the storytelling relationship helps to *create* the individuals who belong to this field. Unlike some "great" works of art which can produce a feeling of separation and even alienation, the story is a popular form which allows for authentic communication between different individuals. Benjamin goes on to describe the attitude of the listener:

> The more self-forgetful the listener is, the more deeply is what he listens to impressed upon his memory. When the rhythm of work has seized him, he listens to the tales in such a way that the gift of retelling them comes to him all by itself. This, then, is the nature of the web in which the gift of storytelling is cradled.[7]

In the end, there is no final separation between the storyteller and the listener, for the listener is also a potential storyteller who hands down his own version of the story to others. And through storytelling the collective experience of a people is passed on from one generation to the next.

What does the story convey? On this point, Benjamin notes that the real story offers something useful—usually some kind of moral or counsel that will help listeners in their own lives: not "the meaning of life" which is too grandiose, but "the moral of the story" which is certainly more practical:

> All this points to the nature of every real story. It contains, openly or overtly, something useful. The usefulness may, in one case, consist in a moral; in another, in some practical advice; in the third, in a proverb or maxim. In every case the storyteller is a man who has counsel for his readers. But if today "having counsel" is beginning to have an old-fashioned ring, this is because the communicability of experience is decreasing. In consequence we have no counsel either for ourselves or for others.[8]

This is the crux of Benjamin's argument. By "counsel," he means wisdom—not factual information or anything merely *objective*, but a living truth which can be absorbed and reflected upon and later communicated to others. But the art of storytelling is dying out because wisdom itself is in decline. Individuals are separated from each other: The workshop has given way to the factory—more recently to the cubicle and the workstation—and this entails the decline of the interpersonal encounter which should promote the communication of wisdom.

Benjamin emphasizes that the true story is open-ended, and in this way it provokes reflection and inspires recollection. Herodotus, Leskov, and Hebel are good storytellers because they don't try to explain or justify, and they resist the temptation of a psychological account. The same would also be true of Kafka, whom Benjamin admired, even praising his parables as "fairy tales for dialecticians."[9] To illustrate his general point, Benjamin uses an example from

Herodotus: Psammenitus was the king of Egypt; the Persian king Cambyses defeated Psammenitus and to humble him he made Psammenitus watch the victory procession which included Psammenitus's own daughter and his son on the way to execution. Through all of this, Psammenitus remained mute and motionless, but when he saw one of his elderly attendants among the prisoners he broke down "and gave all the signs of deepest mourning."[10] Like many others, Montaigne was fascinated by this story and wonders how it was that Psammenitus was able to control himself through every trial until he saw his servant.[11] Was it simply the final straw or the consequence of relaxing tension after his own children had gone by, or is there another way to understand his mental collapse? I think the point is that such a story is like a parable—it is a loose, underdetermined narrative which requires the activity of the listener or the reader to make sense of things by incorporating its meaning into the context of her own life.

Benjamin does not say this, but presumably this is why some of the great teachers of the world, including Jesus and the Buddha, use parables to impart their wisdom. In Christianity, the story of the Good Samaritan is unforgettable and encourages thought on what it means to be a good neighbor: Other people, including a priest and a Levite, failed to help the man who had been beaten and left for dead on the side of the road, but the Samaritan stopped, took him to an inn, and paid for his recovery, and he did all this without hesitation and without even thinking about what his "duty" required.[12] In Buddhism, the story of Kisagotami is about a grieving woman who is told that the Buddha will restore her child if she can collect mustard seeds from a household that has never been troubled by death; she goes unsuccessfully from one house to another until eventually she realizes that her grief is not exceptional because suffering is the ultimate reality of life.[13] This is not the solution to a riddle, but a piece of practical wisdom that helps us to live, and it presents itself most forcefully *without* an explanatory hypothesis. Indeed, wisdom is not a fixed content, or a piece of information, but the ability to apprehend and integrate the lessons of storytelling and life itself. As Benjamin puts it:

> There is nothing that commends a story to memory more effectively than that chaste compactness which precludes psychological analysis. And the more natural the process by which the storyteller forgoes psychological shading, the greater becomes the story's claim to a place in the memory of the listener, the more completely is it integrated into his own experience, the greater will be his inclination to repeat it to someone else someday, sooner or later.

However, Benjamin finishes this passage by warning us, "This process of assimilation, which takes place in depth, requires a state of relaxation which is becoming rarer and rarer."[14] In his essay on the storyteller, he offers some reasons why this is the case.

First, as a general comment, Benjamin quotes Valéry on the speeding up of modern life and our aversion to any kind of painstaking process that requires patience or proceeding slowly: "The patient process of nature ... was once imitated by men," Valéry notes:

> Miniatures, ivory carvings, elaborated to the point of greatest perfection, stones that are perfect in polish and engraving, lacquer work or paintings in which a series of thin, transparent layers are placed one on top of the other—all these products of sustained, sacrificing effort are vanishing, and the time is past in which time did not matter. Modern man no longer works at what cannot be abbreviated.[15]

Benjamin agrees that we now have real difficulty in sustaining reflection on what cannot be immediately produced. In fact, he says, we are losing our ability to endure long open-ended time, for the openness of idleness or inactivity goes against the frenzied pace of modern life. Interestingly, Benjamin frames this discussion in terms of boredom, which he views quite positively as one of the conditions for that openness which storytelling requires. And he comments: "If sleep is the apogee of physical relaxation, boredom is the apogee of mental relaxation. Boredom is the dream bird that hatches the egg of experience."[16] "Boredom" suggests openness and a lack of any real involvement with one's immediate surroundings—for this is what can inspire daydreaming and the productive imagination. And with all the distractions and interruptions that characterize modern life, a state of reverie is more difficult to achieve.

More specifically, Benjamin argues that the rise of the novel was a significant blow to storytelling. On the one hand, the modern novel is the product of "mechanical reproduction," and so it contributes to the decline of storytelling and the storyteller's "aura." On the other hand, while storytelling is an interpersonal experience, novel reading (as well as novel writing) is essentially a private affair. Indeed, "the reader of a novel ... is isolated, more so than any other reader ... In this solitude of his, the reader of a novel seizes upon his material more jealously than anyone else. He is ready to make it completely his own, to devour it, as it were."[17] As we have noted, the meaning of our own life is much harder to discern as experience becomes more baffling and less communicable in the modern world. In the novel, the reader is offered a sense of life as a meaningful totality.

And here it seems that we can follow the drama of someone else's life, which leads to private knowledge about an individual hero as a substitute for what we cannot achieve for ourselves. Perhaps this claim is contestable because it ignores the insight that (great) novels frequently provide. But Benjamin is insistent: "The novel is significant," he writes, "not because it presents someone else's fate to us, perhaps didactically, but because this stranger's fate by virtue of the flame which consumes it yields us the warmth which we never draw from our own fate. What draws the reader to the novel is the hope of warming his shivering life with a death he reads about."[18] In this respect, the novel is to be understood as an escape from life or an escape into another life that will never be mine. And so it follows one of the main tendencies of modern life which includes the avoidance of death and other aspects of the natural world. As Benjamin notes, death has withdrawn from life, and now we tend to think of it only as a limit experience: "Today people live in rooms that have never been touched by death, dry dwellers of eternity, and when their end approaches they are stowed away in sanatoria or hospitals by their heirs."[19]

Going against such a tendency, Benjamin affirms that storytelling is rooted in the rhythms of life and death, and he insists, "It is natural history to which … stories refer back."[20] The story—and especially the fairy tale—presents the most complete *integration* of that which is natural with that which is human. Indeed, it preserves the ambiguity of human existence, while it also suggests a practical resolution of difficulties that seemed to be insuperable at the outset. Fairy tales are among the first stories that many of us hear. Through fairy tales, the child cultivates a profound awareness of the natural world and he or she learns some of the ways in which trouble and danger are to be faced. Consider "Cinderella," "Rumpelstiltskin," or "Mulan," all of which emphasize the need to encounter the world with cleverness and audacity. As Benjamin comments, "This is how the fairy tale polarizes *Mut*, courage, dividing it dialectically into *Untermut*, that is, cunning, and *Übermut*, high spirits."[21] Like the parable, the fairy tale promotes a kind of practical wisdom which may be brought to reflective awareness. It indicates the existence of something which goes beyond the apparent "fixity" of the physical world, and it contributes to human happiness by restoring possibilities that were apparently closed.

But all of this is under threat, and so we return to Benjamin's original point about the decline of storytelling, not just because of the novel, but even more so because of the rise of newspapers, magazines, and other popular forms which undermine the very possibility of wisdom. Benjamin sounds quite contemporary here: He claims that the modern age involves the emergence of a new form of communication that challenges both the novel and storytelling. "And this new form of communication," he writes, "is information."[22] Now certainly, we also live in an age of information and this means that communication involves the transmission of facts and reports that typically come with their own set of explanations or justification. As Benjamin puts it: "Every morning brings us the news of the globe, and yet we are poor in noteworthy stories. This is because no event any longer comes to us without already being shot through with explanation. In other words, by now almost nothing that happens benefits storytelling; almost everything then affects information."[23] I think this is the key to what Benjamin describes in the first section of his essay—we are losing our ability to integrate or exchange personal experience and we no longer understand anything *except* information and the explanation of facts. But given the priority of information, how are we to grasp our deepest experiences which cannot fit this model? Let alone communicate these experiences to others? Benjamin's quest for an authentic exchange between people and the possibility of real communication remains relevant. In his essay, he focuses on *news* reports. But what he says may apply equally well to the *electronic* transmission of ideas which also involves a kind of leveling of our own inner lives. In this respect, it can be argued that Benjamin's essay is particularly relevant for discussions of digital culture, and the related themes of *understanding*, *community*, and *embodiment*, which have all been questioned in recent years. This is not to say that Benjamin anticipated contemporary developments; and given his ambivalence toward popular culture, we really don't know what he would have thought about the internet. But the culture we live in is an extension of the culture he knew, and Benjamin's critique of the latter is still remarkably perspicuous.

Understanding, community, and embodiment

In his essay "On Some Motifs in Baudelaire" (1939), Benjamin talks about the modern crowd and the lived experience of the city with its frequent "shocks" and overwhelming stimuli, frenetic movement, jostling, and noise. Baudelaire sought to describe these aspects in his lyric poetry, and according to Benjamin he was able to capture the truth of this experience at the very point that it was withdrawing from conscious awareness, like the trauma of war which is repressed by consciousness and hidden from view. At the end of this remarkable essay, Benjamin summarizes his discussion in terms of the distinction between two different forms of experience: *Erlebnis*, which suggests everyday awareness of separate moments, and *Erfahrung*, which for him implies a deeper sense of participation in cultural forms which transcend the individual and shape her accordingly:

> Baudelaire battled the crowd—with the impotent rage of someone fighting the rain or the wind. This is the nature of something lived through (*Erlebnis*) to which Baudelaire has given the weight of an experience (*Erfahrung*). He indicated the price for which the sensation of the modern age may be had: the disintegration of the aura in the experience of shock.[24]

In modern life, experience is increasingly fragmented; events are detached from their underlying context, and this leads to a reduction in understanding and community. Benjamin's point about the disintegration of the aura also implies the disenchantment of modern life. According to Benjamin, Baudelaire saw this particularly in the emergence of photography as a popular form, and he notes that "photography is decisively implicated in the phenomenon of the 'decline of the aura.'"[25] Thus, a new form of technical reproduction changes the nature of our experience. Presumably, the development of electronic media pushes us further down the same path.

Now all of this helps to clarify Benjamin's account of storytelling as something which involves the collective depth of cultural life—or tradition—as opposed to the individual's own personal experience: *Erfahrung* as opposed to *Erlebnis*. As he puts it: "[Storytelling] does not aim to convey the pure essence of the thing, like information or a report. It sinks the thing into the life of the storyteller, in order to bring it out of him again. Thus traces of the storyteller cling to the story the way the handprints of the potter cling to the clay vessel."[26] In this way, storytelling becomes the source of collective wisdom. In fact, Benjamin's comments here can help us to think about different aspects of modern life as an extension of the world that he describes in his essay on the storyteller. This part of our discussion will be more speculative, but it uses the rhetorical strategy of Benjamin's own text to provoke reflection on some of the most significant themes of our own contemporary world.

First, Benjamin argues that we live in an information age in which knowledge is reduced to news, sound bites, and other discrete morsels of information that require no further interpretation or reflection. He comments: "Information … lays claim to prompt verifiability. The prime requirement is that it appear 'understandable in itself.' Often it is no more exact than the intelligence of earlier centuries was. But while the latter was inclined to borrow from the miraculous, it is indispensable for information to sound plausible."[27] Likewise, information today has become a kind of seamless web—the worldwide web—and individuals are not required to be active with regard to this sort of knowledge; in fact, they are passive recipients who are trained to reproduce information as required. Benjamin develops this idea in his discussion of film in the essay on the work of art. There, he notes that "art will tackle the most difficult and most important [tasks] where it is able to mobilize the masses. Today it does so in the film. Reception in a state of distraction, which is increasing noticeably in all fields of art and is symptomatic of profound changes in apperception, finds in the film its true means of exercise."[28] Presumably, a similar argument can be made about the information given on the internet, and the state of distraction and acquiescence which prevails in surfing the web or accessing websites like Wikipedia which present themselves as "oracles" of information. But we should also notice Benjamin's cynicism at this point: He does not celebrate film as a higher form of art or even as a truly democratic medium; its distinction lies solely in breaking with traditional models of art and aesthetic authority. Both fascists and communists were quick to understand that film is a way of bringing people together and directing their responses, so that collective action will become possible in the future. Filmmakers like Sergei Eisenstein and Leni Riefenstahl were among many who sought to exploit the popular appeal of film that was first developed in Hollywood.

As we have seen, Benjamin provides some background for these claims. He describes the frequent "shocks" of modern life—with the tumult of war, the expansion of the city, and all the rapid transitions of modernity, we are continually distracted by experiences that we cannot integrate and we live in a state of distraction. And we are losing our ability to endure long open-ended time, for the openness of idleness or inactivity goes against the frenzied pace of modern life.[29] All of this is accompanied by the rise of information as the only acceptable model of knowledge or *understanding*. But information is given all at once and it comes complete with its own explanatory framework which repels further interpretation, and so we go from one item to the next without stopping to reflect or mull. Is collective action still possible? In the passage above, Benjamin argues cynically that "the masses" can be manipulated to promote their own revolutionary future. He would probably agree that in this respect nothing has really changed, for in this age of *electronic* information we are still at the point where wisdom has withdrawn so that humanity can be controlled in one way or another. We are losing the power of critical reflection, and increasingly we become part of the "a hive mind" which requires conformity and mocks anything that cannot be reduced to its own perspective.

This is a troubling scenario, but our situation could still change with the recovery of wisdom and the unmasking of other forms of knowledge/information which are part of the leveling process. For example, the cyber pundit Jaron Lanier has claimed that *"information is alienated experience."*[30] He intends this as a slogan that we should live by, and it suggests at least two relevant points that must be considered here. First, we tend to think of "information" as a self-contained body of knowledge that imposes itself upon us, even though it is ultimately derived from human experience. This means that information involves *reification*, for it is something that we have projected outside of ourselves as an independent object, and we have forgotten its social origins.[31] We may think about the oracular status of Wikipedia and other websites, and we may think about another popular slogan—"Information wants to be free"—which is attributed to the writer Stewart Brand. *This* slogan is frequently used by those who are enthusiastic about the internet, but once again it asserts the (false) autonomy of something that really belongs to us.[32]

Second, even though it derives from lived experience, information is typically presented within a uniform template for what knowledge should be like, and this constrains our experience of the world: in Wikipedia, for example, which enframes all human knowledge within the same parameters and rejects all hierarchy, or Twitter, which at this time allows us to package experience in 280 characters or less. The fact is we find it increasingly difficult to grasp that which is *not* given to us in the ordinary categories of thinking, and we find it hard not to appropriate everything in our own conceptual terms, which are increasingly based on information or "the facts of the case." In the essay on Baudelaire, Benjamin points out that lyric poetry has lost its popularity, and this is presumably because the structure of our experience has changed. The essay on the storyteller makes a similar claim about storytelling as opposed to novel reading and other popular forms. But Benjamin's point can be extended into the present—for our understanding is now more completely constrained than ever before by the templates of knowledge and information, so that it is much harder to appreciate poetry, parables, or even the stories that Benjamin affirms.

As a corollary to this, Benjamin dwells on the isolation of the individual in mass society, a phenomenon that sociologists have sometimes referred to as "the lonely crowd." This point echoes Kierkegaard's critique of the present age, in which separate individuals are constrained by the abstraction of "the public," which seems to reduce all views and experiences to the same basic level. For Kierkegaard: "Only when there is no strong communal life to give substance to the concretion will the press create this abstraction, 'the public', made up of unsubstantial individuals who are never united or never can be united in the simultaneity of any situation or organization and yet are claimed to be a whole."[33] This is the so-called wisdom of the crowd or the "hive mind" which presupposes uncritical conformity and isolation at the same time. According to Benjamin, the rise of information as the dominant form of knowledge has led to a reduction in our ability to communicate our experience with others at anything more than a surface level. And the inability to share experiences means that we cannot have done with them or go beyond ourselves to the healing perspective of the *community* that grounds the individual life. Taking this further and into the present time, it is still unclear whether the electronic community—like Facebook—is a real community in any strong sense. It can just as easily be argued that it is a collection of separate individuals who forego personal encounter for the sake of online association. And through such virtual associations the real community is neglected and undermined.[34] The internet has brought amazing benefits, but it has also diminished our lives by disconnecting us from the direct experience of other human beings. This is highlighted by the angry, uninhibited postings of many of those who comment on the internet, which manifest a kind of selfish individualism. Likewise, social networking reduces the complexity of friendship and relationship to fixed identifiable categories which are mapped out in advance, and the lived encounter between two human beings, which should involve the experience of difference and even strangeness, becomes a matter of shared interests and liking.

Now any attempt to criticize the forms of mass culture—film, television, the internet, Facebook, etc.—is bound to appear elitist or even reactionary in nature. But this is the whole *raison d'etre* of Benjamin's *storyteller* who embodies an oblique criticism of modernity. Thus, Benjamin discusses the significance of Leskov. He comments that "the storyteller in his living immediacy is by no means a present force. He has already become something remote from us and something that is getting even more distant,"[35] and "to present someone like Leskov as a storyteller does not mean bringing him closer to us but, rather, increasing our distance from him."[36] But this is important: The whole point of Benjamin's essay is not just to discuss Leskov or even storytelling as such. It is to show how the decline of storytelling is the symptom of a much wider phenomenon connected to the isolation of the individual in private life and the inability to communicate experience or apprehend wisdom—for this has become a feature of modernity. Part of the problem here is that we have separate experiences (*Erlebnis*) which we accumulate, but we don't have the profound kind of experience (*Erfahrung*) in which we are transformed by what we encounter. We are self-conscious and reactive but we do not integrate experience at a deeper level. In different ways, we just try to fend it off without making it our own.

It is significant to note that Benjamin dwells on *embodiment* or the physical aspect of storytelling. For example, he emphasizes the coordination of hand, soul, and eye as the most complete expression of the storyteller's craft:

> After all, storytelling, in its sensory aspect, is by no means a job for the voice alone. Rather, in genuine storytelling the hand plays a part which supports what is expressed in a hundred ways with its gestures trained by work ... That old co-ordination of the soul, the eye and the hand ... is that of the artisan which we encounter wherever the art of storytelling is at home.[37]

In other words, we should say that true storytelling is embodied wisdom, and the storyteller is not just a disembodied voice telling stories. Storytelling involves the lived encounter with a teacher or a wisdom figure who communicates in a singular way to the one(s) that he or she is addressing, both directly and responsively. Thus, in any situation the storyteller must know the right story to tell and have a good enough memory to remember how the story goes. But he or she must also gauge the audience and encourage appropriate responsiveness through eye contact, voice inflection, appropriate pausing, and physical gestures. To *become* a storyteller not only involves listening carefully to stories, but it also requires being mindful of the storyteller's "performance" in front of others. Following one of Benjamin's own distinctions, we could say that the storyteller is like a stage actor but not an actor in a film: For the one is receptive and responsive to every audience, while the other puts together only one performance that is edited and fixed for all time.[38]

Now all of this is apparently at odds with the contemporary experience of cyberspace and the accumulation of electronic information which seems to take place in the *absence* of the body and all its "unnecessary" distractions. This is a controversial theme, but on this point, Hubert Dreyfus notes an important distinction between physical embodiment and virtual life, and he gives good reasons for the priority of embodiment as the basis of authentic wisdom. In his discussion of the internet, Dreyfus comments thoughtfully:

> Our sense of the reality of things and people and our ability to interact effectively with them depend on the way our body works silently in the background. Its ability to get a grip of things provides our sense of the reality of what we are doing and are ready to do; this, in turn, gives us a sense both of our power and of our vulnerability to the risky reality of the physical world. Furthermore, the body's ability to zero in on what is significant, and then preserve our understanding in our background awareness, enables us to perceive more and more refined

situations and respond more and more skillfully ... All this our body does so effortlessly, pervasively, and successfully that it is hardly noticed. That is why it is so easy to think that in cyberspace we could get along without it, and why it would, in fact, be impossible to do so.[39]

This is a position that Benjamin would certainly affirm. For one thing, he thinks of storytelling as an embodied performance in which storytellers must leave their own imprint: "Thus traces of the storyteller cling to the story the way the handprints of the potter cling to the clay vessel."[40] But at the same time, we should add that storytelling also involves those privileged objects and *things* that are the occasion for stories in the first place.

I will speak of this briefly: In his memoir, *Berlin Childhood around 1900*, Benjamin describes childhood places and objects, such as the new telephone, the rolled-up socks in his drawer, and the strip of light under his bedroom door when his parents were entertaining.[41] Seeing these things from a child's perspective makes us see them anew, and in this way these things are wrenched free from the "objective" information world, and they become luminous in their own right. The toys and special places of his childhood, or his collection of books, including first editions and other rare works—all of these things seem to have a story to tell, and this is why he collects and preserves them or talks about them in his own writings.[42] They are literally "soulful" and our experience of such things can deepen our sense of self and our soul which is in attunement with the world around us. It appears from all of this that both the storyteller and storytelling are grounded in the physical world of lived experience which is given to us *here* and *now*. But they cannot flourish in cyberspace, which is disembodied and a kind of nowhere place. And just as life in the city requires repression, absorbing every "shock" and trauma, the internet can also be seen as the ultimate attempt to escape embodiment and collective life.

The withdrawal of wisdom

All of these interrelated ideas—the rise of information as the dominant form of understanding, the isolation of the individual and the withdrawal of community, and the suspicion or even the denial of embodiment—reflect the decline of storytelling, which also indicates the withdrawal of wisdom itself. But we must still ask ourselves, what *is* wisdom? For given the absolute priority of information in the modern age it becomes increasingly difficult to articulate what wisdom is or even to accept the reality of anything that goes beyond the ordinary forms of explanation. The fact is we have become skeptical of wisdom. The information system that characterizes the field of modern knowledge is based on quantity rather than quality. On the internet everything is of equal importance and there is no place for that which is of *primary* significance or *ultimate* concern. By contrast, Benjamin insists that the storyteller embodies wisdom and concludes his essay as follows:

> Seen in this way, the storyteller joins the ranks of the teachers and sages. He has counsel—not for a few situations, as the proverb does, but for many, like the sage. For it is granted to him to reach back to a whole lifetime (a life, incidentally, that comprises not only his own experience but no little of the experience of others; what the storyteller knows from hearsay is added to his own). His gift is the ability to relate his life; his distinction, to be able to tell his entire life.[43]

And then he adds, somewhat ironically, "This is the basis of the incomparable aura about the storyteller."[44] In the other essay of 1936, the aura is the halo associated with the alienating forms of higher culture which intimidate and subjectify people. It is the sign of a false consciousness and a fetishism that must be overcome. But the idea of the aura associated with the storyteller is more positive insofar as it involves the source of genuine wisdom. This could mean practical advice, counsel, a sense of what is and what is not important, or a sense of one's place in nature and the ultimate order of things. For all of these things comprise wisdom. The storyteller is a sage and a teacher—like Socrates, Buddha, Confucius, or Jesus—who offers us spiritual wisdom in stories, parables, and fairy tales. Indeed, without some measure of wisdom our information world would become an overwhelming manifold that we could hardly make sense of at all.

Benjamin is not straightforward on the subject of wisdom, and his discussion is usually indirect as in his account of the storyteller. He also makes it clear that information is not significant wisdom, since it repels the possibility of coming to grips with things, which seems to be essential to wisdom itself. So in this respect, Benjamin may not have a "theory" of wisdom or even a fully-fledged concept, but the possibility of wisdom remains the hidden question in many of his writings, and it shapes the ideal of *Erfahrung* as the experience that develops across history and time. The bottom line is that now we are *losing* wisdom, and this is a tremendous spiritual blow which Benjamin tries to make sense of and responds to.

Can we recover the possibility of wisdom in the modern information age? From his own standpoint, Benjamin seems to expect the worst, although he hopes against all hope for something better. In his essay, he describes a figure that has become increasingly absent from everyday experience: the storyteller as a kind of craftsman who knows how to speak to people and who offers sage counsel which helps us to navigate our lives. He comments that the best writers are those like Leskov, Hebel, Poe, and Stevenson whose work approximates most closely to storytelling as a verbal form, and this suggests the priority of the spoken word and interpersonal communication between the speaker and the listener which is part of a continuing chain of understanding. In many ways, this is a more traditional view of wisdom which involves the master and the student or the teacher and the disciple, in which knowledge or enlightenment is transmitted from the one to the other through parables and teachings that can be absorbed into the context of the student's personal life. I think this goes against the grain of "The Work of Art in the Age of Mechanical Reproduction," which resists the power of tradition as something that must be overcome if progress and enlightenment are ever to be achieved. By contrast, "The Storyteller" is more helpful because it allows us to understand our situation and the withdrawal of wisdom that appears to accompany all of our technological "progress." I have suggested that in this respect, Benjamin is a "spiritual philosopher," because he dwells on the impoverishment of modern life, and the loss of spiritual depth and understanding which characterizes our experience of the world. Of course, Benjamin may not have thought of himself as a spiritual thinker, but as a critic of modern culture he seems to describe our spiritual malaise and the deeper realities that we are losing sight of.

I suggested earlier that "The Storyteller" is neither a revolutionary essay oriented toward the future possibilities of the world, nor a more conservative account that longs for the fullness of the past. In fact, "The Storyteller" is a critique of the present which analyzes the deficiencies of modern life. We probably lack the words to articulate such things, and there is nothing straightforward about the difficulties that we face, but "The Storyteller" gives a very clear account of some problems of modernity: The priority of information, the reduction in the possibilities of experience and communication, the decline of community, and the wisdom that we have lost, often in the name of technological progress, from the age of mechanical reproduction and—we will add—to the internet, smartphones, and beyond.

But in all of this, I think the real storyteller is Benjamin himself. In "The Storyteller," he tells us an elaborate story, which is his *own* story about storytelling: The craftsman and the journeyman are in the workshop, telling stories to an assembled group of workers; then novel reading begins to challenge storytelling, and this is followed by the rise of information and the emptying out of wisdom.

Here and there we have remnants of the old ideal of wisdom in Leskov, Hebel, and possibly even Kafka. But all of this is a *story* that Benjamin tells his readers. In fact, it is also the *strategy* that he uses to restore the possibility of authentic communication and ultimately wisdom itself.[45]

It is sometimes said that Walter Benjamin is an "unclassifiable" thinker: a philosopher, a cultural theorist, a literary critic, and a theologian—he is all of these things and more. I would suggest, however, that one way to understand Benjamin's work is in terms of *storytelling*, and if this is correct then Benjamin's own essay on the storyteller may be a key to his other writings, for Walter Benjamin is a storyteller and a sage who points us toward the possibility of wisdom in difficult times. In this chapter, I have argued that wisdom is a spiritual theme which expresses the strength of our connection to the world, our relationship to others, as well as our knowledge of ourselves. It is difficult to articulate the nature of wisdom, but this is something that Benjamin accomplishes, through indirection, in his account of storytelling as authentic communication and information as a soulless form. It would be wise to remember Benjamin's work whenever we try to speculate on the meaning of contemporary culture or the nature of the future that it points us toward.

5

Jung on Religion and the Sacred

At the beginning of his autobiography, *Memories, Dreams, Reflections*, Carl Jung describes his whole life in terms of a spiritual quest; for in looking back over the course of his lifetime, it is not the outer events or even the people who stand out for him, but the inner journey in which he experienced reality most profoundly: "Only what is interior has proved to have substance and a determining value. As a result, all memory of outer events has faded, and perhaps these 'outer' experiences were never so very essential anyhow, or were so only in that they coincided with phases of my inner development."[1] Later, Jung describes conscious life as an individual blossom that emerges from the immense rhizome of life, which is for the most part invisible and hidden. And yet, this rhizome endures through the decay of individual lives and civilizations, and it represents our *true* life; for it is here that our finite existence comes into contact with a more profound and abiding reality, and it is this connection that makes our lives meaningful.[2] For Jung, this is the origin of the sacred, and it underlies the power of myth and religion to inspire and enhance our sense of who we are.

Toward the end of his autobiography, Jung goes on to write about the importance of preserving a sense of mystery concerning life. He says we should remain open to all that is magical and mysterious in this world, for if we are closed to the mystery our life will be bereft:

> It is important to have a secret, a premonition of things unknown. It fills life with something impersonal, a *numinosum*. A man who has never experienced that has missed something important. He must sense that he lives in a world which in some respects is mysterious; that things happen and can be experienced which remain inexplicable; that not everything which happens can be anticipated. The unexpected and the incredible belong in this world. Only then is life whole. For me the world has from the beginning been infinite and ungraspable.[3]

As far as Jung is concerned, we should not search for consoling answers or try to reduce every difficulty to a scientific problem that has to be solved. For then we will lose everything that transcends the narrow boundaries of science and our ordinary frame of reference. Without the idea of a "secret," there can be no sense of wonder, and our experience of the world will be diminished by the withdrawal of the sacred or what Jung refers to as the *numinosum*, the transcendent element in life.

Jung insists upon the scientific nature of his project, and he presents himself as a scientist and a psychologist. At the same time, however, he condemns the narrowness of scientific reductionism, and he laments the fact that as science becomes more dominant our spiritual life is impoverished, and the world is increasingly "dehumanized." He also emphasizes the danger of rationalization which undermines all the powerful symbols that formerly gave us access to the sacred powers of life: "We have stripped all things of their mystery and numinosity; nothing is holy any longer."[4] The world has become disenchanted; the sacred dimension of life has fallen away; and now we are in the greatest danger from all the destructive powers that were previously contained by religion and other spiritual forms. Jung does not want to turn the clock back to an earlier time, but he values the insights of archaic life, and he sought to recover the sacred dimension of the world. As he wrote in an essay from 1933: "We moderns are faced with the necessity of rediscovering the life of the spirit; we must experience it anew for ourselves. It is the only way in which we can break the spell that binds us to the cycle of biological events."[5] Jung wrote at a decisive point in world history; he experienced two world wars and the coming of the nuclear age; and he saw that we always seem to have the "best" reasons for fighting more wars, so that eventually we may destroy ourselves.

According to Jung, the sacred is evoked by symbols, archetypes, and myths which form our collective unconscious. A symbol is "an expression for something unknown or not yet knowable," and it points us toward a reality that is ultimately mysterious and beyond the everyday world that we belong to.[6] Unlike signs, symbols cannot be exhausted or reduced to a fixed meaning, but they are affective and powerful, and they are redolent of the numinous quality of life. The archetypes are recurrent figures in mythologies from all over the world, and they reflect the most significant human situations. But even though they are within us, they do not really belong to us because they have a life of their own—in dreams, stories, literature, art, etc. A myth offers a deeper representation than the facts or the literal truth, because a myth has a universal human validity, and it is the inner truth of a situation that we respond to. So while we may not embrace myths as literally true, they still express a form of poetic thinking which is more extensive and profound than modern scientific reasoning. Now, however, with the rejection of myth, and the growing ambivalence toward religion—which arises when we insist on taking it *literally*—the wisdom of archaic life is limited to dreaming, and the accumulation of neuroses and symptoms that show our lack of attunement.

Jung never sought to abandon the conscious ego, but he believed that the ego had to renew its relationship to the sacred by *dreaming the myth onwards*:

> Even the best attempts at explanation are only more or less successful translations into another metaphorical language. (Indeed, language itself is only an image.) The most we can do is to *dream the myth onwards* and give it a modern dress. And whatever explanation or interpretation does to it, we do to our own souls as well, with corresponding results for our own well-being.[7]

Without this underlying spiritual renewal, any kind of transformation or "progress" may be accompanied by moral disaster or the oblivion of the soul. In the same essay, he writes:

> Progress and development are ideals not likely to be rejected, but they lose all meaning if man only arrives at his new state as a fragment of himself, having left his essential hinterland behind him in the shadow of the unconscious, in a state of primitivity or, indeed, barbarism. The conscious mind, split off from its origins, incapable of realizing the meaning of the new state, then relapses all too easily into a situation far worse than the one from which the innovation was intended to free it—*exempla sunt odiosa!*[8]

Jung's ideas are complex. He is not a systematic philosopher who moves step by step toward a final conclusion, and one has the sense that even his most basic ideas—concerning ego and archetype, the collective unconscious, etc.—are only provisional perspectives which would be revised at any point if a stronger hypothesis could be found. But he is a powerful thinker; he is oriented toward spirituality, the sacred, and the *psyche* in its original sense as the soul; and he is opposed to the reductive framework of instrumental reason which impoverishes life.

In this chapter, I will look at one of Jung's most controversial works—the *Answer to Job* (published in 1952). This book offers an important critique of religion and modern life; it raises profound questions concerning the problem of evil and the nature of God; and it helps to illustrate Jung's own ideas about the nature of the sacred, archetypes, and symbols, and the theory of individuation. The last of these is especially important: According to Jung, individuation is a fundamental psychic process through which we can achieve wholeness or the spiritual goal of life. For Jung, individuation is a spiritual ideal, and it describes the way in which we can become ourselves.

The answer to Job and other biblical questions

True believers can read the Bible as the revealed word of God, and spiritual seekers can think of the Bible as a wisdom text or part of the perennial tradition that includes the *Daodeching*, the *Bhagavad Gita*, and other works that seem to speak to all people. Others simply disregard the Bible as arcane and irrelevant; for in modern secular society, religion has no privileged standing and everything must be judged in terms of its reasonableness or use value. Jung himself was ambivalent about the existence of God, and though he came from a long line of protestant pastors he complained of his father's narrow views about faith. For Jung, the reality of God and religion cannot be kept separate from everyday life, and it would be a mistake to think of God as a purely transcendent being, since the truth of the God image is kept deep within the soul. We cannot prove the existence of God, and religion is by definition beyond all factual demonstrations, but "God" exists as a psychical fact or a numinous image which corresponds to the archetype of the "Self" or the sense of wholeness. As Jung argues at the beginning of the *Answer to Job*:

> We do not know how clear or unclear these images, metaphors, and concepts are in respect of their transcendental object. If, for instance, we say "God," we give expression to an image or a verbal concept which has undergone many changes in the course of time. We are, however, unable to say with any degree of certainty—unless it be by faith—whether these changes affect only the images and concepts, or the Unspeakable itself.[9]

According to Jung, we are always oriented toward the sacred, even if we consciously reject it. And though we live in a secular society, we may still suffer from spiritual repression and the loss of the sacred, which was formerly expressed by religion.

For Jung, Christianity is endangered, like other religions, because it usually insists upon the *literal* truth of its doctrines from the Creation, to the Incarnation, the Resurrection, and the Assumption to name but some among many. But this is at odds with the modern scientific viewpoint and the established facts of nature, so that such a religion can only survive as a pure avowal of faith. Jung holds a metaphorical view, and he argues that traditional religions, like earlier mythologies, reflect the deepest aspects of the soul and the world. But faith is in decline now and we need to look at religion as a set of symbolic truths that give us access to the sacred. This is what Jung sets out to accomplish in his *Answer to Job*—for by showing how biblical stories can still illuminate our lives he is *dreaming the myth forward* and making those stories more relevant for our own time.[10]

From the outset, Jung appeals to the reader's good will and the principle of charity. For, "The book does not pretend to be anything but the voice or question of a single individual who hopes or expects to meet with thoughtfulness in the public."[11] As Jung predicted, however, many readers rejected his book as blasphemous, and they condemned his arrogance in going against centuries of the Church's teachings on important Biblical themes. But Jung argues that a religion can never be fixed or complete, and he says it would undermine the essence of a living religion if we claimed, dogmatically, that we can ignore any future revelations as well as any new interpretations that differ from those that have prevailed up to this point.

Now of course, any religion can become a sterile set of teachings or a collection of fixed dogmas which are accepted but not really understood, for as long as they are not incorporated at a deeper level into one's life. According to Jung, Christianity has already suffered such a fate, for it has become encrusted with fixed ideas and assumptions that undermine the living spirit of religion and its power to transform us. In *Answer to Job*, Jung wants to challenge some of the most important dogmas and received ideas of Christianity, and he has a personal agenda: He lays out some of the reasons why he can no longer subscribe to the faith of his fathers; he tells us elsewhere how he wrote this book in a single burst of creative energy; and he says that while he would want to rewrite most of his books, *Answer to Job* is the one text that he would leave "just as it stands."[12] His overall strategy is to release the hidden power of the sacred, by wiping away the sediment of tradition and authority that prevents us from experiencing the Biblical text in a more direct and immediate way. In this respect, his ultimate goal is the re-enchantment of the world through the recovery of the spiritual dimension in religion, as well as in nature, art, love, and other kinds of human experience. In what follows, I focus on three separate episodes that Jung discusses: the story of Job and the problem of evil; the incarnation and the Holy Spirit; and the role of Mary, the mother of God. If Jung is right then these ideas and stories are related to each other, and they form part of a greater narrative that challenges traditional interpretations by making connections which others have been unable to see.

To begin with, we can look at Jung's interpretation of the story of Job. This is a story that has always troubled people because the protagonist, Job, is most unfairly treated by God, and there really is no satisfactory resolution. Job is a good man; at the start of the story, he is devout, prosperous, and happy, but then

Satan comes up with a plan to test the depth of his righteousness by making him suffer the worst kind of emotional and physical anguish. The really bad thing is that God agrees to the test. As Jung points out, in this very early book of the Bible, Yahweh and Satan seem to be close companions—in fact they are like father and son; and even though he is held to be omniscient, Yahweh reacts very testily to the suggestion that Job might be unfaithful. As Jung comments:

> Why, then, is the experiment made at all, and a bet with the unscrupulous slanderer settled, without a stake, on the back of a powerless creature? It is indeed no edifying spectacle to see how quickly Yahweh abandons his faithful servant to the evil spirit and lets him fall without compunction or pity into the abyss of physical and moral suffering.[13]

Clearly, something is going on here, but what?

Job acquits himself well. In spite of the protestations of his so-called friends, he knows that he has not done anything wrong, and he pleads to have his day in court with God. As Jung says, the only thing he can be blamed for is his incurable optimism in thinking that he could appeal to divine justice. At the outset, he is preoccupied with his own misery, but as Levinas points out in his own essay on Job, once he starts to reflect on things he comes to realize that for many people—the poor, widows, and orphans—life really is about suffering, and so he begins to learn compassion for others, and this takes him out of his own self-involvement.[14] In the course of the story, Job becomes a better person, whereas God, when he finally responds as "the voice in the whirlwind," seems petulant and spiteful. For a long time, he roars his disapproval of Job and celebrates his own power in creating the world. But even though he is supposed to be just, he seems unconcerned about Job's tribulations, although eventually he restores Job's fortunes. As Jung points out, at a certain point Job realizes that he is not going to get divine justice; and so, with considerable dignity, he accepts God's inconsistency and the reality that God is not a responsible being but a force of nature that one could never trust to be constant or true. In fact, "the paragon of all creation is not a man but a monster!"[15]

In this way, Jung argues that Job achieves a moral triumph over Yahweh, for in spite of Yahweh's blustering and intimidation, and the pointless ordeal that he imposes upon him, Job stands firm, remaining true to himself, and devoted to justice more than ever. At some level, Yahweh realizes this, and he is afraid: "He is afraid of it, for only in face of something frightening does one let off a cannonade of references to one's power, cleverness, courage, invincibility, etc. What has all that to do with Job? Is it worth the lion's while to terrify a mouse?"[16]

Jung catches the psychological nuances here and elsewhere in the story. Why does Yahweh agree to the test to begin with? Why is he angry with Job, who seems to pass this terrible test of faithfulness, and why isn't he angry with Satan who has manipulated him and egged him on to do some fairly awful things? In other parts of the Old Testament, Yahweh rages against mankind, he threatens to destroy them, and sometimes he carries out his threats. He demands that Abraham prove his loyalty by sacrificing his own son, and he is not always reliable or even particularly good. But now that he realizes his limitation through Job, he determines that he will suffer incarnation as a human being. Not because men have sinned, and someone has to pay the price for this; but because he was wrong to punish Job for no good reason, and the incarnation is God's atonement for his own crimes against human beings.

Once again, Jung recognizes the obvious blasphemy here. But he also sees the offensiveness of the traditional story which describes God's motivation in sending his only son—or himself—as a human being to live and suffer among humankind. According to the traditional story, we have sinned so much that we can never repay the debt that we have incurred, and so God in his mercy has to send his only begotten son to pay the price of our sins by dying on the cross. Like Nietzsche in *On the Genealogy of Morals*, Jung objects to the obvious cruelty of the traditional view, which reaffirms the Old Testament image of God as a somewhat sadistic being who demands payment while refusing to consider forgiveness even if it means the death of his own son.[17] As Jung explains:

> On this view, a wrong is imputed to God … if one assumes that it was necessary to torture the son to death on the Cross merely in order to appease the father's wrath. What kind of a father is it who would rather his son were slaughtered than forgive his ill-advised creatures who have been corrupted by his precious Satan?[18]

When it is framed in this way, it is difficult to affirm the necessity of our redemption; and I think Jung is right to ask questions, even though this is a focal point of Christian faith.

How then are we to understand the Incarnation? For Jung, the Old Testament Yahweh is a bundle of different qualities—justice, omnipotence, and omniscience, and also unfaithfulness, anger, and unconcern. But he is becoming more aware of the inconsistencies in his own nature. Other humans, like Job, are morally superior to him, and so "he has to catch up and become human himself."[19] But now, in the person of Jesus Christ, God separates himself from his bad qualities to become the very image of moral perfection. In this way, he will serve humankind as a loving guide, and his atonement for his earlier treatment of Job and other human beings will end with a sacrificial death. As Jung points out, there is a certain logic to all of this: "It is ... as if Job and Yahweh were combined in a single personality. Yahweh's intention to become man, which resulted from his collision with Job, is fulfilled in Christ's life and suffering."[20]

At the same time, Jung notes that there are several points in the New Testament narrative where Christ becomes irascible and upset, and this suggests that the underlying personality of Yahweh is still present, even if for the most part it has been surpassed and replaced by God's new image as the *Summum Bonum*. Christ is absolute goodness; but as Rudolf Otto argues in his classic work on *The Idea of the Holy*, we lose much of the power of the sacred when it is reduced to the power of the good.[21] For Otto, the bottom line of religion is the experience of the *mysterium tremendum* which is both attractive and repellent at the same time; it is a reassuring experience, he says, but it is also quite terrifying, and it calls our whole being into question. It is linked to the good, but it cannot just be limited to the good because it has a dark side as well. With the Incarnation, however, Yahweh seems to cast off his dark side or his "shadow." But in the end, this aspect is bound to reassert itself, because it has been repressed, although it is lying low for now.

On this point, Jung refers forward to the *Book of Revelation*, where the Lamb of God, formerly so meek and so mild, becomes a monstrous horned animal who opens the Seven Seals, thereby unleashing the four horsemen of the Apocalypse and every other kind of cosmic catastrophe upon the world.

> His Christ-image, clouded by negative feelings, has turned into a savage avenger who no longer bears any real resemblance to a savior ... The grotesque paradox of the wrathful lamb should have been enough to arouse our suspicions in this respect. We can turn and twist it as we like, but, seen in the light of the gospel of love, the avenger and judge remains a most sinister figure.[22]

The point here is that the Incarnation was not ultimately successful. And we should not strive to be perfect because perfection is a false ideal that leads to one-sidedness and the absence of wholeness. As Jung points out, whatever we refuse to deal with or push away from ourselves will only re-establish itself at a deeper level: "But in the unconscious is everything that has been rejected by consciousness, and the more Christian one's consciousness is, the more heathenishly does the unconscious behave, if in the rejected heathenism there are values which are important for life—if that is to say, the baby has been thrown out with the bath water, as so often happens."[23] Here, Jung may have in mind St.

John (who according to tradition wrote the gospel of love as well as the Book of Revelation), St. Paul ("if thine eye offend thee pluck it out"), and the early church fathers, including St. Augustine and others who preached the sinfulness of sex and the need to practice an austere asceticism. This is also the flip side of the gospel of love with the hatred of our human limitations and the *need* to feel imperfect or broken.

This point is worth developing: In Christianity, perfection is the usual goal and we are told to live in imitation of Jesus Christ. But we are not perfect, and so we repress whatever we do not want to accept about ourselves, and we live our lives with a strong sense of our own inadequacy because we can never measure up to the ideal of perfection. Perfection is one-sided and incomplete, but Jung argues that *wholeness* is a much more relevant ideal. Certainly, it requires reflection and self-understanding, for it involves living a life that unifies all the different aspects of who we are—spiritual, physical, emotional, male and female, etc. Completeness may always be "imperfect" in some respects, but as Jung observes, perfection is always incomplete "and therefore represents a final state which is hopelessly sterile."[24] And again: "No path leads beyond perfection into the future—there is only a turning back, a collapse of the ideal, which could easily have been avoided by paying attention to the feminine ideal of completeness."[25] In his own work, David Tacey argues that this is an important distinction which helps us to understand the appeal of contemporary spiritual movements: For if *religion* seeks an approximation to perfection and celebrates such an ideal, then *spirituality* is more about living a balanced and complete life, in which one establishes a relationship to ultimate reality and meaning.[26]

In this respect, Jung's solution is to look for the possibility of a new incarnation that would transcend or complete the earlier two stages of God's assertiveness and his perfection. But he does not affirm this in opposition to the Bible's teaching, and he notes that even before the crucifixion Christ himself promises his disciples that he will send them another comforter or an "advocate." This is the Holy Spirit, or the Paraclete, who is the third aspect of the Trinity. As Jung writes: "The future indwelling of the Holy Ghost in man amounts to a continuing incarnation of God. Christ, as the begotten son of God and pre-existing mediator, is a first-born and a divine paradigm which will be followed by further incarnations of the Holy Ghost in the empirical man."[27] One of the problems with the original Incarnation is that Christ is not completely human—even though he died on the cross, he was born without sin, and he was the product of a union between God and the exceptional Mary, who was also born without sin. But now, the Holy Spirit is to enter human beings with all their raw humanity, their virtues and their vices, their minds and their bodies, so that through the Holy Spirit we may achieve the final integration of all our human qualities, including the shadow side of our nature which is usually disowned or projected on to others. Jung quotes from the Gospel of John where Christ says, significantly: "He who believes in me, will also do the works that I do; and greater works than these will he do."[28] This suggests that the divine principle can enter into all of us, which means the original incarnation was not a unique and exceptional event. It continually renews itself, and there is always the possibility of a *further* revelation, which shows the unfolding of Christianity as a living religion as opposed to a set of teachings that are fixed once and for all time.

So in the end God becomes man and man discovers God within himself. Clodagh Weldon observes that to some extent Jung is looking at Biblical stories through the lens of his own psychotherapy.[29] For in his *Answer to Job*, he moves from Yahweh (as the unconscious life) to Christ (as conscious self-assertion, or ego) to the Holy Spirit (which corresponds to integration). For anyone familiar with Jung's theory, this whole movement involving the three persons of God is an example of what he refers to as "individuation." Individuation is a process involving self-understanding and the experience of personal growth, and it is the way in which we integrate all the different aspects of ourselves to become a whole human being. It is an important idea in Jung's psychoanalytical theory, and we will return to it later. Perhaps it will be said that Jung imposes this framework on a text which is basically foreign to it. But insofar as it illuminates the text and makes sense of some difficult passages—such as God's treatment of Job or sending his own son to suffer an agonizing death instead of simply forgiving us—I think it builds support for the credibility of his own theoretical position and the framework that he uses.

In the *Answer to Job*, Jung spends some time trying to recover a hidden feminine tradition which is there in the Bible, although it is seldom the focus of our critical attention. In Proverbs, for example, Yahweh has Sophia, who is the feminine personification of wisdom and a part of the divine personality taken separately from the unity of God. Sophia was with God at the creation of the world: "When he marked out the foundation of the earth, then I was by him, like a master workman, and I was daily his delight."[30] She gives him advice and leads him on to self-reflection. Later, Israel is explicitly referred to as Yahweh's "bride."[31] And Jung refers us to many references in the Bible and the Apocrypha in which a feminine principle is hypostasized as a part of the divine. Not surprisingly, however, Jung is most interested in the depiction of the Virgin

Mary, and he is encouraged by the doctrine of the Assumption which the Pope had recently proclaimed—in 1950—as one of the Catholic articles of faith.

Jung argues that for the most part, Christianity is lacking a strong feminine archetype that would appeal to our spiritual need. Christianity is a patriarchal religion, but there are tantalizing glimpses of the feminine—in Sophia, in Lilith, the woman who apparently precedes Eve as Adam's wife, and especially in Mary who becomes the mother of God. The problem is that Mary is no ordinary woman: She was held to be a virgin, in spite of being Christ's mother; according to the doctrine of Immaculate Conception she was born without sin; and according to the Assumption, she was taken up into heaven immediately after her death. Mary does not have to wait for the resurrection, but goes immediately to the heavenly court where she intercedes for all human beings. In this regard, the Pope's proclamation is just the final acknowledgment of a popular understanding:

> One could have known for a long time that there was a deep longing in the masses for an intercessor and mediatrix who would at last take her place alongside the Holy Trinity and be received as the "Queen of Heaven and Bride at the heavenly court." For more than a thousand years it has been taken for granted that the Mother of God dwelt there, and we know from the Old Testament that Sophia was with God before the creation.[32]

From the perspective of symbol and archetype, if not from the official perspective of theology, Mary becomes God, or Goddess, and for Jung this is not just the birth of a new god, but "the continuing incarnation of God which began with Christ."[33] In this way, the divine principle of the feminine is acknowledged, and given a place of honor, which may correspond to our own intuition concerning such things. Today, we are more likely to see the divine feminine in nature, and this is what inspires so much of our concern and devotion to the natural world. We are finally beginning to understand that nature is not just a resource to be used selfishly, and concern for the environment—with pollution, species preservation and overdevelopment, etc.—follows from cherishing nature as a loving parent who cares for us. So even if God created nature, *she* is now revered as the good mother who gives us her bounty and provides us with our home, and when she—the Goddess—is threatened by ecological catastrophe, or abuse, it sparks a sense of outrage.

Once again, there is a more general point here concerning the dangers of repression: Freud always dwelled on the problems associated with sexual repression, but for Jung there are other kinds of repression that we also need to be mindful of. Christianity and Western culture in general have suffered from the repression of the feminine, and this supports the view that contemporary religions are one-sided. This means that women cannot always recognize themselves in the images and symbols of the divine, and any religion can become a masculine preserve. In writing about the doctrine of the Assumption, for example, Jung celebrates the recent papal declaration. But then he adds, "It leaves Protestantism with the odium of being nothing but a *man's religion* which allows no metaphysical representation of women."[34] Other things that have been repressed in Western culture include *the body*—or the physical as opposed to the spiritual; *nature*, which has always been treated as an object to be dominated and controlled; and *evil*, or any negative aspects of ourselves or our culture that we just do not want to deal with. Jung saw the real danger associated with *spiritual* repression. When we live in a secular society, everything that is real has to be measureable, and materialist explanations are often the only ones that are acceptable. Religion is in decline because it is heavy with received ideas and dogmas, and established paths which its adherents are supposed to follow. In such a situation, spirituality is repressed; we are drawn into addiction and other kinds of avoidance, and it becomes difficult to pursue an authentic spiritual life.

Responses to Jung

When Jung's book first appeared it was subject to a lot of criticism and some devastating reviews. Many religious supporters and defenders of the faith were upset by Jung's work because it seemed to make a mockery of traditional religious ideas—including, most scandalously, the goodness of God—by reworking Biblical narratives along the lines of Jungian psychology. Most well known here is the review by Father Victor White, who had been one of Jung's close correspondents, but White broke with him over this book.[35] Focusing on the dark side of God was bad enough, but calling for new incarnations of God beyond Jesus Christ was a final blasphemy that could never be accepted. White had always hoped that Jungian psychology would offer a new path to the transcendent, and it is possible that Jung's general position could have encouraged such a reading.

At the end of *Answer to Job*, for example, Jung seems to equate the reality of God with the archetype of wholeness. He never affirms that the one really is the same as the other, but given the limitations of human understanding—as laid down by Kant, for example—it seems that we can never know ultimate reality which must forever remain transcendent to human experience. But the figure of God is also inside of us, and according to Jung it corresponds to the archetype of the Self, which is the higher reality that encompasses the ego, the unconscious, and all the determinations of psychical life. And like all archetypes it is experienced as a separate being that is "split off" inside of us with an energy of its own:

> Strictly speaking, the God-image does not coincide with the unconscious as such, but with a special content of it, namely the archetype of the self. It is this archetype from which we can no longer distinguish the God-image empirically ... Faith is certainly right when it impresses on man's mind and heart how infinitely far away and inaccessible God is; but it also teaches his nearness which has to be empirically real if it is not to lose all significance. Only that which acts upon me do I recognize as real and actual. But that which has no effect on me might as well not exist. The religious need longs for wholeness, and therefore lays hold of the images of wholeness offered by the unconscious, which, independently of the conscious mind, rise up from the depths of our conscious nature.[36]

But this is much too problematic for the traditional believer like Father White, who wrote, with some ambivalence, that:

> a Christian reader should hear, beneath all the provocation, behind the seeming mockery of all he holds most sacred and most dear, a profoundly moving cry of anguish, a reproachful sign of distress. But he should also observe that, destructive and childish as much of this book seems to be, its aims are eminently constructive, and that its challenge to ourselves and our contemporaries is imperative and urgent.[37]

It is clear that White was torn between the strength of his own traditional faith and the compelling force of Jung's psychological critique which he could not simply reject out of hand. The result is a review in which his personal anguish is evident.

In the *Answer to Job*, Jung is not opposed to religion and the power of the sacred to inspire and enhance our lives. But he seems to be taking on all of those theologians who believe that religion is reasonable and that Christianity is just a matter of common sense. And if we accept this standard of reasonableness, then we may have to allow that Jung offers an original and compelling new interpretation of the Bible, which has never received anything like a convincing or a reasonable response. The final point is more speculative and pertains to faith: If religion and spirituality are truly living forces, then it makes sense to think of the Incarnation as something that is still at work in the world—and as we have seen, there is scriptural support for such a claim. Jung argues that if God and the sacred are regarded as wholly transcendent, then they can never have any relevance for living human beings. This is because, in the language of Kant, we cannot know the noumenon and we are limited to appearances. Even so, Jung claims that God or the God image can be experienced from within. For apart from the ego there is the (Jungian) Self, which is the Oneness of our being, and this may or may not be equivalent to what we call "God." Jung comments: "We cannot tell whether God and the unconscious are two different entities. Both are border-line concepts for transcendental concerns."[38]

What I think this means is that we can *experience* the divine but we can never completely know it because we can only *know* things in relation to the categories that we project onto the world. Within this context, however, Jung is making the important point that "incarnation," "enlightenment," or whatever we choose to call it is something that can happen repeatedly. In Christianity this is achieved through the working of the Holy Spirit, for "the indwelling of the Holy Ghost, the third Divine Person, in man, brings about a Christification of many."[39] But at the same time, as Jung goes on to clarify at the end of his book: "That is to say, even the enlightened person remains what he is, and is never more than his own limited ego before the One who dwells within him, whose form has no knowable boundaries, who encompasses him on all sides, fathomless as the abysms of the earth and vast as the sky."[40] Here, the point is that there are always reasons to be grateful; spiritual and religious life will continue because there is no *final* revelation; and in this way, the image of the Divine is refined and enhanced through an unfolding process which corresponds to "individuation" in the life of a human being. And God, the sacred, the Absolute, or Ultimate Reality can be experienced from within.

Individuation

In his essay on "The Relations between the Ego and the Unconscious," Jung defines the concept of individuation in the following way: "Individuation means becoming an 'in-dividual', and, in so far as 'individuality' embraces our innermost, last, and incomparable uniqueness, it also implies becoming one's own self. We could therefore translate individuation as 'coming to selfhood' or 'self-realization.'"[41] Now on the face of it, this may suggest a kind of narcissism or self-involvement to the exclusion of collective goals, but Jung is at pains to distinguish individuation from individualism, and he points out, quite reasonably, that our "social performance" actually depends upon the fulfillment of our personal nature. Elsewhere, he comments: "As the individual is not just a single, separate being, but by his very existence presupposes a collective relationship, it follows that the process of individuation must lead to more intense and broader collective relationships and not to isolation."[42] Jung's account may suggest an uncritical doctrine of authenticity in which the true self is discovered underneath "the false wrappings of the persona" and separated from the suggestive power of primordial images. But individuation is an active process in which the individual emerges more fully into the light of day, and this is both a matter of creation and a process of discovery, along the lines of the artist who produces a work of art—although in this case the work of art is the life itself. The end result is an individual who is no longer self-absorbed, but enlarged and enhanced through his or her relationship to the underlying and "superordinate" Self, which includes both the personal and the collective unconscious:

> In this way there arises a consciousness which is no longer imprisoned in the petty, oversensitive, personal world of the ego, but participates freely in the wider world of objective interests. This widened consciousness is no longer that touchy, egotistical bundle, of personal wishes, fears, hopes, and ambitions which always has to be compensated or corrected by unconscious counter-tendencies; instead, it is a function of relationship to the world of objects, bringing the individual into absolute, binding, and indissoluble communion with the world at large.[43]

And this would be the achievement of individuation.

Individuation is one of the keys to Jung's work. And it derives from the insight that our psychical life is inherently purposeful in nature. Of course, the ego may resist because it does not see the big picture, and it is comfortable with how things are. But the Self, which is the center of our whole being, registers the need for a change at decisive times in our life, and this impulse comes from within; it is not simply a response to external events:

> On the contrary, there is a host of experiences which seem to prove that the unconscious is not only spontaneous but can actually take the lead. There are innumerable cases of people who lingered on in a pettifogging unconsciousness, only to become neurotic in the end. Thanks to the neurosis contrived by the unconscious, they are shaken out of their apathy, and this in spite of their own laziness and often desperate resistance.[44]

For example, I may dream about death when it is really time to make some changes in my life, and I may lose interest in other things that I had formerly viewed as important. And this initiates the process of individuation in which we come to grips with our one-sidedness and recover our sense of wholeness.

In his lectures on religion and psychology, Jung gives the example of one of his patients, an older man, and a scientist, who became convinced that he was dying of cancer and maintained this belief, even though every test showed that he was perfectly well. Jung came to believe that the man's phobia and his neurosis were a message from his deeper Self or psyche that his own conscious ego could not at first accept. Up until that time, the man had lived a completely rational and well-ordered life, but this one-sided existence had become a kind of spiritual death. As Jung puts it, "He has forced everything under the inexorable law of his reason, but somewhere nature escaped and came back with a vengeance in the form of an unassailable bit of nonsense, the cancer idea."[45] So while he was successful in worldly terms, he could not go on living this way because he was cut off from spiritual life, and healing would only be possible if the man accepted the message that he was being given and changed his life accordingly:

> What, then, shall we say to our patient with the imaginary cancer? I would tell him: "Yes, my friend, you are really suffering from a cancer-like thing, you really do harbor in yourself a deadly evil. However, it will not kill your body, because it is imaginary. But it will eventually kill your soul. It has already spoilt and even poisoned your human relations and your personal happiness and it will go on growing until it has swallowed your whole psychic existence. So that in the end you will not be a human being any more, but an evil destructive tumour."[46]

The symptom of cancer phobia was not in itself a sickness because it was warning him of a deeper problem that he had to deal with at once. In effect, it was saying to him, "You must change your life!" And even though he resisted at first, he eventually came to realize the superior wisdom of the unconscious. The case suggests that it is entirely possible to become mentally or physically ill because of a lack of meaning or an impoverished spiritual life.

In this example, the man's cancer phobia initiates the process of individuation by moving the individual away from his one-sidedness and toward wholeness. There are other cases where Jung describes the importance of dreams for bringing people to this significant turning point; and in literature, a well-known example of a different sort appears in Tolstoy's story, *The Death of Ivan Ilych*: Ivan Ilych was a civil servant who lived a completely dull and routine existence devoted to his official duties and the social round. But he was finally shaken out of this wretched contentment once it became unavoidably clear to him that he was going to die soon, even though, as he continually insisted, he had not done anything wrong. At the end of his life, Ivan finally came to terms with his own "unlived life" and made some amends. As Jung understood, and as Tolstoy's story seems to confirm, the psyche is inherently purposive and oriented toward spiritual life and meaning. It is not just a passive register of memories and desires, because it actively shapes and compensates the conscious ego—in dreams, symptoms, and forebodings—and it draws us on toward psychic balance and wholeness.

Jung came to realize that the process of individuation may happen whether we want it to or not, because we naturally change and evolve over the course of a lifetime, especially in the second half of our lives when we are no longer so ego directed. Perhaps at this point we have made our mark on the world and explored the limits of self-assertion, and we are drawn to the greater reality of which the ego is only a part. Now, we can take hold of the individuation process in a more deliberate and mindful way, through "critical understanding," which involves a dialogue between the conscious ego and the unconscious to interpret the wisdom of the deeper Self. And this includes whatever is given to us in symptoms or in dreams, which the conscious self can *amplify* and make sense of.

In the light of Jung's argument in the *Answer to Job*, it would seem that individuation is related to the archetype of God or wholeness in the collective unconscious, so that individuation may actually be the divine part of human life and a source of our cosmic significance. As we have already noted, Jung comments toward the end of his book that "the indwelling of the Holy Ghost, the third Divine Person, in man brings about a Christification of many."[47] But this does not mean that we can all become gods, for Jung thinks that individuation is actually quite rare; and, at the same time, "even the enlightened person remains what he is, and is never more than his own limited ego before the one who dwells within him, whose form has no knowable boundaries, who encompasses him on all sides."[48] However, this suggests that the divine and the human are intermingled, and that God, the sacred, the Absolute, or ultimate reality and meaning can be experienced within an individual life through the process of individuation, in which we recreate ourselves as balanced and complete human beings.

Jung is a spiritual thinker who takes religion seriously, and he contemplates a return to the sacred and the archetypal forces of life. In his *Answer to Job* he describes the unfolding of God's nature as this is described in the Bible, and he dwells particularly on the story of Job and the Incarnation. In Christ's account of the Holy Spirit he sees the possibility of new incarnations, for it seems that the divine is not only outside of us, but it can also become a part of who we are. I have argued in this chapter that for Jung, God's self-unfolding corresponds to what he describes elsewhere as the process of individuation, for in each case the goal is one of wholeness and the fulfillment of our own unique being. In this respect, individuation can be viewed as a spiritual activity in which we cultivate the divine within ourselves and so we may continue the process of the incarnation.

Today, Jung is often ignored by scholars in the academy, and he does not appear to have a place in psychology, philosophy, or religious studies. Jung emerged from the psychoanalytical movement, and in many ways his emphasis on spirituality is a direct response to Freud's biological reductionism and the elevation of libido. But now his work seems to be at odds with modern science and contemporary postmodernism which emphasizes our fragmented nature and the absence of grand narratives that could make sense of our collective human experience. Even so, Jung is an audacious thinker who knows science, medicine, ancient and medieval alchemy, non-Western religion, Christianity, and philosophy in depth. In the end, he remains one of the most important spiritual philosophers of the modern age. His work will endure, and he will continue to inspire us at the deepest spiritual level.

6

Hillman on Spirit and Soul

Spirituality is difficult to articulate, and it may be held that any attempt to put it into words must be a kind of falsification. This is because spiritual experience seems to transcend our rational concepts, and spiritual reality appears to be discontinuous with ordinary life. Also, there are no objective measures of spirituality, and because some people believe that whatever cannot be measured does not exist, they conclude that there is no spiritual truth—which is to say that everything about spirituality is purely subjective or emotional. With the decline of religion and the rise of reductive scientific views, traditional ideas about spirituality are increasingly being challenged. In fact, the very possibility of spirituality is under threat, and so we need new perspectives on spiritual life that would make sense to us, especially if our goal is to recover a sense of the sacred.

In this chapter, I will review some of the received ideas about spirituality, including "spirit," "soul," and "self-overcoming," and I will focus my discussion on James Hillman, a post-Jungian thinker and a psychoanalyst, whose work is provocative but also extremely helpful for thinking things through. Hillman is critical of the traditional standpoint on spirituality, but at the same time he affirms the reality of spiritual experience, and he provides an engaging perspective on the elements of spiritual life. This is important, for with the rise of consumer culture, and the refusal to take spiritual life seriously, it seems that we are suffering from the absence of the sacred—and this has diminished our experience and disenchanted the reality of the world. Hence, it becomes necessary to re-vision the basic categories of spiritual life just to see if spirituality is still relevant and viable. In what follows, I will not presuppose a specific definition of spirituality; and in the spirit of Jung, I will pursue an immanent as opposed to a transcendent perspective which allows for the possibility of living a spiritual life, regardless of one's beliefs about God or the nature of ultimate reality. The work of James Hillman is of particular interest here, insofar as he offers an explicit reading of spirit, soul, and self-overcoming from an immanent phenomenological standpoint. To a great extent, spirituality and religion overlap, but the growing number of people who identify as "spiritual but not religious" illuminates some of the shortcomings of organized religion, as well as the limitations of traditional secularism as a philosophy to live by. It also reflects the emergence of a "post-secular" culture in which spirituality can be taken seriously for its own sake and not just as an adjunct to religion. From this, it follows that spirituality can be viewed as a unique form of experience.

Before turning explicitly to Hillman, however, I want to look at three basic themes that are traditionally associated with spirituality: First, there is the idea found in many different wisdom traditions that spiritual life begins with the death of the ego; for this is what allows us to escape from the narrow horizons of our own selfish existence and to participate in the greater reality that we belong to. In Christianity, we are supposed to abandon our own selfish will and follow the will of God. In Buddhism, we are taught to reject the idea of the self as a separate self-contained being and cultivate compassion which involves a sense of the interconnectedness of all beings. In Hinduism, the ego is an illusion; it is just a dream that we can awaken from, while the underlying Self, or Atman, is one with Brahman which is the ultimate unconditioned reality. Here, then, in all of these different wisdom traditions, the underlying view is that we cannot make any spiritual progress unless we can overcome the selfish ego which prioritizes its own particular goals and ambitions, for this ego makes it so much harder to connect with the greater reality that we all belong to. More examples could be given—Stoicism or Daoism, etc.—but the basic point is that spiritual life presupposes self-overcoming.

The second idea is that spirituality involves an escape from ordinary values such as power, money, and personal success, and a focus on more ultimate concerns, such as living a meaningful life or apprehending the truth of ultimate reality. In Plato's story of the Cave, which illustrates the human condition, the prisoners are chained to a bench and completely preoccupied by the shadows in front of them on the cave wall. This suggests that we are slaves to all the received ideas and prejudices that we have inherited from our culture; although if we can make our way out of the Cave, we will experience enlightenment and connection to the highest good.[1] According to legend, the Buddha spent the first part of his life as a prince in a great palace. He enjoyed his life, but one day he went out and encountered a sick man, an old man, and a dead man, and for the first time he realized the problem of suffering that he had avoided up to that point. He could have returned to the palace and lived comfortably for the rest of his life, but instead he became a spiritual seeker who sought answers to some basic questions: How should I live? Does suffering undermine the value of life? And how can we achieve nonattachment? In this way, it is possible to escape the spiritual oblivion that characterizes much of our lives.

The third idea about spirituality is related to the other two, and it says that spirituality is to be understood as a kind of quest or a journey which goes from the lowest realm up to the highest level of being. Thus, as we have noted, Plato's story of the Cave epitomizes spiritual life. We live in a cave, and we are fixated on shadows. But it is possible to free ourselves from received ideas and to make our way upward toward the light of the Good, or absolute being. As we will see, this ascent toward the truth is frequently repeated in other spiritual narratives, including St. Augustine's account of his heavenly vision at Ostia, and this is felt as a peak experience which signifies our escape from history, the world, and our ordinary self.

In this chapter I will question each of these spiritual ideas—the necessity of self-overcoming, the rejection of everyday goals and concerns, and the ascent toward the *higher* realms of being. I do not want to reject spirituality itself or the value of a spiritual life; but through Hillman we need to re-examine some of our fixed ideas concerning spirituality, and especially significant themes like "spirit," "soul," and "self-overcoming" which shape so much of our thinking about the nature of spiritual life.

Nietzsche, Jung, and Hillman

To begin with, we can consider two kinds of criticism that can be made against spirituality. The first kind of critique would involve looking at spirituality from a political or an economic perspective, while the second kind of criticism would involve thinking about the internal coherence of spirituality when this is measured against its own inherent ideal. Of course, both kinds of criticism can be valid, but in this chapter my focus is on the second type of criticism which explores spirituality as an authentic field that we have neglected or misunderstood. But first, we can consider the external critique that examines spirituality from a more skeptical standpoint.

To a great extent, our everyday life is shaped by the categories of politics and economics, but there appears to be a significant conflict between the "spiritual" and the political realms. As we have noted, spirituality seems to involve self-cultivation and enhancement which leads us away from the cave of everyday life, while politics can be understood as the "science" of the cave which tries to determine the best kind of life in the cavern that we live in. Spirituality seems oriented toward individual achievement, whereas politics requires the promotion of the community itself. Spirituality may involve the refinement of the soul and our devotion to spiritual virtues; but from such a narrow perspective, we cannot grasp the basic forms of society, including the laws and institutions that shape our social life and determine our own wellbeing.

And yet such arguments are not completely convincing, because they pose a false dilemma: Do we really have to choose between spirituality and politics? Sometimes the two are in tension with each other, but the fact is there are plenty of individuals who are both spiritually *and* politically gifted, and they use their spiritual strength to fight for social and political causes like justice and equality. In the most outstanding cases—Martin Luther King, Dorothy Day, Mahatma Gandhi or the Dalai Lama, and so on—their spiritual strength makes them the most effective leaders of the political struggles they are involved in. In fact, many movements—against poverty, and for peace, civil rights, and the good of the environment—are both spiritual and political, and the more spiritual they become the more effective they will be as they are inspired by something much deeper than personal gain or any sort of selfish fulfillment. So while spirituality may sometimes seem remote from "real world" concerns, there is plenty of overlap between spirituality and politics, and we needn't think of spirituality as a kind of escapism or as a retreat from life in general.

Similarly, we do not have to embrace the basic Marxian view that spirituality (along with religion) is the opium of the people which allows us to put up with injustice and oppression in this world. Like Marx, we may regard economic conditions as absolutely fundamental, but the fact is, not everything is reducible to economic factors, and this includes spiritual responses such as compassion, forgiveness, kindness, and love. At the same time, however, it is clear that some forms of spirituality have been appropriated and commodified by capitalism: There are expensive seminars and retreats, books, classes and tapes, and spiritual masters who charge exorbitant fees to promulgate their spiritual wisdom, and everything seems to have a price, including the spiritual wisdom that we *thought* was literally priceless. In a similar way, Slavoj Žižek argues that contemporary New Age spirituality—or what he calls Western Buddhism—is just another way of dealing with the relentless acceleration of modern life. Basically, it tells us to "go with the flow," and as such it is an "accomplice" of what it apparently disdains:

> Instead of trying to cope with the accelerating rhythm of technological progress and social changes, one should rather renounce the endeavor to retain control over what goes on, rejecting it as an expression of the modern logic of domination—one should, instead, "let oneself go," drift along, while retaining an inner distance and indifference towards the mad dance of this accelerated process, a distance based on the insight that all this social and technological upheaval is just a non-substantial proliferation of semblances which do not really concern the innermost kernel of our being.[2]

Žižek points out that such a response only furthers the agenda of global capitalism.

For the time being, we can keep this critique in mind, for it anticipates similar claims about spirituality in the absence of "soul" and the more grounded possibilities of human life. Against Žižek, however, I assume that authentic spiritual experiences are possible—including compassion, reverence, mindfulness, wonder, and a sense of the sacred or the sublime—and that not everything derives from rational self-interest. There are some things that are necessary for life, but there are other things that make life worth living. And it is a dogmatic position which rejects the validity of spiritual experience from the outset. In this chapter, I am more interested in the possibility of a spiritual critique that challenges traditional ideas *from within*—and this means questioning spiritual formulations, not to repudiate spirituality in its entirety, but in order to recover a more authentic account of spiritual life that corresponds to our experience of the world.

Several thinkers come to mind here, including Nietzsche, Jung, and especially Hillman. In *Beyond Good and Evil*, Nietzsche makes a point of calling for new versions of the soul hypothesis:

> Between ourselves it is not at all necessary to get rid of "the soul" at the same time, and thus to renounce one of the most ancient and venerable hypotheses— as happens frequently to clumsy naturalists who can hardly touch on "the soul" without immediately losing it. But the way is open for new versions and refinements of the soul-hypothesis; and such conceptions as "mortal soul," and "soul as subjective multiplicity," and "soul as social structure of the drive and affects," want henceforth to have citizens' rights in science.[3]

As we have seen, in spite of his atheism, Nietzsche is a profoundly spiritual thinker. Jung follows Nietzsche in criticizing traditional religion while affirming the power of myth and the sacred, but he is also painfully aware that the reality of the sacred is threatened by scientific materialism and its reductive point of view.

Hillman is the third thinker in this line; he contrasts conflicting ideas about "spirit" and "soul," and he strives to disentangle the one from the other. Hillman is an important thinker—and a "spiritual philosopher"—and in what follows, I will focus on his work to convey what I believe is a compelling view of spirituality. This *internal* criticism of traditional spiritual forms may enhance our understanding of spirituality by affirming aspects that have been neglected in the past. And if, as I think, a meaningful life is connected to spiritual themes, then it would be important to review basic spiritual terms such as "spirit," "soul," and "self-overcoming," and this is precisely what Hillman does. On this view, spirituality does *not* entail withdrawal from the world, but only a more profound involvement with it; and by clarifying the proper relationship between spirituality and the self, it suggests that an authentic spiritual life involves self-enhancement as opposed to self-loss, and a return to suffering in the "valley" from the "peak" of spiritual achievement and bliss.

James Hillman was a psychologist in the Jungian tradition who wrote extensively on archetypal psychology, polytheism, and the imaginal basis of consciousness.[4] He tends to be overlooked by contemporary philosophers despite being one of the most insightful of all the depth psychologists. For some years, he was the director of Studies at the Jung Institute in Zurich, and while he embraced Jung's basic views on the collective unconscious and other themes, he was also critical of Jung's ideas and can reasonably be described as a post-Jungian thinker. Jung had been concerned about the loss of meaning in modern life; he wrote some popular books, including the aptly titled *Modern Man in Search of a Soul*, and in his final work, "Approaching the Unconscious," he laments the disenchantment of the world and the decline of myth and symbols that made life meaningful in the past. Jung was a dedicated scientist, but he also distrusted the narrow formulations of science, as he searched for a deeper spiritual vision:

> As scientific understanding has grown, so our world has become dehumanised. Man feels himself isolated in the cosmos, because he is no longer involved with nature and has lost his emotional "unconscious identity" with natural phenomena. These have slowly lost their symbolic implications ... No voices now speak to man from stones, plants and animals, nor does he speak to them believing they can hear. His contact with nature has gone, and with it has gone the profound emotional energy that this symbolic connection supplied.[5]

In this respect, as we have seen in the previous chapter, Jung sought to recover the power of the sacred through the renewal of religion and myth as living forces in this world.

Like Jung, Hillman shares this general concern for the spiritual oblivion of modern life, and the need for re-enchantment through myth, poetry, art, and all the other forces of the imagination. For Hillman, so many of our problems derive from viewing the world in terms of opposites—physical/spiritual, mind/body, reason/emotion, etc.—and this has delimited our experience. Now we have the *spiritual* which is rooted in the rational, intellectual mind, and which is typically viewed as the opposite to whatever is merely physical. But in the past, the *soul* was viewed as the powerful source of creativity and imagination, inspiring the intensity of life, and this has now been lost. As Hillman puts it:

> Our distinctions are Cartesian: between outer tangible reality and inner states of mind, or between body and a fuzzy conglomerate of mind, psyche, and spirit. We have lost the third, middle position which earlier in our tradition, and in others too, was the place of the soul: a world of imagination, passion, fantasy, reflection, that is neither physical and material on the one hand, nor spiritual and abstract on the other, yet bound to them both. By having its own realm psyche has its own logic—psychology—which is neither a science of physical things nor a metaphysics of spiritual things.[6]

In this respect, as we will see, Hillman celebrates the idea of "soul-making" as the proper antidote to all that is soul-destroying in modern life. He has many important works, including *Revisioning Psychology*, *The Dream and the Underworld*, and *The Soul's Code*, but I will focus on just one outstanding paper that he published in 1975. In this paper, he looks at the difference between spirit and soul; he rejects spiritual transcendence, and he argues for the priority of the soul over the spirit.[7]

Spirit and soul

The full title of Hillman's paper is "Peaks and Vales: the Soul/Spirit Distinction as the Basis for the Differences between Psychotherapy and Spiritual Discipline." In this essay he lays out some of the most basic features of "spirit" and "soul" as we typically understand them, and he shows how spirituality has become the privileged term which affirms itself through the abandonment of the other term, which is *psyche* or soul. Hillman also offers a brief history of these two concepts in the Western (Christian) tradition, claiming that in the New Testament the increasing emphasis on *pneuma* over *psyche* is profoundly significant. As Hillman notes, *pneuma* is typically translated as spirit, while *psyche* is more usually translated as *soul*. Of course, modern translators are by no means unanimous, but for Hillman, the decided preference for *pneuma* in the New Testament represents a movement away from the soul (or *psyche*) which is the essence of our lived embodiment.[8] It is also a movement toward the disembodied spirit which is usually associated with self-consciousness or an immaterial existence.

Hillman claims that this teaching, which apparently began with St. Paul, culminated with the Fourth Council of Constantinople in 869 when the traditional trichotomy of body, soul, and spirit was officially rejected. He writes with a sense of outrage:

> What the Constantinople Council did to soul only culminated a long process beginning with Paul, the Saint, of substituting and disguising, and forever after confusing, soul with the spirit. Paul uses *psyche* only four times in his Epistles. *Psyche* appears in the entire New Testament only fifty-seven times compared with two hundred seventy-four occurrences of the word *pneuma*. Quite a score! Of these fifty-seven occurrences of the word *psyche*, more than half are in the Gospels and Acts. The Epistles, the presentation of doctrine, the teachings of the school, could expose its theology and psychology without too much need for the word soul. For Paul four times was enough.[9]

A little further on, he explains the significance of these findings:

> Because our tradition has systematically turned against the soul, we are each unaware of the distinction between soul and spirit—therefore confusing psychotherapy with spiritual disciplines, obfuscating where they conflate and where they differ. This traditional denial of soul continues within the attitudes of each of us, whether Christian or not, for we are each unconsciously affected by our culture's tradition, the unconscious aspect of our collective life.[10]

Hillman frames this discussion in terms of the difference between psychology and spirituality as two conflicting ways of dealing with all the difficulties in our lives. The spiritual approach seeks the goal of transcendence and unification beyond all the sufferings of this world, and it seems to have very little use for feelings, personal memories, and relationships which would show how grounded we are in this life. By contrast, psychology, as the study of *psyche*, requires coming to terms with every vicissitude and the anguish of our everyday existence. And so it must focus on the soul, which is connected to both the spirit *and* the body as the deepest part of who we are. This is the part of us that is drawn to meaning and love, and which seeks a connection to eternity *and* mortality. To be clear on this point, Hillman is not asserting the absolute reality of spirit or soul as objects in the world (although his discussion is relevant to those who would make such an assertion). Rather, he is proposing another way of thinking about spirituality that does justice to both the spiritual and the soulful elements of human life.

And he calls his essay "Peaks and Vales" because he wants to show that these are two significant dimensions that can be thought about separately, even if they are actually inseparable from each other, like the mountain and the valley.

Now on the face of it, both of these terms, *pneuma* and *psyche,* could be translated as "spirit" since they seem to have a similar meaning; there is also some dispute about what actually happened at the Fourth Council of Constantinople.[11] Even so, it must be allowed that there are some passages in the New Testament where St. Paul and others differentiate *pneuma* from *psyche*, and this suggests that they subscribe to the view that the spirit is the higher part of the soul, which is divine, while the soul and the body are inferior and relate to our own worldly self. In 1 Thessalonians 5:23, for example, Paul writes: "Now may the God of peace Himself sanctify you completely; and may your whole spirit [*pneuma*], soul [*psyche*], and body [*soma*] be preserved blameless at the coming of our Lord Jesus Christ."[12] This passage describes a straightforward trichotomy in which spirit, soul, and body can be distinguished from each other. Likewise, in 1 Corinthians 2:14, St. Paul comments: "But the natural [*psychikos*] man receiveth not the things of the Spirit [*Pneumatos*] of God: for they are foolishness unto him: neither can he know *them*, because they are spiritually [*pneumatikōs*] discerned." Both here, and elsewhere, as Peter Tyler notes, the person in Christ receives *pneuma* which then alters the *psyche*.[13] Finally—although there are more examples—in the Epistle of James, chapter 3, the divine wisdom from above is contrasted with *psyche* which is a lower, unspiritual form of understanding:

> But if ye have bitter envying and strife in your hearts, glory not, and lie not against the truth. This wisdom descendeth not from above, but *is* earthly, sensual [*psychikē*], devilish. For where envying and strife *is*, there *is* confusion and every evil work. But the wisdom [*Sophia*] that is from above is first pure, then peaceable, gentle, *and* easy to be intreated, full of mercy and good fruits, without partiality, and without hypocrisy.

In this respect, it can be argued that for some early Christians (including St. Paul), the spirit is viewed as the higher part of the soul or that which is furthest from physical existence. And because of this, everything that is associated with physical existence—including sickness, emotion, sex, dreams, breathing, and even diet—becomes unimportant and basically irrelevant to spiritual life. Hillman makes a strong case that we are the heirs of this tradition, and we are still suffering because of it.

Today, the words "spirit" and "soul" are more likely to be viewed as synonyms, but it is significant that there are some contexts in which we would typically say "spirit" and others where we would usually say "soul." The New Age writer

Deepak Chopra offers the following explanation from a very different spiritual standpoint:

> Often the two words are used interchangeably, but when they are differentiated, the usual distinction is that the soul is a more personalized aspect of our individuality that carries our history and tendencies through time, whereas the spirit is our pure essence that expresses our universality. Our spirit is our divine spark, without any qualification or limitation to it.[14]

This is not a stipulative definition, but an observation of how these terms are actually used. And it is significant that Chopra's New Age view seems to conform to Hillman's distinction. But while Chopra would probably be one of the targets of Žižek's earlier critique, Hillman is not susceptible to the same arguments. In fact, Hillman offers his own critique of this kind of spirituality, by turning the soul against the spirit while affirming the value of a spiritual life as a part of this life, here and now. Nothing is *proved* here one way or the other, but this is not crucial because Hillman's essay works as a polemic; it seeks to separate psychology—which should be all about *psyche*—from Christianity, Buddhism, and New Age writings that use spirituality as an escape from real life. In his essay, Hillman admits that he is "speaking with hatred and urging strife."[15] In other writings he is more sympathetic to spiritual possibilities than he appears to be here, but in "Peaks and Vales" his goal is to restore the spiritual balance by reaffirming what contemporary spirituality has tried to ignore or even dismiss.

On the one hand, then, there is the spiritual dimension which is supposed to correspond to the peaks of human experience associated with ecstasy and self-overcoming. The spirit is strong, active, solitary, and it aims for unity and transcendence. On the other hand, there is the soul dimension which corresponds to the vales or valleys and the deepest kind of experience, often associated with suffering and a profound sense of our entanglement in the world. The soul is passive and it feels things deeply, it is open to others, and it is grounded in life. And while spirit aims *high* and gives us the bliss of a peak experience, the soul is *deep* and reflects the suffering and the anguish of human life. In fact, we are sometimes afraid of *losing* our soul, and the soul, but not the spirit, is often in torment, and unable to escape from itself.

Hillman points out that in most accounts of spirituality and spiritual life, certain themes are emphasized while others are downplayed or rejected. In Plato's story of the cave, for example, there is an active striving toward the peak goal of enlightenment which represents the achievement of the individual, while the cave of everyday life is scorned as the realm of spiritual oblivion. But the

Cave story is only one among many spiritual journeys that move from darkness to light, from suffering to bliss, and from life immersed in the lower world to the peak of eternal Wisdom. There is also the spiritual experience which St. Augustine had when he was with his mother at Ostia, and which St. Augustine describes as follows:

> Our colloquy led us to the point where the pleasures of the body's senses, however intense and in however brilliant a material light enjoyed, seemed unworthy not merely of comparison but even of remembrance beside the joy of that life, and we lifted ourselves in longing yet more ardent toward that which is, and step by step traversed all bodily creatures and heaven itself, whence sun and moon and stars shed their light upon the earth. Higher still we mounted by inward thought and wondering discourse on your works, and we arrived at the summit of our minds; and this too we transcended to touch that land of never-failing plenty where you pasture Israel for ever with the food of truth. Life there is the Wisdom through whom all these things are made, and all others that have been or ever will be; but Wisdom herself is not made: she is as she always has been and will be for ever.[16]

Dante moves from the Inferno to Paradise. Petrarch ascends Mont Ventoux.[17] St. John of the Cross has his dark night of the soul and ascends Mount Carmel. In this way, spiritual life is supposed to go from multiple preoccupations (all the shadows in the cave) to a unified sense of being, inspired by the one radiant principle, which could be God, the Good, or some other form of the absolute. St. John of the Cross explains it in this way:

> He who truly arrives there
> Cuts free from himself
> All that he knew before
> Now seems worthless,
> And his knowledge so soars
> That he is left in unknowing
> Transcending all knowledge …
> And if you should want to hear:
> This highest knowledge lies
> In the loftiest sense
> Of the essence of God.[18]

Now Hillman does not discuss the example of Plato's cave, or St. Augustine, or St. John of the Cross, but in his paper he does quote from a letter, supposedly written by the Dalai Lama, to show how these ways of thinking permeate both

Western and non-Western perspectives, and this would suggest that there is a kind of spiritual imaginary that is common to different cultures. Following Hillman, I quote from the letter below. I am not convinced that it was written by the Dalai Lama, but even as a fictional account it does not negate the basic claim that much of our thinking about spirituality runs along similar lines, elevating the spirit to the peaks and leaving the soul to brood in the desolation of the valley. The letter reads, in part, as follows:

> The relation of height to spirituality is not merely metaphorical. It is physical reality. The most spiritual people on this planet live in the highest places. So do the most spiritual flowers. ... I call high and light aspects of my being *spirit* and the dark and heavy aspect *soul*.
>
> Soul is at home in the deep, shaded valleys. Heavy torpid flowers saturated with black grow there. The rivers flow like warm syrup. They empty into huge oceans of soul.
>
> Spirit is a land of high, white peaks and glittering jewel-like lakes and flowers. Life is sparse and sounds travel great distances.
>
> There is soul music, soul food, soul dancing, and soul love. ...
>
> When the soul triumphed, the herdsmen came to the lamaseries, for soul is communal and loves humming in unison. But the creative soul craves spirit. Out of the jungles of the lamasery, the most beautiful monks one day bid farewell to their comrades and go to make their solitary journey toward the peaks, there to mate with the cosmos. ...
>
> No spirit broods over lofty desolation; for desolation is of the depths, as is brooding. At these heights, spirit leaves soul far behind.[19]

This is an extraordinary passage. It certainly confirms the essential division between spirit and soul, with one higher and the other lower; one concerned with the cosmos and the other concerned with the world; one focused on individual achievement and the other on communal life. But it is unlike anything else that I have read by the Dalai Lama, and I wonder if it could be authentic. I am not saying that Hillman fabricated the letter, which originally appeared in the collection: *Tales of a Dalai Lama* by Pierre Delattre. But the important point is that Hillman describes an important distinction here; and once it is pointed out to us, I think it has to be acknowledged as a real one. Speaking charitably, we must also keep in mind the rhetorical thrust of Hillman's essay which, despite appearances to the contrary, is not an exercise in scholarship. It is rather an attempt to unsettle us by undermining some very fixed ideas that we may have about the nature of spirituality and the forms of spiritual life.

Suffering, the soul and the gods

I will consider some of these ideas in more detail. According to Hillman's argument, which I am exploring here, spirituality—whether Buddhist, Hindu, Christian, or New Age—is associated with transcendence and the abandonment of the ordinary self that is too difficult or too damaged to deal with. The spirit does not want to deal with personal suffering. It is opposed to brooding; it warns us against petty resentments and spite, and so we refuse to own these things which could be of the highest importance because they are the most revealing of who we are. By contrast, psychology—or at least a post-Jungian philosophical psychology—deals with the *psyche* or soul, which is neither self-consciousness nor material reality but a third region of individual being which originates images of myth, fantasy, and poetry. In this respect, the care of the soul involves caring for the self that spiritual life wants to abandon—and this is the everyday self which is entangled in the world and different relationships, and which suffers from ordinary afflictions like jealousy, dissatisfaction, a sense of failure, yearning, misery, and lack.[20] We should notice, however, that these are the things that give us a strong sense of who we are. So should we try to forget about our pain and our trauma? Or is it even possible to leave these things behind us in our ascent to the peak? As Hillman writes, with some disdain: "Can this [everyday self] be left at the door like a dusty pair of outworn shoes when one goes into the sweet-smelling pad of the meditation room? Can one close the door on the person who brought one to the threshold in the first place?"[21]

Elsewhere, Hillman emphasizes that our suffering is important because it sensitizes us and it gives us a powerful sense of who we are and how the world is. For example, melancholy is a significant emotion because it clarifies the world for us; it allows art and beauty to enter into us, and in this way it helps us to experience our own depth of soul. In this regard, even trauma is important, not just because it shapes personal identity, but because it gives us a profound sense of our own individual being. Hillman comments: "We may imagine our deep hurts not merely as wounds to be healed but as salt mines from which we gain a precious essence and without which the soul cannot live." And he goes on to explain:

> Viewed from the perspective of salt, early traumas are moments of initiation into the sense of being a me with a subjective personal interior. We tend to fixate on what was done to us and who did it: resentment, revenge. But what psychologically matters is that it was done: the blow, the blood, the betrayal ... A trauma is a salt mine; it is a fixed place for reflection about the nature and

value of my personal being, where memory originates and personal history begins. These traumatic events initiate in the soul a sense of its embodiment as a vulnerable experiencing subject.[22]

Hillman suggests that in this way we come to know ourselves as unique individual beings. But it is not all about tragedy, and the same kind of point could presumably be made about the ecstasy of being in love. For love, more than most things, gives us a very strong sense of being alive, and this is why we crave it and delight in it so much, even when love is difficult and we find ourselves gripped by anxiety and despair. All of this opens up a strong sense of self which is not merely ego inflation but a feeling of personal existence, or even destiny. And this experience of *soul* cannot be assimilated or reduced to the categories of spiritual life.

In his essay "Peaks and Vales," Hillman alludes to a letter that Keats wrote to his sister and brother in 1819 in which the poet says that "the world is a vale of soul-making." This line becomes one of Hillman's favorite mottoes, and in his essay he seems to cry out when he writes: "Come down from the mountain, monks, and like beautiful John Keats, come into the vale of soul-making."[23] I take "soul-making" to be the opposite of "soul-destroying"; and for Jung, Hillman, and other spiritual philosophers, the soul-destroying aspects of contemporary life would include the proliferation of information and technology, and the decline of those religious and spiritual perspectives that could establish a sense of the sacred. Keats views the world as the place where each human soul can become what it is meant to be, and he spells out the core of this philosophy in his letter: We should not think of the world as a vale of tears, but as a vale of soul-making in which we become who we are:

> Call the world if you please "The vale of Soul-making." Then you will find out the use of the world ... I say *Soul making*—Soul as distinguished from an Intelligence. There may be intelligences or sparks of the divinity in millions—but they are not Souls till they acquire identities, till each one is personally itself. Intelligences are atoms of perception—they know and they see and they are pure, in short they are God.—How then are Souls to be made? How then are these sparks which are God to have identity given them—so as ever to possess a bliss peculiar to each one's individual existence? How, but by the medium of a world like this? ... Do you not see how necessary a World of Pains and troubles is to school an Intelligence and make it a Soul? A Place where the *heart* must feel and suffer in a thousand diverse ways! Not merely is the Heart a Hornbook, It is the Minds Bible, it is the Minds experience, it is the teat from which the Mind or intelligence sucks its identity. As various as the Lives of men are—so various

become their Souls, and thus does God make individual beings, Souls, Identical Souls of the sparks of his own essence.[24]

The passage suggests that our intelligence is nothing personal, and it does not belong to us. But the soul is our own, and the pathos of the soul and its labyrinthine depths makes us the unique, unrepeatable beings that we are. In this respect, suffering is crucial, not so much as a test of spiritual endurance, but as the great teacher that reveals us to ourselves.

Hillman downplays the religious connotations of "soul," but he seems to affirm Keats's philosophy as his own. He points out that spirituality is embarrassed by the individual self and tries to repress it or lose it—as when the novice is instructed not to dwell on his previous life, his hurts or his petty troubles. But from the soul's perspective, the spiritual ascent is a kind of abandonment, and it is also a mistake. According to psychology and psychotherapy, we must deal with our problems in patient analysis, by reflecting on the minutiae of our everyday life, our emotional responses, and even the most painful experiences. But to think that we can do away with all of this at a stroke is foolish and unrealistic, and it isn't even desirable because we *are* the complex web of experiences that we live through, and this is something that cannot be wiped away. We are each a part of history and we each have our own personal history that we cannot escape from. How much more important, then, to recover our life and to find the stories that make sense of it, than just to abandon ourselves to the One because soul work is too difficult and upsetting! In this way, Hillman tries to restore the importance of the soul, after a prolonged period of neglect. And he provides us with a starting point for re-visioning spirit and soul, in contrast to "modern" ideas about spirituality as self-consciousness that aspires to the absolute.

According to Hillman, the soul is inherently linked to the imagination, which is all about creativity, including artistic creation as well as the everyday creativity that goes on in dreams and other aspects of our personal life. And even though it is the social dimension which tends to shape and organize our experience, the power of imagination is our individual response to the world and the affirmation of who we are. It allows us to encounter art, nature, and love, as it sensitizes us to receive these things; and at some level, we already *know* that without imagination the soul will die. Hillman has a sense of wonder about the world, and his own "archetypal psychology" is an attempt to re-animate things by recovering a sense of enchantment. This is not to be done by reducing everything to a single fixed principle or by merging with the absolute, but by affirming the multitude of possibilities which make the world a sacred place. In this passage, for example,

Hillman affirms polytheism as the celebration of multiple perspectives against the monotonous One:

> Anima, as Jung said, is an equivalent of and a personification of the polytheistic aspect of the psyche. "Polytheism" is a theological or anthropological concept for the experience of the many-souled world. This same experience of multiplicity can reach us as well through symptoms. They too make us aware that the soul has other voices and intentions than the one of the ego. Pathologizing bears witness to both the soul's inherent composite nature and to the many Gods reflected in this composition ... Here my point is that soul-making does not deny Gods and the search for them. But it looks closer to hand, finding them more in the manner of the Greeks and Egyptians, for whom the Gods take part in all things. All existence is filled with them, and human beings are always involved with them.[25]

Here, Hillman is describing some of the basic features of his own archetypal psychology, and this confirms the value of his thinking as a resource for re-visioning psychology beyond the reductive scientific model. He would certainly agree with Nietzsche that monotheism—of any kind—is basically "monotonotheism," for it challenges diversity and the possibility of different spiritual paths, and it affirms the same God for everyone.

Now of course, there is more to Hillman's account of the soul than just his discussion in this one short essay. Like Jung, Hillman also affirms the idea of the *anima mundi*—or the "world soul"—which challenges the very idea of the soul as a private possession that is somehow separate from the rest of nature. As he comments elsewhere: "The artificial tension between soul and world, private and public, interior and exterior thus disappears when the soul as *anima mundi*, and its making, is located in the world."[26] Hillman also likes to quote a fragment from Heraclitus that seems to underline this view: "You could not discover the limits of the soul even if you travelled every road to do so; such is the depth of its meaning."[27] For the soul has a *cosmic* dimension which exceeds the narrow horizons of the individual self. Following Jung, Hillman argues that the soul is itself a cosmos which is just as vast as the physical universe. It seems to overlap with the physical universe, and at the same time it underlies everything.[28] Much of our spiritual distress derives from our loss of connection to the psychic totality of the world, which goes along with the illusion that the soul is just a limited part of the self. Some might view this perspective as simply mysticism, but it helps to explain why we are so concerned about the natural world and our need to heal it. And it implies that the meaningful character of the world is not just a projection that we are ultimately responsible for.

Now there are significant differences between Hillman and Jung: As we have seen, Jung prioritized the wholeness and unity of the psyche as an absolute goal, and he developed the concept of "individuation" to clarify the possibility of becoming a more balanced and complete human being.[29] By contrast, Hillman subscribes to "polytheism" because he is suspicious of any attempt to recover the unified self, especially the Jungian idea of the Self as a unifying force that lies beyond or behind the *psyche*. For Hillman, our inner life is characterized by a diversity of conflicting impulses and images from the ground of the imagination itself. Other writers have criticized Hillman for his insistence on this radical plurality of being, and I think the point is well taken.[30] But underlying the celebration of what he calls "polytheism," Hillman's basic point is that everything in this world is miraculous and marvelous; only we lose a sense of how enchanted this world is when we climb the mountain peaks to gaze with reverence and wonder at the One.

"Peaks and Vales" was originally written for a popular anthology that was conceived as "a vital book for people in trouble, in pain, or in quest of a more fulfilling life," and the whole work is organized as a kind of debate over the relative merits of "Sacred Tradition" as opposed to "Psychotherapy."[31] Hence Hillman, no less than Žižek, is quite ready to ridicule some of the excesses of New Age spirituality, and he makes a broad stroke attack on Christianity, Buddhism, and other spiritual paths that remain critical or unimpressed by the value of psychotherapy. But while he rejects these spiritual traditions here, it is important to note the frequent affirmation of the spiritual quest in some of his other works in terms of the Jungian *puer* concept which corresponds to youthful enthusiasm, bringing joy into life. Perhaps it would be best to say that a truly accomplished person would have to be grounded both in spirit and in soul, and his or her life would testify to *both* of these conflicting tendencies. I have no doubt that Hillman would accept this conclusion, although it is not clear whether he would accept the unity of body, soul, and spirit since "unity" is an ideal that he challenges with some vehemence. What can be said is that Hillman's insistence on soul over spirit helps to illuminate the spiritual significance of everyday life, the spiritual aspect of the body, and the importance of anxiety, suffering, and melancholy which allow us to feel the real depth of the world—and *this* is something that an obsession with the mountain peaks obscures.

We are often taught that depression and despair are the enemy, and we are encouraged to do everything that we can to resist them or deny them. Contemporary spirituality, especially of a New Age variety, does not have much room for feelings like sadness, melancholy, or despair, and it tends to avoid the reality of death, by drawing on dubious metaphysical assumptions or by seeing it as just the continuation of life. It is also becoming much more difficult to experience the magical and miraculous aspects of this life; for as we become both the consumers and the *products* of modern society, we are increasingly leveled and "lost." For Hillman, the remedy lies in the recovery of the soul's depth, and the re-enchantment of the world, and this can be accomplished through the power of imagination which can be viewed as a key to the sacred. As David Tacey comments: "We have failed to understand that imagination and myth are windows into, not escapes from reality."[32] All this pertains to the way in which we encounter the world, and it calls for an *immanent* justification, along the lines that Hillman gives us.

Like Nietzsche, Hillman grasped the profound depth of this life and the absolute generosity of the present moment. Like Jung, he saw that the world is mysterious although science is no longer capable of apprehending the sense of its mystery, and he sought a third position between complete materialism and the belief in an independent spiritual substance. From this perspective, which for the time being we can call "imagination," Hillman saw how spirituality had become vapid, impersonal, and literally soul-destroying. He did not aim to undermine spirituality, but to turn it right side up. And so he questions self-overcoming; he challenges the spirit; and he returns us to the soul.

7

Foucault on the Care of the Self

Starting with Pythagoras, Socrates, the Stoics, and the Epicureans, there is a long tradition of philosophy as a way of life which emphasizes self-cultivation in order to achieve spiritual mastery and attunement to the highest values. According to Pierre Hadot, these thinkers regard philosophy as a kind of spiritual medicine that can cure the afflictions of the soul.[1] In more recent times, the "self-help" movement can perhaps be viewed as a popular version of the same basic project. In the nineteenth century, Samuel Smiles's pioneering work, *Self-Help*, was a huge bestseller; and in the mid-twentieth century, Norman Vincent Peale's *The Power of Positive Thinking* struck a popular chord.[2] More recently, with the emergence of the New Age spiritual movement, there are many popular works that emphasize self-enhancement by living in accordance with different precepts that are supposed to make one happier or better: *The Four Agreements* by Don Miguel Ruiz, *The Power of Now* by Eckhart Tolle, or *The Seven Spiritual Laws of Success* by Deepak Chopra to name but some among many.[3] Of course, these works are of varying quality, and some would argue that the self-help movement is just another aspect of contemporary capitalism that commodifies everything, including our spiritual life. Even so, I think these thinkers are responding to the same spiritual need—which is to take charge of our lives and to live a genuine existence in the face of self-deception, habit, and the pressures of social conformity. Some might complain that the desire for spiritual enhancement is actually a kind of narcissism which reflects a selfish desire for empowerment more than anything else. But I do not think we can make such a blanket claim. Socrates, for one, views self-cultivation in the context of an honorable and authentic life which could presumably be of value to others. And at some point self-cultivation can become self-overcoming, where selfish concerns are quite secondary.

I offer this background because I think that Foucault's work on the care of the self belongs to the same general tradition of thought. For Foucault, the care of the self is an explicitly spiritual theme, and while it is self-oriented, I do not think it is intended in any *selfish* sense, as a project of the ego or the domination of self over others. Rather, as we saw in the last chapter, we may be making a false assumption if we think that spirituality entails losing oneself and one's own personal history in order to enjoy transcendence from the self and the world. For Foucault, the care of the self involves the cultivation of oneself as a human being, and in this way life celebrates itself through us. This is a theme that develops gradually in Foucault's writings; he does not have a full-blown theory of the care of the self, and he died before he could think through all of his intuitions. Nevertheless, his discussion—which begins with his work on the ancient Greeks and Romans, and moves through Kant and Baudelaire—illuminates this important spiritual theme, and it remains compelling. As we will see in what follows, the spiritual is not the same as the ethical, which emphasizes the universal aspect of duty. But neither is it a purely aesthetic choice, like being a dandy or fixating on a personal style to the exclusion of all else. We might think that Foucault, of all people, would be the first to repudiate spirituality as an impossible escape from real life. But for him, such a project becomes an example of philosophy as a kind of spiritual practice.

In *Madness and Civilization, Discipline and Punish*, and *The History of Sexuality: Volume One*, Foucault speaks out for the dispossessed of history—the mad, the criminal, and the deviant—and he elaborates the ways in which we are produced and organized as docile bodies, or responsible subjects, in the prison house of modern society. Foucault's writing is both powerful and subversive; and by making us aware of the *genealogy* of truth, he creates a space in which life is no longer encumbered by the meanings it had previously acquired. Even so, Foucault remains cautious about the possibility of human liberation. In *The History of Sexuality: Volume One*, for example, he seems to challenge the idea that human liberation is even possible, if it is only a reversal of perspectives that remains within the orbit of what it seeks to escape from. Witness the case of "Walter," the anonymous nineteenth-century author who wrote a multivolume account of his own sexual life. Was he really liberated and free, or isn't Foucault right to suspect that "Walter's" sexual affirmation and his readiness to tell everything was the effect of a much deeper structure of domination and control?[4] In the West, since at least the time of Christianity, sex has functioned as our basic truth and the key to who we are; and repression and liberation, prudery and pornography, all belong to the same insistent regime. It is not clear how we should deal with this impasse, for if every response to power is always already circumscribed by it, then, as many commentators have pointed out, there is no real freedom and resistance is pointless.[5] And the *spiritual* life—which involves turning away from ordinary material concerns to matters of ultimate concern—can only be viewed with suspicion as another form of imaginary liberation.

But this is not the end of the story, and in Foucault's final books—*The Use of Pleasure* and *The Care of the Self*—the discussion of power and knowledge is supplemented by self-cultivation or "the care of the self" as the focus of his concern. Looking at ancient Greece and the later Hellenistic/Roman period, Foucault shows how the discourse of sex is part of a larger formation that is centered on self-cultivation, or care of the self, rather than adherence to strict moral codes. But even though Foucault talks about the possibility of freedom in this context, it is still a limited kind of freedom which involves the intricacies of self-fashioning and "creating oneself as a work of art," and on the face of it this would seem to be a pale substitute for social and political action. As we will see, however, the "care of the self" is a significant ethical ideal which also forms the basis of Foucault's account of spiritual life.

In this chapter, I examine Foucault's ideas concerning the care of the self. First, I review some relevant themes in *The Use of Pleasure* and *The Care of the Self* which illuminate the underlying context of Foucault's ideas. Then, I look at some objections to the care of the self as a significant value. Finally, I look at the care of the self as the focus of Foucault's views on spirituality. Foucault's later work provides the basis for a secular spirituality which is especially relevant today, but most discussions of Foucault have failed to deal with the positive perspective on spirituality that is found in many of his later writings. This chapter attempts to say more on this theme.

Foucault on sex and power

Foucault's thinking on the care of the self is contained in numerous interviews that he gave, the transcripts of several courses he taught at the Collège de France, and the second and third volumes of his history of sexuality that were published just weeks before his death in 1984. In *The Use of Pleasure*, Foucault focuses on sex in ancient Greece in the fourth century BCE, and he singles out three themes for particular attention: *regimen, household management,* and *the courting of young men.* According to Foucault these were problematic fields that provoked considerable anxiety as well as an immense amount of reflection and medical/philosophical advice. Writing about sexual regimen, for example, Foucault describes all the different strictures associated with the sexual act, including climate, the seasons, time of day, food, and so on. But even though sex was highly circumscribed within this society by medical and moral authorities, the intention was not to forbid certain practices, but to cultivate a harmonious relationship to sexual life through the proper care of the self:

> The sexual act did not occasion anxiety because it was associated with evil but because it disturbed and threatened the individual's relationship with himself and his integrity as an ethical subject in the making; if it was not properly measured and distributed, it carried the threat of a breaking forth of involuntary forces, a lessening of energy, and death without honorable descendants.[6]

Hence, we could say that the attention paid to sex was part of the more inclusive care of the self whose goal was something like temperance or the achievement of self-control. And all of this was for the good of the community as well as the perfection of the individual self.

Foucault defines the care of the self in terms of "those intentional and voluntary actions by which men not only set themselves rules of conduct, but also seek to transform themselves, to change themselves in their singular being, and to make their life into an oeuvre."[7] Perhaps the significance of this ideal remains contestable from the modern point of view, but it is a value that we recognize when it is pointed out to us. In the *Apology*, for example, Socrates berates his fellow Athenians because they do not take care of themselves: "Best of men," he asks, "aren't you ashamed of caring about acquiring the greatest possible amount of money, together with reputation and honours, while not caring about, even sparing a thought for, wisdom and truth, and making your soul as good as possible?"[8] The same idea is prevalent in later Hellenistic and Roman thought, where the imperative of caring for oneself became so widespread it was, according to Foucault, "a truly general cultural phenomenon."[9] In this respect, Foucault is drawn to a discussion of different spiritual practices of the time, such as: meditation and self-examination; using reason to overcome the fear of death; or anticipating the death of loved ones in order to undermine grief in advance. Early Christians also emphasized the necessity of self-cultivation through different spiritual exercises; for as Foucault observes:

> What is called Christian interiority is a particular mode of relationship with oneself, comprising precise forms of attention, concern, decipherment, verbalization, confession, self-accusation, struggle against temptation, renunciation, spiritual combat, and so on. And what is designated as the "exteriority" of ancient reality also implies the principle of an elaboration of self, albeit in a very different form.[10]

The difference here is between the ancient *askesis* or spiritual discipline of the self, which aimed at self-cultivation and the achievement of a beautiful life, and related Christian practices which were ordered in terms of self-abnegation for the sake of personal salvation, but both are versions of the care of the self as Foucault understands it.

For Foucault, a more significant distinction concerns the difference between these early technologies of the self—Greek, Roman, or Christian—and the moral codes that have more narrowly structured personal existence especially since the beginning of the modern period. Ethics can be grasped in terms of moral laws, or it can focus on the virtuous behavior of individuals. As Foucault puts it:

> In certain moralities the main emphasis is placed on the code, on its systematicity, its richness, its capacity to adjust to every possible case and to embrace every area of behavior ... the ethical subject refers his conduct to a law, or a set of laws, to which he must submit at the risk of committing offences that may make him liable to punishment ... On the other hand, it is easy to conceive of moralities in which the strong and dynamic element is to be sought in the forms of subjectification and the practices of the self. In this case, the system of codes may be rather rudimentary. Their exact observance may be relatively unimportant, at least compared with what is required of the individual in the relationship which he has to himself.[11]

Today, we are so accustomed to thinking about sex and morality in terms of rules and prohibitions that we often misapprehend the care of the self or we reject it as an *ethical* possibility since it is held to be "purely aesthetic." In this respect, Foucault's final works recall Nietzsche's *On the Genealogy of Morals*, for in each of these books the author seeks to recover a forgotten possibility of ethics—the account of "Master morality" in Nietzsche's case or the care of the self in the case of Foucault—as a way of reorganizing our thinking concerning moral life.[12] Thus, the care of the self offers a compelling way of thinking about morality and it avoids the abstract legislation of principles which reduces ethics to an impersonal theme. It is an ethics which focusses on character rather than rules, and in this respect, the return to the care of the self parallels the emergence of "virtue ethics" and the rejection of "morality as law" by many in the Anglo-American philosophical tradition.[13] Like Nietzsche, Foucault focuses on a past possibility in order to inspire the present and even the future of humankind.

Foucault's last book, *The Care of the Self*, looks more closely at the Hellenistic and Roman world of the second century AD. Once again, the focus is on sexual life and the need for self-mastery in this aspect of our being. But Foucault notes a shift in the way that sexual issues and themes are now articulated. For the ancient

Greeks, the love of boys was considered natural because any beautiful work of nature whether male or female was attractive and necessarily evoked desire. The problem was that highborn men were supposed to practice self-mastery, and to be a ruler over others presupposed that one was capable of practicing control over oneself. Likewise, the male was supposed to be active and masterful in all things, but if the boy yielded to his lover, his future standing as a ruler over others was compromised. In *The Care of the Self*, Foucault claims that by the second century the problem concerning boys was no longer pressing, and the most important issue, which Stoic philosophers addressed, concerned the proper relationship between husband and wife. For the early Greeks, such a relationship involved a simple division of labor in which each had their own appropriate role to play. But for the Romans, the goal was to establish a loving and harmonious union between the two parties who were partners in a significant ethical relationship:

> With regard to wives and to the problematization of marriage, the modification mainly concerns the valorization of the conjugal bond and the dual relation that constitutes it; the husband's right conduct and the moderation he needs to enjoin on himself are not justified merely by considerations of status, but by the nature of the relationship, its universal form and the mutual obligations that derive from it.[14]

Foucault's genealogy of sexual themes seems to underline the sense in which there is nothing "natural" here, only a shifting network of different ideas and anxieties that help to create the individuals who are shaped by these concerns.

In his last works, *The Care of the Self* and *The Use of Pleasure*, Foucault describes some of the exercises that Stoics and other philosophers used in order to shape the self and to maintain its equilibrium. He also notes that Christianity included a variety of spiritual practices, for: "*askesis* in its different forms (training, meditation, tests of thinking, examination of conscience, control of representations) eventually became a subject matter for teaching and constituted one of the basic instruments used in the direction of souls."[15] Under Christianity, however, sex received a negative connotation as an evil that signified our fallen nature. Foucault suggests elsewhere that in the Middle Ages, sexual practices, desires, and pleasures were codified in much greater detail, in confessors' manuals and other works. And he claims that these matters were gradually absorbed into a moral calculus that determined the rightness or wrongness of every action, as well as every desire and feeling.[16] The Counter Reformation in particular inspired "meticulous rules of self-examination" which led to the increasing problematization of this aspect of our lives: "Everything had to be told.

A twofold evolution tended to make the flesh into the root of all evil, shifting the most important moment of transgression from the act itself to the stirrings—so difficult to perceive and formulate—of desire."[17] Sex was also a point of concern and anxiety in classical antiquity, but Foucault insists that it was never regarded as an evil in itself. In fact, different forms of love, including the love of boys, were not considered wrong for as long as they did not lead to self-abandonment and the failure to maintain self-mastery in one's life.

In his final lectures at the Collège de France, Foucault remains pessimistic about these "states of domination" and the subtle technologies of subjectification which increasingly characterize modern life. But at the same time, he affirms the spiritual possibilities of philosophy and other ways of life in terms of human *freedom*. As he comments in one of his final interviews:

> In its critical aspect—and I mean critical in a broad sense—philosophy is that which calls into question domination at every level and in every form in which it exists, whether political, economic, sexual, institutional, or what have you. To a certain extent, this critical function of philosophy derives from the Socratic injunction "Take care of yourself," in other words, "Make freedom your foundation, through the mastery of yourself."[18]

The care of the self as a modern ideal

The care of the self is an ancient ideal, but to what extent can it continue to inspire modern life? In *The Use of Pleasure*, Foucault introduces a four-point framework for apprehending different ethical formations in terms of their *ethical substance, mode of subjection, ethical work*, and the *telos* of the subject.[19] The ethical substance could include pleasures, desires, or actions; the mode of subjection—the reason for being moral—was the care of the self rather than God's will or the necessity of the moral code; the ethical work involved spiritual practices such as writing, meditation, self-examination, thought experiment, etc., while the telos of all this was not salvation or fame, but living a life that was worthy of being honored and held in memory by others. Now this framework suggests that while the different moments of an ethical formation must influence and illuminate each other, they can also be separated from this total context and be considered by themselves. Hence, it is certainly the case that Foucault has no desire to return to the ancient world and he describes the gross inequality of that age, and especially the subordination of women, as "quite disgusting."[20] But there is *something* about the care of the self that he finds inspiring and perhaps even capable of enhancing our own lives in the present: Today, the existence of God and the "fact" of the moral law are by no means accepted by everyone, and one of the problems with ethics in modern times—noted by Nietzsche, Anscombe, and others—is that it seems to diminish us instead of inspiring us. Morality is now the sense of duty that weighs us down, and something that is felt to be *outside* of us instead of an inner necessity. As Foucault explains:

> Moving from Antiquity to Christianity, one passes from a morality that was essentially a quest for a personal ethic to a morality that was obedience to a system of rules. If I have taken such an interest in Antiquity, that is because, for a whole series of reasons, the idea of morality as obedience to a code of rules is now in the process of disappearing or has already disappeared. And this absence of morality calls for—must call for an aesthetic for existence.[21]

By framing the opposition between the two perspectives in this way, Foucault seems to imply that the one is an antidote for the other. And so we may ask ourselves whether the care of the self could renew life by inspiring individual fulfillment within the present. And more importantly for this book, what is the *spiritual* significance of the care of the self?

We shall return to these questions. But first, I want to consider three significant objections to Foucault's account which can help to specify his position more clearly. These are objections that are frequently brought up by Foucault's critics, and it would be important to respond to them here: (1) The ontological objection: The care of the self is a self-regarding ideal that emphasizes the fabrication of the self as something like a fixed work of art, and this is a fundamental misapprehension of the nature of selfhood. (2) The ethical objection: The whole orientation of the care of the self is self-involved, and far from being an alternative ethical ideal, it appears to undermine the basis of ethics which is first and foremost the care of others. And (3) The historical objection: Foucault's final work is simply a misreading of ancient texts and ideas, and it is pointless to return to Greece and Rome to resolve contemporary problems. By responding to these three objections, it will be possible to bring out the strength of Foucault's position and the significance of the care of the self as a "remedy" for modern life.

In describing the care of the self, Foucault uses phrases like "an aesthetics of existence," "being the artist of one's own life," or "living one's life as if it were a work of art." But is this anything more than self-cultivation, or "striking a pose," along the lines of Baudelaire or Oscar Wilde? Foucault is quite aware of the possibility of misinterpretation here, and at the beginning of his lectures on *The Hermeneutics of the Subject,* he warns us against the negative interpretation of the care of the self, as a kind of escapism from life into the despair of total self-involvement:

> All these injunctions to exalt oneself, to devote oneself to oneself, to turn in on oneself, to offer service to oneself, sound to our ears rather like—what? Like a sort of challenge and defiance, a desire for a radical ethical change, a sort of moral dandyism, the assertion-challenge of a fixed aesthetic and individual stage. Or else they sound to us like a somewhat melancholy and sad expression of the withdrawal of the individual who is unable to hold onto and keep firmly before his eyes, in his grasp and for himself, a collective morality (that of the city-state, for example), and who, faced with the disintegration of this collective morality, has naught else to do but attend to himself. So, the immediate, initial connotations and overtones of all these expressions direct us away from thinking about these precepts in positive terms.[22]

Foucault is right to think that "the care of the self" *suggests* narcissism, in the sense that one seems to feel entitled to special consideration. But it also seems to imply that the self is a fixed object, like a house or a car that must be cared for, and this provokes the ontological objection. For example, in one interview, Foucault suggests that the self could be viewed as an "art object": "But couldn't everyone's life become a work of art?" he wonders, "Why should the lamp or the house be an art object but not our life?"[23] Now talking about the care of *the* self certainly suggests that the self is a preexisting thing, and at first this seems reasonable. For example, we talk about "being true to ourselves," and this implies that the self—or the true self—is something deep inside of us that we tend to neglect or ignore. Indeed, we are at risk of being "inauthentic" if we don't try to be ourselves. This line of thinking recalls a famous passage in the *Enneads* where Plotinus compares the care of the self to the sculptor who releases the beautiful form that is already present within the stone: Philosophy is therapy, and the goal of philosophy according to Plotinus is to recover one's true self:

> How then can you see the sort of beauty a good soul has? Go back into yourself and look; and if you do not yet see yourself beautiful, then, just as someone making a statue which has to be beautiful cuts away here and polishes there and makes one part smooth and clears another till he has given his statue a beautiful face, so you too must cut away excess and straighten the crooked and clear the dark and make it bright, and never stop "working on your statue" till the divine glory of virtue shines out on you, till you see "self-mastery enthroned upon its holy seat."[24]

This is a powerful image. But in spite of Plotinus's intention, the passage invites us to identify "ourselves" with the "sculptor self," as well as the "statue self" that the sculptor creates. The truth is that we are both active and passive in relation to ourselves. In fact, the self *is* this self-relationship, and this means that self-cultivation has to be an ongoing process and "the self" is *not* a separate, self-contained thing. Foucault understands as much, and for him the care of the self is a continual movement of self-appropriation and self-fashioning, but not the recovery of a fixed self that already exists, at some level, as my own unique possibility of being.[25]

Here, the example of Buddhism is helpful. Buddhism is a religion, but it is also a practical philosophy which involves the cultivation of positive feelings and emotions such as love, compassion and mindfulness, and the avoidance of negative feelings and emotions, including anger or hatred. This is achieved through various spiritual exercises, including meditation and self-examination, or setting intentions for oneself as in Stoicism and other ancient schools of philosophy. Buddhism encourages the continual care of the self and self-enhancement toward the good, but at the same time Buddhists deny the reality of a fixed self as an error of thinking. There is no self. "The self" is just a convenient fiction—from which it follows that the care of the self does not have to be understood in terms of self-discovery or acquiring an authentic self that would be our ultimate truth. On the contrary, as Foucault himself points out, living your life as if it were a work of art involves self-cultivation where "the self" is a continual work in progress. There is no authentic or hidden self that we are supposed to uncover, and no determinate ideals of sovereignty that are bound to constrain our thinking in advance.

How is this relevant here? In his late essay "What Is Enlightenment," Foucault quotes Baudelaire to the effect that "modernity does not liberate man in his own being," but in fact it does the opposite: As Foucault has shown, in modern society the structures of power/knowledge create docile subjects whose freedom is narrowly regulated by contemporary norms. Through all the disciplinary procedures of modern life, in schools, prisons, factories, and offices—as well as through advertising, television and other media, etc.—we are trained to be ourselves, continually organized, conditioned, and corrected to be normal. In this context, more rules and more laws cannot help us; life is already weighed down by rules and spiritually diminished, and our only recourse is to refuse the identities that have been foisted upon us and create ourselves anew. In his essay, Foucault notes: "Modern man, for Baudelaire, is not the man who goes off to discover himself, his secrets and his hidden truth; he is the man who tries to invent himself. This modernity does not 'liberate a man in his own being'; it compels him to face the task of producing himself."[26] This is the same ideal of self-fashioning that Foucault describes in his final works as "the care of the self," and it suggests that we must reimagine and transform the present, including ourselves and our fixed ways of thinking; for the moral rules and regulations that we once lived by are no longer as applicable or binding. Hence, it is important to repeat that Foucault's main concern is not to return us to the ancients—about whom he is quite ambivalent—but to shake us free from the subject-ivation of *modern* life which produces the individual as a limited being. And the final goal is simply to live a meaningful life, following the ancient philosophers who practiced self-cultivation not for the sake of salvation or earthly rewards, but just to achieve a beautiful existence. As he notes in *The Use of Pleasure*:

> Therefore in this form of morality, the individual did not make himself into an ethical subject by universalizing the principles that informed his action; on the contrary, he did so by means of an attitude and a quest that individualized his action, modulated it, and perhaps even gave him a special brilliance by virtue of the rational and deliberate structure his action manifested.[27]

Clearly, this is not to be understood in a narrow aesthetic sense or in opposition to moral considerations; for it is a life that is unique, attractive, and compelling to others on a variety of different levels. None of this is formalized, however, and according to Foucault there is no blueprint or set of conditions for what it means to care for the self in any precise way. Even so, for Foucault, the care of the self is an empowering ideal that we can find ourselves compelled to respond to.

But there is another difficulty: For even if we accept that the care of the self offers an alternative way of thinking about morality, there is still the problem that the care of the self is all about oneself as opposed to others, and those others, it is said, should be the primary concern of morality. This is the ethical objection, and Foucault's response is clear: Even though the care of the self is necessarily self-oriented, it is not a form of self-indulgence. For the ancient Greeks, the care of the self as *sophrosyne* was regarded as an indispensable condition of public life because it was understood that whoever could not control himself, like the tyrant in Plato's *Republic*, could never legitimately rule over others. And the man whose sexual passions were unconstrained could never be the ruler of a family or a household. In the case of the later Romans, the care of the self involved knowing and fulfilling one's duties toward others, including one's spouse, children, slaves, and fellow citizens. As Foucault explains in one of his final interviews:

> But if you take proper care of yourself, that is, if you know ontologically what you are, if you know what you are capable of, if you know what it means for you to be a citizen of a city, to be the master of a household in an *oikos*, if you know what things you should and should not fear, if you know what you can reasonably hope for and, on the other hand, what things should not matter to you, if you know, finally that you should not be afraid of death—if you know all this, you cannot abuse your power over others. Thus, there is no danger.[28]

So on this reading, the care of the self does not stand opposed to the care of others, for the one evokes and implies the other.

In fact, Foucault argues that the care of the self is ontologically prior to the concern for others. This does not mean that the self has a higher value than anything else—including one's family, friends, fellow citizens, or even the state. It simply means that both logically and psychologically, the care of the self is a precondition for the care of other people. Foucault affirms that caring for others follows naturally from caring for oneself because one cares for oneself as a parent, citizen, friend, or member of the human community (in the case of Stoics). And in promoting our own individual virtues we are thereby enhancing our connection to the community and to others. This may seem problematic, especially when the moral priority of the other is frequently affirmed—and here we may think of philosophers such as Levinas who insist upon the primacy of "the other." But there is another strand in Western philosophy that challenges this perspective, and this is what Foucault affirms.

Kant, for example, recognizes the priority of individual sovereignty when he points out that autonomy is a precondition for ethics, and when he says that our duties to ourselves are logically prior to our duties toward others. In his *Lectures on Ethics*, he claims: "The autocracy of the human mind, with all the powers of the human soul in so far as they have a bearing on morality, is the principle of our duties towards ourselves, and on that very account of all other duties."[29] As an example, he claims that telling the truth is primarily a duty that we owe to ourselves, and "it follows that the prior condition of our duties to others is our duty to ourselves."[30] For Kant, the imperative of autonomy can be understood as the original calling which is supposed to summon each individual to the task of sovereignty, for it commands us to take command of ourselves. In his own essay "An Answer to the Question: What Is Enlightenment?" Kant insists: "Sapere Aude!" which means: dare to know, "have courage to use your understanding," and make your existence your own.[31] Indeed, it could be said that it is only through the possibility of acting in one's own name that the individual can ever emerge as a specific or a singular individual in any significant sense. In this respect, something like autonomy must be regarded as foundational for the establishment of ethics or any system of values—including spiritual values—that requires the cultivation of the individual. Or as Foucault puts it: "Care for others should not be put before the care of oneself. The care of the self is ethically prior in that the relationship with oneself is ontologically prior."[32]

As we have seen, the care of the self suggests a return to virtue ethics, in which the cultivation of specific virtues—including courage, justice, temperance, and wisdom—is a form of self-fashioning that helps to orient our basic attitudes toward other people. This is "self-regarding" but not necessarily *selfish*, since it is the necessary condition for remaining open and available to others. Significantly, for Foucault the care of the self as self-formation is also a space of freedom in which we can gather ourselves to live and act according to our own will. Foucault is not saying that we are free to choose anything we want to, and he rejects existentialism which emphasizes the burden of our absolute metaphysical freedom. We are not "condemned to be free," as Sartre would have it, since freedom is, more realistically, something that we must cultivate through the attentive care of the self.[33] It is also a kind of "concrete liberty" which reacts against the context of the moment by affirming it or rejecting it—like the soldier who chooses to obey or disobey orders, or the believer who chooses the explanation of faith over other possibilities. In this sense, Foucault argues that the individual shapes himself in terms of "the models that he finds in his culture and are proposed, suggested, imposed upon him by his culture, his society, and his social group."[34] But this is also the point at which we affirm our freedom as we constitute ourselves in response to all that is fixed and given.

Finally, the historical objection: Some classical scholars have rejected Foucault's discussion of the ancient world as misleading or inaccurate, although others have been more sympathetic.[35] Foucault admits that he is not a classicist but he has tried to make sense out of a huge amount of classical material, and he offers an interpretation that highlights some aspects that are not usually given prominence. Once again, the most obvious parallel is with Nietzsche. In *The Birth of Tragedy*, Nietzsche infuriated classical scholars by proposing a new account of Greek tragedy structured in terms of the "Dionysian" and the "Apollonian" as explanatory categories that help to illuminate the Greek world. But his ultimate aim was to inspire his readers toward a different kind of future than the one entailed by the mediocrity or "wretched contentment" that seemed to prevail in his own time. By looking back to the past, Nietzsche sought to recover the possibility of a higher kind of future. Foucault's recovery of significant themes in Greek and Roman life has a similar kind of goal—the unsettling of established ways of thinking and the emergence of a new perspective that casts doubt on the legality of the code or the morality of law as the only *ethical* possibility. This new perspective offers a compelling account of the past, and it elaborates another way of thinking about moral life; and in this way, it allows us to move beyond our present self-understanding to affirm the possibility of human freedom and a spiritual life.

For some commentators, Foucault's reading of ancient texts is compatible with his original discussion of power/knowledge and it provides an account of what was missing in his earlier work—namely, the subject as co-creator of her own life and the possibility of personal transformation. In different interviews, Foucault points out that after his early attempts to understand knowledge, discursive formations, and the functioning of power, the individual subject remained undertheorized in his work, and it is this that he turns to in his final published writings—*The Use of Pleasure* and *The Care of the Self*. Hence, it can be urged that these works do not represent a betrayal of his fundamental insight (on power/knowledge) but the completion of a framework of understanding that allows us to grasp the standpoint of modern life. At the same time, we may want to go even further and say that Foucault's later works involve a development—if not a reversal—that goes beyond the apparent dead end of his earlier works. In *Discipline and Punish* and *The History of Sexuality: Volume One*, the individual subject is posited as a fixed determination and a product of the forces that create it. Personal identity is itself a constraint and a form of subjection—and hence the doubt concerning "Walter," mentioned earlier in this chapter. But in his final books, essays, and interviews, Foucault elaborates a space of personal freedom—through the care of the self—which allows us to some extent to challenge the identities that are fixed upon us and to reinvent ourselves. For when the subject becomes aware of the power relations that surround and threaten her, she also becomes aware of her own possibilities of action and response. And this inspires the possibility of self-transformation and spiritual renewal as a movement away from received ideas and goals. Freedom is not absolute, and there is no necessity of social or political progress. But as the Greeks and Romans understood, we are free within certain parameters—according to the Stoics, some things are up to us while other things are not up to us—and by reconnecting with the care of the self we can recover the possibilities of "autarchy," "autonomy," or "self-mastery," which are the conditions of freedom as much as its fulfillment. This is also an opening on to spiritual life as the quest for a more purposeful existence which affirms belonging, as opposed to separation and death.

The care of the self as a spiritual goal

At this point, we have considered some objections to Foucault's account of the care of the self. We have evaluated these objections, and I think we must conclude that the care of the self is an ideal that remains relevant to contemporary life. But as well as being an ethical project, the care of the self is also a *spiritual* goal and it is this that we must now discuss. In his last two books, Foucault treats the care of the self as an ethical concept, but in various interviews and essays, he refers increasingly to the care of the self as a spiritual undertaking and a key to spiritual life. And this makes sense: Ethics can be considered as one part of human life involving our duties and responsibilities to self and others. But spirituality affirms the wholeness of each human existence—not just our ethical behavior, but the commitment of our whole being to a higher reality or truth, and this is what drives Foucault's account of the care of the self. Of course, much depends upon how we determine the nature of spirituality, but here, in accordance with some earlier suggestions, I propose that a spiritual life includes at least three different aspects.[36] First, a spiritual life involves a movement away from the ordinary goals and preoccupations of everyday life, such as wealth, power, and status, as well as openness to higher values and truths that make life more fulfilling. This is not avoiding life, but rejecting all those received ideas that are inherently life-denying. Second, a spiritual life involves some kind of quest or journey toward the truth and "ultimate" meaning, and like every important quest, this may be very challenging since it calls one's own self into question. Third, a spiritual life is an integrated life that involves our whole self; it is not a hobby or a secondary interest apart from the rest of our existence. And the individual who is spiritually committed is devoted to the higher values that he or she feels compelled to follow and sometimes even die for. We can now gauge to what extent Foucault's account of the care of the self follows a spiritual trajectory, using these three determinations as our guide.

First, the questioning of received ideas and everyday values. Following Pierre Hadot, Foucault argues that ancient philosophy is all about living one's life in the right way, and it is certainly not limited to intellectual speculation. In *The Use of Pleasure* and *The Care of the Self*, Foucault offers sustained discussions of several ancient philosophers, including Socrates, Marcus Aurelius, and Epictetus who devoted themselves to living wisely and well. He also makes it clear that thinkers like Socrates rejected the everyday values of the cave because they considered the care of the self or soul as the most important value of all—more important than fame, money, and even personal safety. In his later work, Foucault tends to conflate the "ethical" and the "spiritual" and the care of the self becomes the point at which both of these emerge. As he comments in one interview: "By spirituality I mean—but I'm not sure this definition can hold for very long—the subject's attainment of a certain mode of being and the transformation that subject must carry out on itself to attain this mode of being. I believe that spirituality and philosophy were identical or nearly identical in ancient spirituality."[37] Foucault's concern with spirituality in his final courses at the Collège de France gives rise to some very powerful analyses of *parrhesia* or "fearless speech" as an ideal in Cynic, Socratic, and Stoic philosophies. Today we would talk about "speaking truth to power," but this involves the same kind of courage that allowed Socrates to speak his mind to the authorities and prompted Diogenes, who refused to be in awe of any human being, to tell Alexander to *move out of the sun*. As Kant reminds us, telling the truth is an ethical requirement; but at the same time, devoting oneself to the truth involves accepting truth as a *spiritual* value or something that is greater than we are and that we must defer to. Being ready to die for the truth is to affirm a spiritual perspective on human existence, and it implies that a spiritual life is possible. It is not to be viewed as an "illusory" form of liberation—which is what we might have expected from Foucault's earlier work.

Second, the individual quest for higher truths and values: As we have seen, philosophers like Socrates were prepared to die for their values, and they made their own personal safety a secondary consideration in affirming the truth, however inconvenient, to others. The Stoics and Epicureans offered compelling philosophies to live by, but as Hadot points out, each of the ancient philosophical schools had its own ideal, and individuals were supposed to overcome personal desires for the sake of an impersonal goal that was the same for everyone.[38] Of course, this does not fit with Foucault's account of self-cultivation, for as soon as we insist on fixed goals and *rules* for self-formation we move closer to the universal morality of law that he wanted to escape from. In the end, Foucault says that all of this work must remain an *experiment* to determine what is still possible in modern life and to push the limits of our understanding of it. He also insists that the goal of "truth-seekers" is not just to know more things. It is to recover the openness of the world and a sense of belonging to *the truth*, which can effect a personal transformation. "After all," he asks:

> What would be the value of the passion and knowledge if it resulted only in a certain amount of knowledgeableness and not, in one way or another, and to the extent possible, in the knower's straying afield of himself? There are times in life when the question of knowing if one can think differently than one thinks,

and perceive differently than one sees, is absolutely necessary if one is to go on looking and reflecting at all.[39]

Foucault was critical of the ancients, but he was more critical of the moral codes that undermine individual sovereignty and organize our reflections in advance, and he was profoundly concerned with the anomie of modern life: We have become habituated to ourselves. We have become like the products that we happily consume, and in this respect we are losing our freedom and any possibility of what he refers to as our "spiritual life." But in this respect, the *renewal* of the care of the self is a return to the original goal of philosophy, which is to cultivate a way of life through questioning, reflection, and various spiritual exercises. And this, as Nietzsche might say, is an "experimental" life, which is inspired by a basic trust in existence and one that is certainly worth living.[40]

Third, the spiritual life is an integrated life, which means that it involves the ongoing goal of personal transformation as the focus of our existence. This would include not only the intellectual, but also the emotional, physical, and other aspects of the self that must be cultivated and trained from one day to the next as our own life's work. On this point, Foucault comments suggestively in one of his final interviews: "Among the cultural inventions of mankind there is a treasury of devices, techniques, ideas, procedures, and so on, that cannot exactly be reactivated but at least constitute, or help to constitute, a certain point of view which can be very useful as a tool for analyzing what's going on now—and to change it."[41] The treasury of devices that Foucault describes would certainly include many of the practices that are associated with Buddhism, Christianity, and ancient philosophical traditions such as Stoicism, Cynicism, Epicureanism, and the rest. And they would include meditation, self-examination, the anticipation of death, prayer, and other ways of setting purposeful intentions for oneself. It is certainly possible that such devices can be co-opted by the truth regime of power. But Foucault is clearly inspired by their liberatory potential as spiritual practices, for they help to disengage the individual from the received ideas and models of existence that he or she is supposed to subscribe to.

In this way, Foucault elaborates the care of the self as an ethical project while at the same time he also comes to think of the care of the self as a significant spiritual goal. And insofar as his discussion conforms to the general account of spirituality that I have proposed, I think we have to view the care of the self as an important spiritual ideal. In recent years, spiritual concerns have become more prominent than before. Many people now enjoy a comfortable lifestyle with abundant moral possessions, but they find that their lives are impoverished. They do not possess the meaning that they wish they had and so they look for spiritual meaning. But while they search for a spiritual path, they are often less interested in traditional religions because the latter have strict faith requirements and they seem to offer fewer possibilities for personal experiment and growth. All this points to the need for a more personal spirituality—one that would have more appeal as traditional religions become inflexible and resistant to change. In his discussion of the care of the self, Foucault develops the outlines of a "philosophical spirituality" which could also become the basis of a more popular spiritual expression, especially since it encourages spiritual growth and transformation without insisting on fixed religious practices or beliefs.

By opening new perspectives on the forms of our experience, and challenging us to think differently, Foucault's work promotes a kind of joy, for it liberates us from received ideas and fixed determinations, and in this way it creates a space of freedom. Now, as Nietzsche would put it, "All the daring of the lover of knowledge is permitted again"; for life becomes full of possibility and an *experiment,* as Foucault recovers the impulse behind philosophy and the origin of spiritual life. And in this way, Foucault's account of the care of the self illuminates the authentic possibility of self-determination as a spiritual goal that we can aspire to.

8

Derrida on Mourning

For many ancient philosophers, the fear of death is irrational, and one of the most important philosophical tasks is to come to terms with one's own mortality. The Stoics say we should accept whatever happens as the will of the cosmos, and we should not bewail death, but embrace our fate as a part of the order of things. For Epicurus, death is of no concern to us, for while we exist death has not yet come, but when death has come we no longer exist, and so nothing can actually hurt us. Lucretius argues that death is a part of nature, and since nature is basically good, to rail against the shortness of one's own life is to be out of attunement with nature or life itself. But in all of this, it is always one's *own* death that is the problem; the death of *others* is not such a crucial matter, and this seems to beg the question. According to Seneca, for example, it may be quite natural to experience grief when a loved one dies, but it does not really change anything, it cannot bring the loved one back, and so we should minimize our sorrow and avoid public displays of grief which only show our weakness. Marcus Aurelius and Epictetus both tell us that we should try to forestall the shock of the loved one's death by anticipating such a possibility in advance, so that when it happens we will already be immune: "If you kiss your child or your wife, say that you are kissing a human being; for when it dies you will not be upset."[1] All the same, this attitude seems strained because it views the death of the beloved as something that I must be protected from. And it sees grief and mourning as a kind of self-loss, and something that is harmful to me, rather than a genuine response to the fate of the other, which is surely the most important thing.

In fact, my own death may not be my greatest concern. The death of my friend or my child may actually be a much greater cause for anguish, and we may even say—quite honestly—that if we could change places with the deceased then we would gladly do so. Our own existence and sense of self is completely bound up with our relationship to others, so when we lose someone we also lose an important part of ourselves. We cannot simply recover this by loving someone else. In this respect, there is a real shift from concern for my own death to mourning the death of others, and among recent philosophers, Derrida responds to this spiritual issue at the most serious level.

For the Stoics, the death of the other is something that distracts me from my own authentic path, and it is treated as a problem that must be overcome. In other words, mourning is understood to be a process that can finally lead to "freedom" and self-recovery. In this chapter, I will begin with Freud's account of mourning, because I think that Freud's theory is similar to the ancient philosophical view. For Freud, mourning is something that should come to an end, sooner rather than later, for it is the expression of a terrible wound in the psyche, but life goes on and the self must recover and renew itself. In opposition to Freud, I will then look at Roland Barthes who seems to think that the opposite is true—for life really cannot go on after the death of the loved one and any recovery is a betrayal of the one who has died.

The main part of this chapter looks at Derrida's view of death and mourning against the background of Freud (and Barthes) who view mourning differently. Derrida is a profoundly spiritual philosopher, and in his work he frequently deals with spiritual themes, including forgiveness, religion, and the gift. His discussion of mourning is powerful and compelling, and it is a good example of what I would call "philosophy as a spiritual practice." Derrida uncovers the spiritual dimension of mourning which goes beyond its ethical aspects, and he shows how mourning involves memory, testimony, gratitude, faithfulness, and care for those who have departed from us. Derrida keeps Freud and other psychoanalysts at the forefront of his thinking; but in his work on mourning he shows how it is possible to have a spiritual connection with the dead—not in terms of spiritualism or anything like that, but as a continuation of the relationship with those who have passed away and who are no longer present in any ordinary sense, but not completely absent either. The other lives on inside of us, and it is up to us to keep them present in mind.

The end of mourning

Why do we mourn? Do we owe it to the dead? But the dead are gone. They have ceased to exist or they exist in another place, and in either case they will not return. They do not need our grief or our compassion. Sometimes we say, "If he was here with us today ...," but the point is he is not here. We have lost him and we are lost without him, and so it seems that we must be grieving for ourselves and our own situation. People say, "I am sorry for your loss," but this is not right either because it makes the survivor, rather than the departed, into the central figure. And if the goal is just to get over our own pain, we must eventually abandon the departed whom we claim to love, and this would be like killing him for a second time. So why do we mourn? Obviously, through mourning we slowly erase the pain of our loss. But how does the work of mourning achieve this? And is there a deeper, more spiritual perspective on mourning that goes beyond the prescribed rituals that we are supposed to follow whenever somebody dies?

In "Mourning and Melancholia," Freud describes mourning as unproblematic in comparison to melancholia, which is its pathological relation. According to Freud, the goal of mourning is to free ourselves from the emotional bonds that tie us to the beloved who has died so that we can invest that love elsewhere. The choice is between following the one who has died or disengaging ourselves from the departed, so we can resume our interest and our involvement in life. Freud describes mourning as a kind of reality testing in which we painstakingly recall every memory and every wish associated with the one who has departed. The loved one is no longer with us but, as Freud points out, it is extraordinarily difficult for anyone to willingly abandon a libidinal position, "even when a substitute is already beckoning to them."[2] Thus, there will be resistance, but gradually we come to accept at a deeper level that the beloved has died and our relationship has ended:

> Normally, respect for reality gains the day. Nevertheless its orders cannot be obeyed at once. They are carried out bit by bit, at great expense of time and cathected energy, and in the meantime, the existence of the lost object is psychically prolonged. Each single one of the memories and expectations in which the libido is bound to the object is brought up and hypercathected, and detachment of the libido is accomplished in respect of it.[3]

According to Freud's abbreviated account, the mourner loses interest in the outside world. At the same time she dwells on those memories and hopes which involve the departed, and in this way she creates a strong sense of the departed which counters the reality of his passing. But eventually, there is a shift in perspective as reality intrudes, and the mourner comes to accept the death of the departed while she maintains an ideal internalized image of him. Freud is still a bit uncertain of this analysis, however, and he concludes by commenting:

> Why this compromise by which the command of reality is carried out piecemeal should be so extraordinarily painful is not at all easy to explain in terms of economics. It is remarkable that this painful unpleasure is taken as a matter of

course by us. The fact is, however, that when the work of mourning is completed the ego becomes free and uninhibited again.[4]

What is wrong with this picture? First, Freud assumes that mourning, like every other activity, is basically selfish or self-regarding. What, he seems to ask, would be the point of loving someone who is dead? Such a libidinal investment is useless since there can be no return on one's investment. And yet we do continue to grieve for the departed and we choose to embrace suffering rather than abandoning those who have died. How can we explain this from the standpoint of "the economy of suffering" that Freud refers to more than once in his paper? The obvious response to Freud is to say that this very standpoint is itself a presupposition that must be abandoned. Mourning is for the self and we must learn to let go and continue our lives without the beloved, but mourning is also for the other, for the one who has died. We do what we can to commemorate, and the absence of the other is distressing. But this is a pain that we choose to embrace and we would not want it taken away from us. Mourning in this sense is not a useful investment or even a useful withdrawal of our time and love, as Freud would have us believe. Second, Freud's account assumes that other people are substitutable for each other. Why can't we just abandon the departed and invest our libido in another? The answer is that mourning, like romantic love, is focused on the uniqueness of the other person, and now that he is gone we are flooded by memories of him. And we betray him, and our relationship together, if we choose to forget him and focus our feelings on another. Freud reads mourning as a process of abandonment which is entirely self-oriented. Our relationships are treated as so many useful investments, and in this way we lose sight of the value and the uniqueness of the one who has died. But there is something wrong with treating mourning as just a form of disinvestment. At the very least, it implies a lack of personal loyalty and devotion which calls the authenticity of these relationships into question.

In "Mourning and Melancholia," Freud is actually more interested in melancholia. The latter is not a process with a fixed goal but a fixation or a state of being in which we deal with an object-loss—such as a failed romance—by heaping blame upon ourselves as worthless and responsible for what has happened. He comments, "In mourning it is the world which has become poor and empty; in melancholia it is the ego itself."[5] Freud grasps melancholia as a way of keeping a relationship alive, in spite of the departure of the other, by *identifying* with the other person. Thus, the scorn and anger that I feel toward myself actually derive from the ambivalence of my feelings toward the one who has gone; and in despising myself I allow myself to despise him. As Freud explains:

> The free libido was not displaced on to another object; it was withdrawn into the ego. There, however, it was not employed in any unspecified way, but served to establish an identification of the ego with the abandoned object. Thus the shadow of the object fell upon the ego, and the latter could henceforth be charged by a special agency, as though it were an object, the forsaken object. In this way an object-loss was transformed into an ego-loss and the conflict between the ego and the beloved person into a cleavage between the critical activity of the ego and the ego as altered by identification.[6]

This means that we can preserve our connection to the one that we have loved and lost through introjection or identification with him. The other is gone but we hang on to our relationship by internalizing it within ourselves.

In later work, however, Freud seems to claim that melancholia is *not* opposed to mourning since it is a fundamental aspect of mourning itself. He even speculates at one point in "The Ego and the Id" that "it may be that this identification [with the departed] is the sole condition under which the id can give up its objects."[7] Thus, we deal with the departed by internalizing some aspect of him. For example, we put the other to rest by framing a stable image of him inside of ourselves which promotes our equanimity, or we may even take on some of the qualities of the one who has died. Later analysts (including Nicolas Abraham and Maria Torok) have insisted on the difference between *introjection* and *incorporation* as two different strategies that allow us to cope with bereavement.[8] The former involves "healthy" integration and self-appropriation in coming to terms with loss, while the latter involves creating a monument or a "crypt" within ourselves to keep the dead hidden away in order to avoid our grief. In each case, however, we appropriate the departed as a part of ourselves, and we hang on to them through identification or interiorization. There is plenty of evidence for this, both clinical and anecdotal: As we get older, we start acting like our mothers or fathers who are now deceased or we take up hobbies and interests that are associated with those we have lost. As Derrida remarks in *Memoires for Paul de Man*:

> Memory and interiorization: since Freud, this is how the "normal" "work of mourning" is often described. It entails a movement in which an interiorizing idealization takes in itself or upon itself the body and voice of the other, the other's visage and person, ideally and quasi-literally devouring them.[9]

Once again, however, this makes mourning into a process of appropriation in which we gradually overcome the otherness of the other and reduce him to a fixed image. Now the other can never astonish us or surprise us again because he or she is safely present as a part of our own identity. In effect, the relationship with the departed has ceased.

Finally, in "The Ego and the Id," Freud proposes a more relational account of selfhood when he claims that "the character of the ego is a precipitate of abandoned object-cathexes and that it contains the history of those object choices."[10] In other words, we are the history of our relationships, and this suggests that the self is not so separate or at odds with the others that it encounters and invests with libido. Our own self is the product of others, and so losing the other is to lose a sense of who we are. This is why when someone that we love dies we feel lost and cast adrift, and we experience a sense of abandonment because we have lost a part of ourselves. This is certainly an advance over the position that Freud held in "Mourning and Melancholia," and it makes it easier to understand the great "riddle" of mourning once we abandon the earlier economic standpoint. But in each case, whether we recover ourselves by making new emotional investments, or by appropriating the other or some aspect of the other within ourselves, we lose the sense of an ongoing relationship with the other person. For other writers, as we will see, this is precisely what we should strive to maintain.

Attachment and betrayal

We can now consider another approach to bereavement—apart from abandonment and incorporation—one that involves extreme attachment and the refusal to let go of the departed. There are "pathological" cases where, for example, the parents leave their child's room exactly as it had been when she died and they do everything to avoid referring to her "death." Likewise, Roland Barthes identified so much with his own grief that he scarcely wanted to go on living without it. Barthes's final work, *Camera Lucida*, is a personal meditation on photography which is at the same time a work of mourning for his mother who died shortly before he wrote this book. His personal grief is mingled with his reflections on photography, but this discussion becomes a part of his mourning process insofar as it intensifies the anguish that he feels. Barthes does not try to hide the profound love that he feels for his mother, and he wants to share this with us. He is preoccupied with her and the grief that he feels for her, and only this allows him to cope with the reality of her passing. But it is a loss he does not expect to recover from:

It is said that mourning, by its gradual labor, slowly erases pain; I could not, I cannot believe this; because for me, Time eliminates the emotion of loss (I do not weep), that is all. For the rest, everything has remained motionless. For what I have lost is not a Figure (the Mother), but a being; and not a being, but a quality (a soul): not the indispensable, but the irreplaceable. I could live without the Mother (as we all do, sooner or later); but what life remained would be absolutely and entirely unqualifiable (without quality).[11]

In fact, Barthes does not want to recover from this loss, since it would be an act of betrayal against the mother whom he loved so dearly.

Barthes's discussion in *Camera Lucida* focuses on the photograph as a *memento mori*. Barthes is not a photographer himself, but he is fascinated by the power of photographs to elicit a sense of mortality and grief through the revelation of death. According to Barthes, every photograph has a *studium*, an ordinary frame of reference that places the picture within its cultural context, while at the same time, every photograph can have a *punctum* which is the detail in the photograph that affects and wounds us. For Barthes, the *punctum* is an unintentional effect of the photograph—the pure working of chance—which surprises us with its poignancy and power. As he notes: "A photograph's *punctum* is that accident which pricks me (but also bruises me, is poignant to me)."[12] Barthes illustrates this with Alexander Gardner's photograph of Lewis Payne who attempted to assassinate the US Secretary of State in 1865. Payne is shown in his death cell prior to his execution. He is still a young man, but soon he will be dead:

> The photograph is handsome, as is the boy: that is the *studium*. But the *punctum* is: he is going to die. I read at the same time: *This will be* and *this has been*; I observe with horror an anterior future of which death is the stake. By giving me the absolute cast of the pose (aorist), the photograph tells me death in the future. What *pricks* me is the discovery of this equivalence.[13]

This has been, and this will be, and in fact it has already happened. The *punctum* hurts us because it refers to lost time which can never be recaptured. The photograph shows what has been or the moment which is always already dead and gone. It is the same with the photograph that he finds of his mother as a little girl: It contains the sign of her future death, as well as our own future death which is thereby invoked. As Barthes puts it:

> In front of the photograph of my mother as a child, I tell myself: she is going to die: I shudder, like Winnicott's psychotic patient, over a catastrophe that has

already occurred. Whether or not the subject is already dead, every photograph is this catastrophe.[14]

And

> it is because each photograph always contains this as the imperious sign of my future death that each one, however detached it seems to be to the excited world of the living, challenges each of us, one by one, outside of any generality (but not outside of any transcendence).[15]

The photograph involves the return of the dead. It transforms the dead into the living but it also frames the living on the side of the dead.

The photograph is an open wound, but it can also be comforting. When someone dies, we often look at old photographs of the deceased—but what exactly is it that we are looking for? Is it an image to remember him by, before we forget what he looks like? Or are we somehow trying to recover the person who has gone to grasp their essential being? A photograph of someone is a fragment or a trace of that person; it is their image at a certain point in time which provides a metonymical connection to her. And this suggests the possibility of a re-encounter with that person, which provokes our longing. But the moment fixed by the photograph is gone forever, and so we experience the melancholy of having missed the one who was there. In *Camera Lucida*, Barthes describes searching for his late mother: Looking through old family snapshots he forces himself to experience again and again the anguish of his loss. But at last he discovers a photograph of his mother as a child that seems to capture her essential being. It is also from a time before he ever knew her—and this makes sense, since a picture from a later period would fail to live up to the reality that Barthes himself knew:

> In this veracious photograph, the being I love, whom I have loved, is not separated from itself: at last it coincides. And mysteriously, this coincidence is a kind of metamorphosis. All the photographs of my mother which I was looking through were a little like so many masks; at the last, suddenly the mask vanished: there remained a soul, ageless but not timeless, since this air was the person I used to see, consubstantial with her face, each day of her long life.[16]

All of this—the desperation, the anguish, and longing to find her again (even if only in a photograph)—is part of his mourning process. But it is not meant to "get over her." It is rather to experience the pain of her absence as the closest thing that he has to experiencing her presence. For in this way, at least, he remains connected and related to her.

The anguish that Barthes describes ultimately derives from the pleasure of affirming the other—addressing her and remaining open to her while at the same time she cannot be present because she is gone. It is the same with romantic love when the lover experiences the absence of the beloved (her withdrawal, her disdain) as the only way in which she can still be present to him. Barthes says that he could say, like Proust's narrator at his grandmother's death: "I did not insist only upon suffering, but upon respecting the originality of my suffering."[17] For this originality is just the reflection of what was absolutely irreducible in her. Mourning is an impersonal ritual that is repeated by countless others, but we may insist on the uniqueness of our own grief, because mourning, like love, is focused on the uniqueness of the beloved who is "the one and only." Freud says that such mourning must eventually come to an end. But for Barthes, grief and mourning are interminable: The pain of bereavement must be experienced over and over again, so that we can never get over our loss.[18] Indeed, the end of mourning would be an act of betrayal, like the lover who abandons his love instead of affirming it by enduring all the difficulties of their relationship. Barthes is driven to follow his mother into the grave, and he refuses all compromises with death. Indeed, if mourning is viewed as an attempt to mediate death and to overcome its sting through disinvestment or appropriation, then he must avoid it at all costs by remaining one with his grief. Barthes took care of his mother during her final illness. He nursed her, and she became his own "little girl." He writes, "Ultimately, I experienced her, strong as she had been, my inner law, as my feminine child."[19] In this way, he says that he engendered his own mother, which was his way of "resolving death." But now, there is nothing left for him to do, and so he finishes: "From now on I could do no more than await my total, undialectical death."[20] He died, of complications following an accident, just a few months after his book was published.[21]

All of which brings us to what Derrida has called the impossibility of mourning. Neither letting go nor hanging on are appropriate ways of dealing with our grief. Mourning does not end in "triumph" (as Freud sometimes seems to suggest), and neither does it have to end with the triumph of death (as Barthes seems to conclude): For in both cases we lose our relationship to the departed. Mourning is inherently problematic, and yet we must mourn; but whatever we do we seem to violate the ethics of mourning. For example, in his memorial essay on Barthes, Derrida refers to "the double wound of speaking of him, here and now, as one speaks of one of the living or of one of the dead. In both cases I disfigure, I wound, I put to sleep, or I kill."[22] So how should we mourn? And what does showing respect for the dead really involve? Somehow, mourning always creates anxiety, and we are never quite sure about the principles of mourning and whether or not we are doing the right thing.

On the impossibility of mourning

In *Memoires for Paul de Man* and *The Work of Mourning*, Derrida memorializes departed friends and describes the complex ambiguities of mourning that constrain us. Each of his essays is directed toward a particular friend or colleague who had recently died, including Barthes, de Man, Foucault, Marin, Kofman, Deleuze, Levinas, Lyotard, and several others. But while each essay is a tribute to a unique individual, there are some general themes and principles that recur throughout these discussions and these are what we can focus on to begin with. Derrida himself is drawn to the theme of mourning. In fact, mourning gradually emerges in his work as a trope that describes our relationship to the past, including the history of philosophy which we cannot just set aside or hang on to as if it were the final word.[23] In Freud, as in Hegel, Kant, and other Enlightenment thinkers, there is always the possibility of resolution—the *end* of analysis, the *end* of history, or the end of mourning—and self-appropriation at a higher level. But in spite of what Freud implies, mourning is not a process of sublimation. Mourning is for the self, but it is also for the departed, who is neither "present" nor "absent" in the ordinary sense of these terms. Likewise, as Derrida explains, the border between the living and the dead is never entirely closed:

> Upon the death of the other we are given to memory, and thus to interiorization, since the other, outside us, is now nothing. And with the dark light of this nothing, we learn that the other resists the closure of our interiorizing memory. With the nothing of this irrevocable absence, the other appears as other, and as other for us, upon his death or at least in the anticipated possibility of a death, since death constitutes and makes manifest the limits of a *me* or an *us* who are obliged to harbor something that is greater and other than them; something *outside of them within them*.[24]

This is a strange topology, since it implies that we contain more than we actually are. And those who are dead are by no means gone, for they seem to have a life of their own as they continue to shape our sense of who we are.

Derrida worries about the ways in which we betray the dead by not responding in appropriate ways to their passing. Thus, in *Memoires for Paul de Man*, he describes a "possible mourning," which successfully interiorizes the other, as opposed to an "impossible mourning," which fails to incorporate the other and thereby preserves his alterity. Ironically, the *possible* mourning involves appropriation and assimilation and it is thereby a betrayal of the other. The *impossible* mourning seems to respect the otherness of the other, and Derrida's own acts of mourning, in various essays, involve self-conscious reflection on the failure of mourning as appropriation. But if impossible mourning actually succeeds, it is only successful because it also falls short. It is never done with because it cannot negotiate the other. Where, then, is the most unjust betrayal? The possible mourning is an appropriation of the other, but the impossible mourning lets the other slip away. In fact, there are no triumphs here, only a list of all the different ways in which mourning can fail:

> What is an impossible mourning? What does it tell us, this impossible mourning, about an essence of memory? And as concerns the other in us, even in this "distant premonition of the other," where is the most unjust betrayal? Is the most distressing, or even the most deadly infidelity that of a *possible mourning* which would interiorize within us the image, idol, or ideal of the other who is dead and lives only in us? Or is it that of the impossible mourning, which, leaving the other his alterity, respecting thus his infinite remove, either refuses to take or is incapable of taking the other within oneself, as in the tomb or the vault of some narcissism?[25]

Derrida relies on the distinction between introjection and incorporation to explain the difference between a possible and an impossible mourning. But, of course, he would be the first to argue that such a distinction cannot be sustained; and in either case the other is effectively abandoned.[26]

Narcissism, appropriation, and abandonment are only some of the dangers that Derrida describes: In mourning we are also bound to speak and testify on behalf of the other; but at the same time, we cannot speak *for* him or fail to consider his own words. Whatever we say, we know in advance that our words will always fall short, and so we find ourselves at a loss. The departed is not here, and it seems wrong to pretend that he is here; but it is also wrong to say that he has "gone," since the task of mourning involves commemoration, which means keeping his spirit and his memory alive. In mourning we declare our debts, but in saying how much we owe to the departed we are bound to *limit* them, and this is also unacceptable. Finally, in speaking of the deceased, we want to say "we," but what right do we have to use this word, now that the loved one has passed away?

As we have seen, Derrida is quite uneasy with the Freudian standpoint which comprehends mourning in terms of "assimilation," "appropriation," or "incorporation," for such metaphors appear to dissolve the other into the context of the self. Instead, he thinks we should recognize that the other is always already inscribed at the heart of the self, for the self is the sum of all its relations with others. Thus, in *Camera Lucida*, Barthes describes his mother as his "inner law," suggesting she was already in him before he was himself. Likewise, we cannot just incorporate the other, for it is the latter who gives me to myself, and mourning only further undermines my self-mastery. The other has died, and henceforth he can only live on inside of us; but at the same time he is also beyond us, and he seems to gaze at us with a look that calls us back to ourselves. As Derrida explains in his essay "By Force of Mourning," which is addressed to Louis Marin:

> The one who looks at us in us—and *for whom* we are—is no longer; he is completely other, infinitely other, as he has always been, and death has more than ever entrusted him, given him over, distanced him, in this infinite alterity. However narcissistic it may be, our subjective speculation can no longer seize and appropriate this gaze before which we appear at the moment when, bearing it in us, bearing it along with every movement of our bearing or comportment, we can get over our mourning *of him* only by getting over *our* mourning, by getting over, by ourselves, the mourning of ourselves, I mean the mourning of our autonomy, of everything that would make us the measure of ourselves.[27]

This is an important point: On the face of it, it would seem that in mourning, we attempt to recover the other or reappropriate our relationship into the project of our own life. But the departed represents an impossible limit and a boundary which cannot be overcome. In mourning we experience death and the other as inappropriable: We are thrown back on ourselves, and we are completely diminished by grief. In this respect, mourning thereby destroys the possibility of autonomy and transcendence at a higher level. And in spite of what Freud says, it is not true that through the work of mourning we can finally recover our own self-mastery, for this is not possible and even if it was, it would be a betrayal.

Derrida focuses his discussion of mourning on our obligations to the departed, in opposition to Freud who focuses on the recovery of the self. Barthes dwells on the enormity of his grief which seems to cancel the possibility that mourning could ever achieve anything. So far, I have endorsed Derrida's view. But at this point, the question is, how are we to articulate the ongoing encounter between self and other which authentic mourning seems to entail? I think we have some pieces of the puzzle: Derrida (like Barthes) realizes how the loss of the other involves an intensification of the self that remains—when the beloved dies we are thrown back upon ourselves with a strong sense of our own existence, separate and alone. We cannot just forget, abandon, or appropriate the other, but nor can we just return to ourselves after a suitable period of mourning, because we are forever changed by the death of the one we love. This is not a point that Derrida dwells on. He accepts that mourning involves honoring the departed and continuing our relationship with her in some way. But it also involves the reappropriation of the self: Not restoring the old self, as Freud suggests, but remaking ourselves after the death of the other which has undermined our sense of who we are.

In fact, Freud, Barthes, and Derrida open up three different perspectives on mourning, and together they illuminate the dialectics of mourning which remains profoundly problematic. Freud's possible mourning ends with the destruction of the other, while Barthes's version of mourning implies the abandonment of the self. But Derrida is able to straddle the divide between self and other, and he recovers the self in order to honor the other and avoid some of the pitfalls of mourning. Sometimes it seems that he is caught in a loop, moving between possible and impossible mourning as alternatives that presuppose the continuity of the self that we *have* been, in relation to the other who has died. Derrida agonizes over mourning, but it must also be admitted that mourning the *possibility* of mourning is not yet mourning itself. Paradoxically, his own work of mourning—assuming that it is successful—would have to be an example of what *he* says cannot be done. Perhaps we are bound to assume that authentic mourning is possible because this is what we owe to the departed, and ought implies can. At the same time, however, we may also have to conclude that the conditions of mourning are in conflict with each other, and so they are finally impossible to fulfill: Mourning is interminable and mourning is impossible. Derrida focuses on the anxiety of mourning and he describes the ways in which mourning can go wrong. But he seems to neglect the positive determination of mourning, and he avoids the remaking of the self which follows the mourning process.

As we have noted, mourning involves self and others—but not just the other who has died, but all of the others—the survivors—who live in the community that we belong to. Mourning can be a private affair, but there is also public mourning in which we commemorate the departed and begin to renew ourselves in relation to other people. Freud describes mourning as a purely personal process of extreme alienation and self-recovery. He does not mention the public and ritual aspects of mourning that help restore the mourner to the community by enclosing personal grief within a social frame. Now it may seem that Derrida's essays on mourning are also limited, personal works. But we should not forget that these are books and memorial addresses, and as such they are delivered to an audience, they are published, and they are public avowals of grief which involve apostrophes to the dead in the presence of others. And so, Derrida performs the act of mourning in a public setting, in relationship to others—including readers, fellow mourners, and friends.

One final point to make here is that the work of mourning takes time. If Derrida is right it may even be "interminable." Mourning cannot be rushed; indeed, it may well be an endless labor that continues in some form for the rest of our lives. It takes its own time, and it can never be dispensed with. In this respect, there is something deeply wrong with the Stoic sage who exhorts a woman, who has suffered the death of her husband and both of her sons, to put aside mourning and continue with her life. Seneca accepts that mourning is "natural," but he claims that Marcia's excessive mourning is pointless—it does not bring the dead back, and so he says that she should follow reason by abandoning her grief. But this advice seems like thoughtless problem solving, which lacks a spiritual understanding of how these things work:

> If tears can vanquish fate, let us marshal tears; let every day be passed in grief, let every night be sleepless and consumed in sorrow ... But if no wailing can recall the dead, if no distress can alter a destiny that is immutable and fixed for all eternity ... then let grief, which is futile, cease.[28]

Here, Seneca prefigures Freud's position, and his discomfort with grief and mourning is perhaps typical of the Western intellectual tradition.

By contrast, we may consider a different, non-Western perspective: In the *Analects*, Tsai Wo [or Yü] asks Confucius about the customary three-year mourning period for one's parents. Tsai Wo complains that

> even a full year is too long. If the gentleman gives up the practice of the rites for three years, the rites are sure to be in ruins; if he gives up the practice of music for three years, music is sure to collapse.

Tsai Wo is anxious to return to special food and finery within a year, but his attitude shocks Confucius: "How unfeeling Yü is. A child ceases to be nursed by his parents only when he is three years old. Three years mourning is observed throughout the empire. Was Yü not given three years' love by his parents?"[29] Confucius understands the absolute importance of mourning as a way of structuring grief, reconfiguring one's place in the world, and continuing the relationship with the departed so that there may be continuity in spite of bereavement. In the *Analects*, mourning is fraught with anxiety, just as it is in Derrida. But Confucius insists on its importance; indeed, at one point he makes the strong claim that mourning is the proper measure of selfhood: According to Tseng Tzu: "I have heard the Master say that on no occasion does a man realize himself to the full, though, when pressed, he said that mourning for one's parents may be an exception."[30] All of which supports the claim that mourning is not a secondary concern, but a crucial ingredient of personal identity and self-determination. But this is also what Derrida argues for in different places. For example, in his discussion with Elizabeth Roudinesco he seems to claim that mourning is absolutely central to philosophy and his own work in particular:

> For a long time now I myself have been "working" at mourning—if I can put it that way—or have been letting myself be worked by the question of mourning, by the aporias of the "work of mourning," on the resources and the limits of psychoanalytic discourse on this subject, and on a certain coextensivity between work in general and the work of mourning. The work of mourning is not one work among others. All work involves this transformation, this appropriating idealization, this internalization that characterizes "mourning."[31]

For Derrida, mourning is not a marginal theme but a focal point of spiritual life in which philosophy comes to grips with the most difficult questions concerning that which is radically and completely *other*.

Following the death of Paul de Man, Derrida observes that all of our relationships are tinged with mourning, and the unspoken truth of every friendship is that one of us will live to see the other one die. In *Memoires for Paul de Man*, he speculates that the absence of the other—in death or in the anticipation of death—might actually be the origin of the inner life from which we derive our memory and our "soul." For, he writes:

> The "me" or the "us" of which we speak then arise and are delimited in the way that they are only through this experience of the other, and of the other as other who can die, leaving in me or in us this memory of the other. This terrible solitude which is mine or ours at the death of the other is what constitutes that relationship to self which we call "me," "us," "between us," "subjectivity," "intersubjectivity," "memory." The possibility of death "happens," so to speak, "before" these different instances and makes them possible … the "within me" and the "within us" *do not* arise or appear *before* this terrible experience.[32]

Now Derrida's speculation at this point is itself a homage to de Man, and the whole book, *Memoires for Paul de Man*, involves a rethinking and coming to grips with some of de Man's basic ideas in the context of the memorial address. This continuing conversation with another thinker, one whom he knew and loved, becomes the affirmation of an ongoing relationship with the departed, and it suggests the possibility of a successful mourning. In fact, all the essays in *The Work of Mourning* can be read in this way: as the provocation of mourning that impels us toward thinking and writing. Contra Freud, mourning is not simply the disengagement from the other and the reappropriation of the self. As Derrida shows us, mourning is to be viewed in terms of a dialogue and engagement with the deceased, which leads to new possibilities of thinking and response. The relationship with the departed is not fixed and sealed with her death; it must continue, like all relationships with loved ones, to inspire and evoke the best in us. And this is what we owe to those who are gone.[33]

In his essay on the "deaths" of Roland Barthes, Derrida describes how the departed—in this case Barthes himself—seems to command a transformation on the part of the mourners who survive him. Perhaps, by responding to this command and by coming to terms with Barthes, as a thinker and as a human being, we can begin to mourn authentically—and this suggests one respect in which the remaking of the self is possible in Derridean mourning. Of course, we cannot always cite the written work of others, but their words and their deeds may be considered as a part of their essential being:

> Roland Barthes looks at us (inside each of us, so that each of us can then say that Barthes's thought, memory, and friendship concern only us), and we do not do as we please with this look, even though each of us has it at his disposal, in his own way, according to his own place and history. It is within us but it is not ours; we do not have it available to us like a moment or part of our interiority. And what looks at us may be indifferent, loving, dreadful, grateful, attentive, ironic, silent, bored, reserved, fervent or smiling, a child or already quite old; in short, it can give us any of the innumerable signs of life or death that we might draw from the circumscribed reserve of his texts or our memory.[34]

As we have seen, it is not a look or a gaze we can ever control or appropriate for the other remains autonomous within me; but at the same time, the encounter with the departed which this passage describes calls us back to ourselves and toward a better life. Mourning challenges the self and puts it on trial. Indeed, it commands self-renewal and self-appropriation if only for the sake of the beloved: He is dead, but we must honor his name and keep him in mind, and we can continue his "work" so that he can live on. In the end, mourning is a *spiritual* relationship because it affirms our continued connection to those who have inspired us to become who we are, and our sense of belonging to a community—or the stream of life—which includes both the living and the dead. And even though mourning requires memory, gratitude and faithfulness, etc., it goes beyond the *ethical* requirement of honoring the dead in an appropriate way. As Derrida grasps, through his own spiritual practice as a philosopher, death interrupts our relationship with the other and it changes the nature of our responsibilities, but it does not end everything between us.

So why do we mourn, and how is mourning to be accomplished? The following is not an adequate response—questions have been raised in this chapter which must remain unanswered—but perhaps we can suggest a path for future reflection. For Freud, mourning is all about relinquishing the past and coming to terms with the reality of the present. There is no sense of time in the Freudian unconscious—all time is present at once, because every past trauma and every wish concerning the future is at work in the present. Hence it is difficult, but we must be realistic and wean ourselves from that which is over and done with. In Barthes, the emphasis is definitely on the past, and, while he denies it, one has the sense that his grief and his preoccupation with photographs are about recapturing the past or hanging on to it so that it does not slip away. By contrast, Derrida gives us a version of mourning which is directed toward future possibilities—not recovering the past or remaining firmly in the present, but, as we will see, opening up the relationship with the departed toward future possibilities, and possibly a new life. Derrida's discussion reflects a profoundly spiritual view, and it is a compelling example of philosophy as a spiritual practice. Here, for the most part, we follow his lead: First, the task of mourning must include self-gathering and self-healing which is something we can usually assume the departed would desire for us. The self that exists in relation to the beloved also dies with the death of the beloved, and so we must reintegrate ourselves through the reorientation of our self toward others. But this is not a triumphant conclusion, as Freud would have us believe, and the work of mourning must also be in some way to continue our relationship with the one who has died, since abandonment is not an ethical possibility. And because he or she is someone we have loved, and presumably still love, the task of mourning must be to honor the relationship between us, by focusing on the uniqueness of that relationship and the uniqueness of the departed. This is done consciously and deliberately and, more often than not, *publicly*, in a spirit of reverence for what the other person has been, and also because he or she has become a part of who we are. Neither Freud nor Barthes affirms this task in terms of projective understanding, but Derrida memorializes those who have died by looking at the future possibilities of our relationship to them. In this way, Derrida challenges the "traditional" account of mourning that runs at least from Seneca to Freud. For whereas Freud's view is self-oriented and Barthes is completely focused on the other, Derrida maintains a *spiritual* perspective that pays attention to the relationship between the self and other, the living and the dead.

9

Irigaray on Love

Luce Irigaray is a philosopher, a linguist, a psychoanalyst, and a feminist; she is also a practitioner of yoga and other spiritual forms. Her writings are profoundly illuminating because they draw upon such a variety of different perspectives. Irigaray questions the traditional formulations of philosophy, and in some of her works she creates her own speculative, poetic discourse to look at things in a more creative light. She argues that our entrenched ideas about mind and body, the physical versus the spiritual, and the priority of the male over the female have split us off from nature, from others, and even from ourselves. But in response, she looks to love as the way to recover a more genuine life, by transforming ourselves into spiritually accomplished human beings. Irigaray speculates that what we know today as philosophy (or *the love of wisdom*) was at one time *the wisdom of love* which focused on caring, and the cultivation of an intimate, loving relationship with another person.[1] As she comments in *The Way of Love*, we have lost the original sense of philosophy as a kind of spiritual wisdom, and now we are left, for the most part, with an impersonal discourse that only speaks to other specialists:

> Confused with a conceptual translation of the real, a formal knowledge, *sophia* is often reduced to a mental exercise, passed on from a master to disciples, of use in populating universities and in having discussions among the initiated but without the impact on our lives that a wisdom presupposes. The presumed friend of wisdom becomes, from then on, one who falls into wells due to an inability to walk upon the earth. His science causes laughter, like that of the other sages just as incapable of governing their life and who nevertheless issue words claiming to instruct us on the most everyday and the most sublime. Between the head and the feet, a continuity is lost, a perspective has not been constructed. And the wisdom of which these technicians of the logos are enamoured is sometimes a knowing how to die, but seldom the apprenticeship to a knowing how to live.[2]

According to Irigaray, contemporary philosophy has become a rather soulless project, and her own writings can be viewed as an attempt to recover the spiritual goal of philosophy. Some critics, like Morny Joy, see this as just another phase in her thinking, but Irigaray's philosophy has always engaged with spiritual themes; only now this has finally become explicit.[3]

For Irigaray, the true paradigm of a loving relationship is the lived encounter between a man and a woman; for as she points out, the sexual difference of male and female seems to permeate the whole of nature—"Nature has a sex always and everywhere."[4] But sexual difference is also basic to culture as well, and men and women have different experiences of the world because of the physical and cultural differences between them. Irigaray describes this duality of subjectivities in terms of a dialectic which allows for the spiritual flourishing of each partner. But this is not a dialectic that can ever lead to a synthesis, for this would involve the end of desire and the spiritual inspiration that can only exist in the space between one person and another. As she says: "Contrary to other philosophers of difference, I start from a real and concrete difference that is, as such, a universal which cannot be overcome without abolishing the universal itself."[5] This means that traditional ideas about romantic love as a kind of "fusion" are ill-conceived, for it is essential to preserve the autonomy of each of the romantic partners. And if Irigaray is right, then human nature is fundamentally *two*: "The *one* no longer remains here the visible or invisible, conscious or unconscious paradigm, which governs rational organization; this organization henceforth takes into consideration the existence of two subjects, irreducible one to the other."[6]

Irigaray is an important spiritual thinker who begins with the spiritual possibilities of human beings in love. She also discusses other spiritual themes, including breathing, teaching, listening, and thinking, and in this way she recovers a basic spiritual wisdom which is not "heaven-sent" since it emerges from everyday life and our own connection with others. From this starting point—the ideal possibility of human relationship—Irigaray moves on to broader themes, including what we owe to others, the nature of hospitality, and how we can share the world. Other thinkers start with the big picture—including theology and metaphysics—and they work their way down to the microcosmic level of personal relations which seem unimportant by comparison. But Irigaray begins with the lived experience of human relationships, and especially the male–female encounter which she views as the paradigm example of difference. Throughout her work she shows how this can enhance our ethical, political, and spiritual development.

Irigaray claims that through self-cultivation, in the context of a loving relationship with another, I can transcend my natural origins by recreating myself as an autonomous and spiritually accomplished human being. In this chapter,

I focus on the spiritual dimension of Irigaray's philosophy of love. First, I look at her relationship to Plato, and her reading of the *Symposium*, which suggests the possibility of a more inspiring account of love than the one that has prevailed in Western culture, and which still affects us today. In this respect, Irigaray is the philosophical heir of Plato, for she returns to the passionate questioning of love; and like Plato, she emphasizes that love is a spiritual accomplishment that begins with the *eros* of physical desire and longing. Next, I look at Irigaray's own account of love and relationship, and the importance of sexual difference as a catalyst for spiritual becoming. Finally, I discuss some of Irigaray's later work which examines important spiritual themes such as breathing, listening, thinking, and teaching. In her essays, and in books such as *Between East and West* and *I Love to You*, Irigaray seeks to unify her own personal experience as a thinker and a practitioner of meditation and yoga, with the Western philosophical tradition that she belongs to. For the most part, philosophers tend to minimize their personal experience, and they claim that one's own life should not intrude upon the *ideas* which are being discussed. But this makes philosophy a more impersonal exercise from which we need to keep an emotional distance. By contrast, Irigaray makes a point of interlacing her own experience with the spiritual themes that she describes, and this follows from the same "wisdom of love" that inspires her turn to the spiritual.

Platonic love

Plato viewed love as the key to the divine, for in love we have the intimation of a higher realm of being which is more important than our own selfish ego. To begin with, love makes us feel dissatisfied with ourselves, for in love we realize just how incomplete we are, and through the beloved we feel drawn toward a higher reality and truth. In the *Phaedrus* and in the *Symposium*, Plato describes how love initiates a spiritual journey toward the higher forms, including Justice, Temperance, and Wisdom, and ultimately the highest form of all, the form of the Good. But of all the different forms, only Beauty shines forth in the midst of the visible world; and so it is individual beauty that draws us away from everyday life toward the higher realm where the forms exist beyond the ravages of space and time.

In the *Symposium*, the love of individual beauty becomes the first step on the ladder of love, and this leads us through several different levels of spiritual accomplishment.[7] The love of individual beauty pulls me out of my own selfish life and inspires me to care for someone else who seems to complete me. But I cannot remain fixated on just one person; the whole point of love is that it opens up the world for me, and the true lover starts to see the beautiful in everything, including nature, and other people that she knows. In this respect, the next step on the ladder of love would be the love of all physical beauty, or a more complete appreciation for the value of the world and everything that has been given to us. After this, Plato describes the third level of love as the love of inner beauty, in which we recognize that someone may have a beautiful soul even if they are physically unattractive. Here, Plato affirms that personal virtue is itself attractive and that we want to be around people who are good because their goodness is something that we find inspiring. In this way, beauty becomes a stepping stone to morality; the physical and the spiritual are profoundly connected to each other—and this becomes an important aspect of Irigaray's own discussion of love.

After the love of inner beauty, we move to the love of higher principles and scientific laws. At this level, we experience a profound sense of wonder, and this is associated with a more complete revelation of the universe, including the moral realm, and the physical marvels that scientists describe. Eventually, we are brought to the highest level, the love of the Good, which is also associated with Beauty and Truth. The Good is the highest principle of all and the ground of our being. It is the goal of our quest, but it is also what inspired us in the first place even though we did not know it. Plato describes it in somewhat mystical terms, but in the context of the *Symposium*, it all makes perfect sense:

> And if … man's life is ever worth the living, it is when he has attained this vision of the very soul of beauty. And once you have seen it, you will never be seduced again by the charm of gold, of dress, of comely boys, or lads just ripening to manhood; you will care nothing for the beauties that used to take your breath away and kindle such a longing in you, and many others like you, Socrates, to be always at the side of the beloved and feasting your eyes upon him.[8]

The last comment implies that physical beauty is not enough, for it would only be a *semblance* of what is really good and truly beautiful. But as Irigaray observes, the physical is thereby devalued, and in this way we may lose the possibility of erotic encounter that could nourish both the body and the soul.

Irigaray writes about Plato's account of love in her essay "Sorcerer Love."[9] Here, she points out that while Socrates presents his philosophy of love as something that he has learned from the priestess Diotima, Diotima herself is not actually present at the banquet, and she is not one of those who makes her own speech in praise of love. In this respect, the *Symposium* continues the philosophical exclusion of women, and for the most part it disdains the male/female encounter as an inferior spiritual relationship. However, Irigaray also notes that in the *Symposium* the question of love is not just an abstract issue. For here we have lovers who are profoundly affected by their love, and they passionately discuss a question that appeals to the deepest part of who they are. The *Symposium* is clearly concerned with the wisdom of love; and in her essay, Irigaray recovers a deeper spiritual perspective on love which is briefly revealed but finally hidden again by Plato's own metaphysical view.

I am sympathetic to Irigaray's reading of the *Symposium*, and I think she shows that there is a significant conflict in Plato's text. As we saw in the discussion above, the ladder of love is goal directed, and one frequent complaint is that for Plato the individual beloved is not valued for his or her own sake but used as a means to an end.[10] Thus, if I love someone who is beautiful and good, then according to Plato this will inspire me to move higher and higher toward the ultimate end of the Good. But if the Good is our goal, then this suggests that individuals may be substituted for each other; and if someone who is better or more beautiful comes along, then it makes sense to abandon the first person for the second just to make more spiritual progress.

For Irigaray, part of the problem here is that we are not dealing with lovers but with the lover and his beloved; and this hierarchical relationship undermines reciprocity between the two of them. It also challenges the loving relationship which must be nurtured for its own sake: "But, if procreation becomes its goal," Irigaray comments, "it risks losing its internal motivation, its fecundity 'in itself', its slow and constant regeneration."[11] On this view, it seems that once you reach the ultimate goal on the ladder of love, you no longer need the beloved, for now you would be spiritually complete. This is what Alcibiades complains about at the very end of the *Symposium*: Socrates is spiritually accomplished but he does not seem to need anyone (including Alcibiades) in his life. He is completely self-possessed, for he has apparently achieved the highest spiritual goal. And Irigaray asks whether this is really the end that we should aspire to:

> What seemed to me most original in Diotima's method has disappeared once again. That irreducible intermediary milieu of love is cancelled between "subject" (an inadequate word in Plato) and "beloved reality." Amorous becoming no longer constitutes a becoming of the lover himself, of love in the (male or female) lover, between the lovers … Instead it is now a teleological quest for what is deemed the highest reality and often situated in a transcendence inaccessible to our condition as mortals. Immortality is put off until death and is not counted as one of our constant tasks as mortals, as a transmutation that is endlessly

incumbent on us here and now, as a possibility inscribed in a body capable of divine becoming. Beauty of body and beauty of soul become hierarchized, and the love of women becomes the lot of those who, incapable of being creators in soul, are fecund in body and seek the immortality of their name perpetuated by their offspring.[12]

So this is the problem with Socrates's account of love in the *Symposium*: It ignores the lived reality of love in favor of the ultimate goal, which lies *beyond* love and beauty as we know it.

At this point, then, we can return to an earlier point in the *Symposium*, for in the wisdom of Diotima there seems to be another possibility of mutual engendering and self-enhancement which is accomplished through the amorous relationship itself. And this is what Irigaray refers to above as being "most original" in Diotima's method. In the early part of her speech, Diotima argues that love is "a longing not for the beautiful itself but for the conception and generation that the beautiful effects."[13] She says that each of us is full of physical and spiritual possibilities; in fact, we are "pregnant" in our being, and so we naturally seek to procreate or have a relationship with another individual who inspires us to bring our potential to fulfillment and thereby in to the world. Some desire to have children and so they will procreate physically (with a man or a woman). But others are pregnant with spiritual possibilities and they seek a relationship with another who will inspire them "to bring forth in beauty." This is the important part of Diotima's speech that Irigaray calls to our attention:

> We are all of us prolific, Socrates, in body and in soul, and when we reach a certain age our nature urges us to procreation. Nor can we be quickened by ugliness, but only by the beautiful. Conception, we know, takes place when man and woman come together, but there's a divinity in human propagation, an immortal something in the midst of man's mortality which is incompatible with any kind of discord. And ugliness is at odds with the divine, while beauty is in perfect harmony. In propagation, then, Beauty is the goddess of both fate and travail, and so when procreancy draws near the beautiful it grows genial and blithe, and birth follows swiftly on conception. But when it meets with ugliness it is overcome with heaviness and gloom, and turning away it shrinks into itself and is not brought to bed, but still labors under its painful burden. And so, when the procreant is big with child, he is strangely stirred by the beautiful, because he knows that beauty's tenant will bring his travail to an end. So you see, Socrates, that Love is not exactly a longing for the beautiful, as you suggested.
>
> Well, what is it then?
>
> A longing not for the beautiful itself, but for the conception and generation that the beautiful effects.[14]

As Irigaray notes, in this passage pregnancy seems to precede intercourse. The idea being that through an enhanced relationship with another person, we may each be inspired to fulfill our deepest spiritual potential. At this point, however, love is no longer viewed as a means to an end, where the goal is to produce children, or spiritual progeny like books and artworks. Instead, love's desire is for love itself, and through the inspiration of love our souls can become fruitful.

Thus, Irigaray recovers the wisdom of love as a mutual engendering between two people in a loving, caring relationship with each other, which is, "never completed, always evolving."[15] Such a relationship can partake of both the physical and the spiritual, but contrary to what Plato says at the end of Diotima's speech, it really does not need to transcend the realm of the physical or the individual beloved in order to reach its goal, which is eternity, here and now. In the *Symposium*, the central relationship is the one between Diotima and Socrates, for as male and female, teacher and student, they represent the different poles that Eros traverses between the two partners. Such a love transforms both of them; it inspires their continual growth, and it continually regenerates the relationship that they share. It is a sacred encounter, and in the end it allows them to achieve their fullest potential through their complete involvement with each other. But as we have seen, this sense of mutual engendering is lost once Diotima moves into the last part of her account. Here, love becomes a means to an end because now there is something beyond love, which is the goal of the lovers and the reason for love's existence in the first place. And with this account of the ladder of love, we finally reach the point where absolute Beauty is apprehended, eternal and unchanging, and we are free of contamination by the physical realm: "And if ... man's life is ever worth the living, it is when he has attained this vision of the very soul of beauty."[16] This conclusion, whether it derives from Socrates, Plato, or Diotima herself, can be read as a disavowal of this world as an impoverished realm which pales in comparison with the pure realm of the forms and disembodied beauty. But *absolute* beauty cannot figure in any account that tries to grasp the meaningful character of human existence, in which both the spiritual and the physical are present here and now.

Irigaray is profoundly influenced by Plato's account of passionate love in the *Symposium*, but she makes a point of challenging some of Diotima's conclusions, which may or may not derive from Plato himself. In particular, Irigaray maintains that love involves the continual interweaving of the physical and the spiritual— the one is *not* a refuge from the other—and their intensification within desire. She also suggests that love has no final goal beyond itself for this would make love into the means to an end rather than an end in itself. The fact is that love is actually the desire for desire, and the perpetual renewal of tenderness, passion, and joy. Loving human relationships are inherently spiritual in character, although this does not mean that they cannot participate in the physical which must now be revalued as the *ground* of the spiritual, as opposed to its opposite. At the end of Socrates's speech, we are told that love ultimately leads to self-sufficiency and the overcoming of love because it has now reached its goal. But for Irigaray, this is a mistake: love is an intermediary between the two lovers, and between the human and the divine, the physical and the spiritual, the male and the female, etc., and without love as a continually inspiring experience we would be spiritually dead and lacking in the power to grow. In the *Symposium*, Diotima has an ambiguous place as the teacher of Socrates, but this suggests the secret power of the feminine which is recovered at the onset of spiritual life. We can now focus on the wisdom of love in Irigaray's own philosophical project.

The spiritual context of love

It should be clear by now that for Irigaray, spirituality is not unworldly; it is not an escape from material existence but a heightening and perfecting of our individual nature within the horizon of everyday life. And insofar as spirituality is related to transcendence in Irigaray's philosophy, it is always an immanent transcendence which transfigures the world that we live in. In an interview, Irigaray describes this as follows:

> Instead of the repression of spirit on body, which is usual in our tradition, I prefer the transformation of body as living matter into spiritual matter … Eastern cultures have disclosed to me this other path. There is no longer a question of dividing spirit and body, the one having to lay down the law on the other, but of transforming a vital energy into a spiritual energy at the service of breathing, of loving, of listening, of speaking and thinking. Such a process transforms, one could say transmutes or transfigures, little by little, our original bodily matter into spiritualized bodily matter, as I explained notably in *Between East and West*. I consider such a spiritual journey as being more adult and also more religious.[17]

Through spiritual practices—including loving, listening, breathing, speaking, and thinking—we may cultivate and refine ourselves so that we become more spiritually accomplished; and in this way, we can experience "immortality" not as another life than the one that we have now, but as the ultimate depth and fulfillment of the present life here and now.

In various works, Irigaray continues her pursuit of love as the accomplishment of spiritual life. For example, her extraordinary book, *Elemental Passions*, takes the form of a female lover passionately addressing her male beloved. In the following passage, for example, she describes two different kinds of love that roughly correspond to the typically male and the (ideal) female form of romantic encounter. The first is associated with love as a form of domination and control, while the second is the love that can be experienced as mutual engendering and enhancement:

> Love can be the becoming which appropriates the other for itself by consuming it, introjecting it into itself, to the point where the other disappears. Or love can be the motor of becoming allowing both the one and the other to grow. For such a love, each must keep their body autonomous. The one should not be the source of the other nor the other of the one. Two lives should embrace and fertilize each other, without either being a fixed goal for the other.[18]

It is important to keep these two versions of love separate. Love as a kind of master–slave relationship is not authentic love, although it could be a front for something else, and love as a complete and ongoing self-sacrifice is probably not love either since it destroys the dialectical relationship between the one and the other, and this is what enhances love as a genuine possibility that continually renews itself. Irigaray's writing in *Elemental Passions* is lyrical and powerful, and it seems only appropriate to use poetic language for the evocation of love. In this respect, her work is both descriptive and *performative*, for it calls upon readers to celebrate love as an important project in their own spiritual life.

In traditional romantic love, beginning with the courtly love tradition, the beloved is worshipped as an ideal being, and so Lancelot gets down on his knees before Guinevere and swears his eternal devotion. In contemporary society, we are the heirs to the same romantic tradition, and our songs, films, novels, and other cultural forms testify to the continued importance of the romantic ideal of love as a quasi-religious phenomenon. In her work, Irigaray challenges this version of passionate love, and she describes love as a spiritual possibility which empowers and enhances each of the lovers:

> Love between man and woman thus becomes the mastery and culture of energy rather than its instinctual expenditure, to be redeemed by procreation here on earth and faith in asexual happiness in the beyond—the path to this being the acquisition of an insensible logos … Love is accomplished by two, without dividing roles between the beloved and the lover, between objectial or animal passivity on the one hand, and generally conscious and valorous activity on the

other. Woman and man remain two in love. Watching over and creating the universe is their primary task, and it remains so.[19]

We could call this a "post-romantic" love to indicate a critical perspective on romantic love which incorporates all that is good in it, while at the same time it transcends some of its traditional aspects. As we noted earlier, for instance, romantic love is often associated with the ideal of fusion in which the two lovers become one by surrendering their own individual lives within the relationship. Irigaray questions this ideal because it seems to her that merging and fusion can be ways of seeking abandonment, in which love becomes an escape from ourselves. Likewise, she insists on the irreducibility of the *two* in relation to each other: "This is not to say that the two become one, but that each follows a specific path so that the relation is possible in the moment and in the long term, despite or thanks to the difference between the two."[20]

In the passage from *Elemental Passions* that I quoted above, Irigaray emphasizes the difference between thinking about love as a kind of possessiveness or ownership, and thinking about love as allowing the other one to be. The possessive love is based on the subject/object relationship which does not really change the subject, while the other kind of love is based on the love between two subjects who care deeply for each other, and who remain open to each other, so that their love is both for the one *and* for the other. Sometimes, Irigaray talks about the importance of wonder as a condition for achieving this goal: Plato says that philosophy begins with a sense of wonder for without a feeling of astonishment at the sheer existence of this world, we would never begin to ask philosophical questions such as "Why is there something rather than nothing?" Similarly, in the case of love, we experience a sense of wonder concerning the other person, and this inspires us and draws us toward the beloved. Wonder implies a full bestowal of attention that allows the other to fulfill her highest potential. And wonder concerning the other must be maintained if the spiritual possibilities of a relationship are to thrive. By contrast, appropriation and domination entail the end of wonder; for once the forms of our encounter are fixed then nothing new can ever happen between us. In this respect, love must cultivate the autonomy of the other as the very condition for its own fecundity and its continued existence. As Irigaray comments: "Recognizing you means or implies respecting you as other, accepting that I draw myself to a halt before you as before something insurmountable, a mystery, a freedom that will never be mine, a mine that will never be mine."[21] Without wonder we may become habituated to the other person and eventually love will die because the inspiration has been lost.

Even so, the ideal of the couple is a neglected spiritual paradigm, especially in the West. Typically, men and women are taught to think that they can experience complete fulfillment as mothers and as "successful" men; but in *Between East and West* Irigaray argues that we can actually achieve this as lovers, for only in this relationship is it possible to fulfill every aspect of our being, including the physical, the emotional, the intellectual, and the spiritual. It is strange that the couple does not have more importance as a spiritual ideal; but in other cultures, such an ideal is understood. For example, in Hinduism there are many representations of Krishna and his consort depicted side by side as two human beings who pursue a spiritual journey together. And Irigaray comments: "The gods of India, moreover, generally appear as a couple: man and woman creating the universe through their familiarity with certain elements, through their love as well, and they destroy it through their passion. We are far from the philosophical-religious representations that have characterized the West for several millennia."[22] Perhaps men have been taught that their personal fulfillment lies in pursuing a career; and in more traditional cultures, women are encouraged to think of themselves as wives and mothers before anything else. But Irigaray makes an important point by giving priority to the loving relationship between two separate individuals who create a space together. And this is a space into which others—children, friends, and strangers—will come to receive the love and caring that has been cultivated and so prepared for them. As Irigaray explains:

> The first and principal task in order to found or refound a family resides in the work of love between a man and a woman, a woman and a man, who, in the name of desire, intend to live together for the long term, to combine, in them and between them, the moment of the birth of attraction with the perpetuation of love, the instant with eternity.[23]

Once again, in this passage, Irigaray's goal is to evoke the very possibility that she is describing.

The love between a man and a woman can become the model for other relationships, including same-sex relationships and friendship of every kind. For Irigaray it is the paradigm case for thinking about difference or otherness in general. She also insists that the sexual (or "sexuate") difference between male and female is the most significant difference of all—for more than any other kind of difference, it is a difference that makes all the difference in the world: It determines how we make love, how we engender children, how we are treated by others, and the extent of our opportunities in life. In this respect, Irigaray views sexual difference (as opposed to class difference or the ontological difference) as the underlying dynamic of history, and at various points she argues that we can only recover the present and the future once we affirm this primary dialectic between the female and the male: "Sexual difference is one of the major philosophical issues, if not the issue of our age. According to Heidegger, each age has one issue to think through and one only. Sexual difference is probably the issue in our time which could be our 'salvation' if we thought it through."[24]

Irigaray's focus on the male/female relation and its fulfillment in love involves a return to personal relationship as the key to spiritual development and enhancement. As we have seen, she rejects the traditional move toward unity or oneness and insists upon the irreducibility of the relationship between the self and other. In this respect, she belongs to a dialogical tradition in philosophy which includes Plato and others. For Plato, the truth emerges in the course of conversation with another, and it cannot be achieved through solitary inner reflection. More recently, Martin Buber and Emmanuel Levinas both emphasize the I–You or Self–Other encounter, and they insist on the primacy of relationship which always precedes the sense of "you" and "me" as separate beings.[25] For Buber, the I and You are equal partners; for Levinas, the Other has priority and calls me into being. Irigaray is influenced by each of these thinkers, but in the end the male/female encounter that she describes is more relevant insofar as it goes beyond the ethical encounter and acknowledges the spiritual *and* the physical as part of a continuum where there is a reciprocal exchange between us. "Not in me," she writes, "but in our difference lies the abyss. We can never be sure of bridging the gap between us. But that is our adventure. Without this peril there is no us. If you turn it into a guarantee, you separate us."[26]

Given the centrality of the personal relationship, it is perhaps not surprising that Irigaray writes about her own personal experience as well offering a philosophical perspective on these themes. In the preface to *I Love to You*, she describes her encounter with Renzo Imbeni, whom she met when they were on the same panel in San Donato, Italy. For Irigaray, it was an exemplary encounter which she describes as exhilarating and fecund. Imbeni showed judiciousness and integrity, and he was able to listen to what she had to say in a way that she found impressive:

> I appreciate these qualities and I try to behave that way myself. They can only really be exercised and especially appear for what they are in reciprocity. They were possible that night in San Donato. Mutual respect occurred between us that few noticed, perhaps, but which was really there, and still is. We did not, for all that, renounce our own selves; otherwise the outcome would not have been as it was. We were two: a man and a woman speaking in accordance with our identity, our conscience, our cultural heritage, and even our sensibility.[27]

Irigaray tells us that as a result of this encounter she was inspired to write her book *I Love to You*. And so, "It is in the form of a book, then, that the outcome of the debate at San Donato will first manifest itself. A book concerning the encounter between woman and man, women and men. An encounter characterized by belonging to a sexed nature to which it is proper to be faithful."[28] In this respect, we may think of her book as the offspring of love which Diotima describes in the *Symposium*, when beauty inspires spiritual renewal and the fulfillment of emergent possibilities of the soul.

In *Between East and West*, Irigaray also describes some of her spiritual practices and the interlacing of two different traditions as her own spiritual achievement; and this is experienced as a personal appropriation of meaning:

> I knew that the body is potentially divine, I knew it notably through my Christian tradition of which it is, in fact, the message, but I did not know how to develop this divinity. Through practicing breathing, through educating my perceptions, through concerning myself continually with cultivating the life of my body, through reading current and ancient texts of the yoga tradition and Tantric texts, I learned what I knew: the body is the site of the incarnation of the divine and I have to treat it as such … The body itself, including in the carnal act, can be deified. That does not mean that it overcomes itself but that it blossoms, becomes more subtly and totally sensible.[29]

Between East and West is in many ways Irigaray's most engaging work for the spiritual perspective that I have been describing in this chapter. Irigaray is drawn to non-Western thought and practices, and her emphasis on related themes, such as multiculturalism, is an extension of her views on sexual difference as the fundamental difference which can lead us to a better future. The subtitle of *Between East and West* is "from Singularity to Community," and in the next part of this chapter I will look at some other spiritual practices which Irigaray specifies as conditions for the spiritual community that is still on its way. These spiritual practices include breathing, thinking, listening, and teaching, and they can be viewed as different aspects of the same wisdom of love that has just been described.

Breathing, listening, thinking, and teaching

In *Between East and West*, Irigaray dwells on the importance of breathing as the basis of all spiritual practices, and this is something that she has studied and cultivated throughout her life. Irigaray points out that in the West, we have a tendency to think of breathing as something purely mechanical, and an important part of our *physical* health. But we lack any spiritual wisdom concerning breathing, which is our first autonomous gesture, and the way in which we take charge of our own life. As she warns us, "As long as we do not breathe in an autonomous manner, not only do we live badly but we encroach upon others in order to live."[30] One of the reasons that we have neglected breathing is because we have been taught to separate the spiritual from the physical; we have been accustomed to think that everything associated with the body should be despised, and so we have come to think—at least in the West—that by neglecting the body we may actually become more spiritual.

In Asian traditions, however, the importance of breath is more completely understood, and at the same time there is not such a disjunction between the physical and the spiritual as two separate realms. An important part of Irigaray's philosophy involves the desire to overturn this false opposition and to show the inherent connection between the physical and the spiritual aspects of our being. For as she realizes, from her own study of yoga and Hindu breathing techniques, the goal must be to cultivate a spiritual body, where breathing can be apprehended as both spiritual and physical in nature: "Becoming spiritual amounts to transforming our elemental vital breath little by little into a more subtle breath in the service of the heart, of thought, of speech, and not only in the service of physiological survival."[31] And this means that through attention to breath we may also achieve a more spiritual existence which allows us to engage more fully with the world.

On one level, taking hold of our own breath in a mindful, self-conscious way is to affirm our autonomy by gathering ourselves within ourselves as separate self-conscious beings; for as she observes, "We are not really born, really autonomous or living as long as we do not take care, in a conscious and voluntary way, of our breathing."[32] At another level, of course, we all share our breath because we all breathe in the same air that surrounds us, and this emphasizes our interconnectedness with each other. Autonomy and connection seem to run together. On the face of it, this stress on personal autonomy may be jarring in the context of spiritual cultivation, especially from an Asian perspective where the emphasis is more on self-overcoming, for the sake of whatever transcends the individual self. Irigaray's goal, however, is to restore a sense of balance between these two perspectives and to affirm what is good in each of them. Sokthan Yeng points out that for Irigaray it is not so much a choice between self and other (as in other Western thinkers) but between our relationship to others and our relationship to ourselves, both of which are significant.[33] For Irigaray, these are reciprocal determinations where the one enhances and is enhanced by the other. As she says elsewhere:

> As far as I am concerned, becoming spiritual signifies a transformation of our energy from merely vital energy to a more subtle energy at the service of breathing, loving, listening, speaking and thinking. This implies going from merely individual survival to the capacity of sharing with the other, and not only goods but breathing, love, words, thought. We thus find again the link with the other(s) but through a personal becoming, which otherwise runs the risk of being paralyzed.[34]

Here, the emphasis on personal becoming as the link to the other helps to clarify the value of autonomy as the relationship to oneself.

Even so, there are some concerns here, and it can be argued that Irigaray's account of autonomy is undertheorized and out of place in work that leans toward non-Western perspectives. Her reflections on "gender" and "difference" are also problematic. In the case of gender, Irigaray's basic and "irreducible" male/female distinction ignores the fluidity of gender and gender identity which has become such an important contemporary theme. What if anything does Irigaray have to say about the plurality of gender, and is her male/female binary repressive or outmoded? Likewise, another question is whether we lose something if we focus on alterity, otherness, and difference? We *are* all different, and it is a thoughtless mistake to erase the other by treating him or her as someone who is exactly like ourselves. But at the same time, the sense that we all have something in common and that we all suffer in some way or another is the beginning of empathy which finally leads to authentic compassion for the other person. And in the end, perhaps only compassion can bring us together as a community. As Martha Nussbaum argues, compassion is the basic social emotion.[35] And yet this insight seems to be at odds with Irigaray's emphasis on the irreducible differences that exist between male and female, between different cultures, and between different people.

We can briefly look at *listening*, *thinking*, and *teaching* as three different aspects of the wisdom of love that Irigaray dwells on. Typically, we might think of listening as a passive affair in which we allow the other person to say what he or she has to say, before we offer a response. But it would be more correct to think of listening as a kind of activity. In listening, we must make every effort to put aside all of our prejudices and fixed ways of looking at the world, for only in this way can we truly hear the other person and the truth that they are speaking. As Irigaray comments, authentic listening is not about fitting the other's truth into my own perspective on things, but it involves being open and willing to change my own perspective in the light of the other person's truth: "Listening-to is a way of opening ourselves to the other and of welcoming this other, its truth and its world as different from us, from ours."[36] It is only too easy to treat the other as an object that must be accommodated, but authentic listening requires me to stay open and be willing to be affected or transformed by the other who remains a subject for me.

Thinking is another spiritual activity. For the most part, and perhaps especially today, thinking seems to be reducible to calculation, for we tend to follow pre-established rules and methods just to think something through and make it part of our world. Thinking then becomes the means to an end, where the goal is to organize and control some aspect of the world or even another person. But once again, we don't allow the object of thought to present itself just as it is. Genuine thinking, as opposed to mere calculation, cherishes the world and whatever is in it by simply allowing it to be, and not reducing it to the subject's own categories. In an essay on this theme, Irigaray argues: "Thinking is the time of turning back to the self. Thinking is the time of building one's own home, in order to inhabit one's self, to dwell within the self."[37] But she adds that thinking always takes place between different paths: "Thinking requires that one remain faithful to one's own path. But this path needs a constant questioning, and questioning opens different possible ways. The problem is what path is to be taken in order to be faithful to one's own path."[38] This means that questioning requires being open to the other and to the other's path; it also means that true thinking is dialogical in character for it presupposes the authentic encounter with the other—especially someone from another sex or another culture who can never be "mine."

Finally, teaching: Today, the advancement of science, globalization, and media techniques has produced an increasingly monotonous viewpoint that brings us closer to a uniform global thinking and the imposition of a "unique thought" which, according to Irigaray, is capable of "abolishing humanity."[39] Against this there is education, which in one sense involves leading someone out (*e-ducere*) from the cave of ignorance, and bringing them to enlightenment. It follows from this spiritual paradigm, however, that education is not so much about training or consuming information so much as it is about personal transformation toward the highest good. And in this respect, Irigaray insists: "The most important thing that a teacher has to pass on is a way of being more than a way of having, a way of being a someone and not a something"; and she explains, "The Eastern masters taught me that transforming myself is the most important undertaking. To accomplish this task, we have to become able to be, to dwell, and not only to amass knowledge and techniques."[40] So in this respect, education in the most profound sense stands opposed to the reduction of humanity to a single state and a uniform condition. Authentic education allows for the possibility of difference and the cultivation of each unique individual as a dialogical partner in the search for truth.

This means that the best teacher is one who remains open to the possibility of learning from her student. For teaching is inherently dialogical, and in this respect it is like love, since it involves caring for the wellbeing of another for the sake of inspiration and fulfillment:

> In a traditional education, the master expounds the truth and the disciple listens to his discourse. If we agree with the fact that the truth is not unique nor universal, the master also has to listen to the truth of the disciple. Of course, I am not alluding here to a mere psychological truth; for example, to some problem which could prevent the student from listening to and learning the ideal truth that I, as the teacher, have to teach him, or her. Rather, I am talking about a comprehensive truth which is proper to each one, and that we have to hear from one another. The master and the disciple have to listen to one another to hear the human truth that they each convey. This preserves the singularity of each one, the two being in relation, and the horizontal relationship between their subjectivities.[41]

In the end, this suggests that the truth of teaching lies in the relationship between the teacher and the student, and this is a spiritual relationship in the sense that Plato describes it in the *Symposium*. It is a dialogue, or dialectic, between two different souls who are equal partners in the search for truth. And this is something that we need to remember, especially when education is reduced to collective "learning outcomes."

We have now come full circle from the initial chapter on Schopenhauer. Schopenhauer turned away from the traditional view that subordinates spirituality to established religion, and he opened up a different non-Western perspective on spiritual life. But Irigaray is justifiably critical of Schopenhauer's pessimism, and his negative valuation of life and love is completely at odds with her own affirmation of these values. For Schopenhauer, love between individual men and women is unimportant since it is only a front for the continual yearning of the will. And since the body is the most obvious manifestation of the will to live, the goal of asceticism should be to punish the body, for in this way we can achieve salvation through the *denial* of the will to live. According to Irigaray, Schopenhauer's metaphysics of the will is crudely reductive and obliterates everything that is spiritually distinctive and valuable in Indian philosophy.[42]

In her own writings Irigaray explores the liberatory potential of this non-Western tradition. For Irigaray, the irreducibility of love to the carnal or the spiritual (as nonphysical) hints at the falsity of traditional philosophical distinctions; and it inspires an appreciation for Asian philosophy, and in particular yoga, which affirms the spiritualization of the body. As she observes in *I Love to You*:

> In these traditions, the body is cultivated to become both more spiritual and more carnal at the same time. A range of movements and nutritional practices, attentiveness to breath in respiration, respect for the rhythms of day and night, for the seasons and years as the calendar of the flesh, for the world and for history, the training of the senses for accurate, rewarding and concentrated perception—all these gradually bring the body to rebirth, to give birth to itself, carnally and spiritually, at each moment of every day. The body is thus no longer simply a body engendered by my parents; it is also one I give back to myself. Likewise, immortality is no longer reserved for the beyond and the conditions for it cease to be determined by one who is other to me. Each woman, and each man acquires immortality by respecting life and its spiritualization.[43]

This is far from Schopenhauer's view of Indian philosophy, although Schopenhauer and Irigaray are alike in wanting to recover Asian wisdom from its oblivion or its misrepresentation by others. The fact is, this wisdom speaks to us, and the global reality of modern life forces us to review our spiritual horizons, and to reaffirm *all* the spiritual possibilities of the world that we belong to.

Conclusion

In this age of consumerism and reductive scientific materialism, spiritual themes have been neglected or ignored, and this is in part because they cannot be measured or *seen*. But in this book I have discussed a number of "spiritual philosophers" who examine spiritual ideas, and if their work resonates with us then we have some reason to think that such "invisible" themes are real. People have always had different beliefs about the nature of ultimate reality, whether the absolute is personal or impersonal, or whether God exists or not. But regardless of all these religious and metaphysical conflicts, I think we are drawn to spiritual fulfillment, along with physical, emotional, and personal fulfillment, just because this is who we are. Spiritual possibilities make our lives more meaningful while their absence is distressing and so we must stay open to a spiritual point of view. In the modern world, the oblivion of spiritual life is unsettling: Fundamentalism is on the rise because it seems to offer a quick solution, while some people resort to addiction or other kinds of avoidance just to minimize the alienation or the anguish that they feel. Against this, however, the spiritual philosophers argue for the reality of the spiritual in love, compassion, generosity, mourning, wisdom, etc., all of which can be experienced in this life, here and now. The problem is that we do not always know how to talk about these things; for we lack the spiritual vocabulary to describe them and their profound effect upon us. And this is why we need the spiritual philosophers, for each of them provides a starting point for reflection. Taken together they illuminate the spiritual view of life.

Aspects of spiritual concern

This book has examined the work of nine spiritual philosophers, and each chapter has focused on a different spiritual theme that one of these philosophers explores in a thoughtful, provocative way. Obviously, a lot depends upon the meaning of the word "spiritual." In the Introduction, I argued that spirituality involves a sense of connection to a higher or a greater reality that we must defer to, and so it requires self-overcoming from the selfish perspective of the ego. In the following chapters, I looked at three different levels of spiritual concern: Some chapters focused on *spiritual virtues*—Schopenhauer on compassion, Nietzsche on generosity, and Benjamin on wisdom—all of which involve self-overcoming and confirm our connection to something higher or greater than we are, including nature, justice, or humankind. But this is not just about "doing one's duty." Usually there are limits to compassion, generosity, or forgiveness, and no moral requirements beyond a certain point. But as *spiritual* virtues, compassion, generosity, forgiveness, and so on relate us to a higher or a greater reality which we can choose to accept, or embrace as the ultimate truth of our being.

Some chapters focused more on *spiritual practices*, which are different forms of spiritual striving—including Derrida on mourning, Foucault on the care of the self, and Irigaray on love. Of course, love and mourning can exist in unreflective forms, but in becoming more mindful of love or the necessity of mourning, etc., we express the desire for connection with others and the greater reality beyond us, and this allows us to experience the complete depth of our existence here and now. In this respect, it has to be said that each of the spiritual philosophers testifies to the value of *philosophy* as a spiritual practice, by illuminating spiritual possibilities through a reflection on spiritual themes. Finally, other chapters looked more closely at *spiritual points of focus*—including Jung on religion, Kandinsky on art, and Hillman on the soul. In all of these examples, we are dealing with significant objects or nodes of spiritual concern, such as art, religion, the sacred, spirit, and soul. Each of these becomes a focal point for spiritual understanding, and the associated discussion is both descriptive and *performative* insofar as it inspires and enhances our own spiritual life. Now this basic classification is by no means definitive, and these distinctions are not precise—if we choose to cultivate compassion, for example, it can be viewed as both a spiritual practice and a spiritual virtue, and the same may be said about love. But I think we can say that much of our spiritual life takes place within this basic formation which includes spiritual virtues, spiritual practices, and spiritual points of focus.

Agreements and disagreements

There is a considerable overlap between different spiritual philosophers, and while there is not complete unanimity, there are some recurrent themes and conclusions. For example, spirituality is often viewed as the active rejection of *materialism*, and this includes the reductive materialism of modern science (or scientism) as well as the materialism of modern consumer culture which eschews spiritual values for the sake of personal success. This can be seen most clearly in the work of Kandinsky and Nietzsche, but it is also an important theme in Jung, Irigaray, and all of those spiritual philosophers who dwell on the disenchantment of modern life. Likewise, spirituality is often viewed as a kind of quest, or a journey toward ultimate truth and enlightenment, and this includes the idea of philosophy as a spiritual quest, for philosophy is critical and it does not just accept the received ideas of tradition in its search for truth and meaning. In this regard, thinkers such as Jung and Foucault emphasize self-cultivation, but far from extolling the value of selfishness, they want to recover the self as the reflection and fulfillment of life, and such a spiritual quest requires a sacrifice on the part of the ego. Again, as we have already noted, spirituality involves the sense of being oriented toward a higher or greater reality such as nature, life, truth, or the divine. We feel a sense of reverence for this higher reality, and this inspires the cultivation of spiritual values, including generosity, compassion, or love, all of which involve self-overcoming. Thus, Nietzsche celebrates the value of generosity in the spiritual context of *life*; Irigaray affirms love as the ultimate spiritual principle that inspires the perfection of our nature, while Derrida clarifies the importance of mourning by showing how it involves our connection to the departed whom we have loved and the enduring value of "the other."

But while there are parallels, there are also significant differences between these thinkers, and it would not be appropriate to offer a unified "spiritual philosophy" as the outcome of this study. Schopenhauer is a pessimist while Nietzsche and other spiritual philosophers are completely affirmative on the value of life. For many spiritual thinkers, compassion is absolutely basic and important, but Nietzsche dismisses compassion as a kind of weakness. Some spiritual philosophers follow tradition by affirming self-overcoming as the key to spiritual life, while others—including Foucault and Hillman—celebrate the achievement of the self as a spiritual possibility. Hillman argues against "the spiritual" as it is traditionally understood, and he affirms the neglected perspective of the soul. Irigaray argues that spirituality involves the spiritualization of the body, although in the West the spiritual and the physical have traditionally been viewed as opposites, and the cultivation of the one appears to diminish the other. Finally, Irigaray emphasizes the fundamental differences between people— gender, culture, etc.—while Schopenhauer claims that as individuals we are all basically the same. There are other issues that the spiritual philosophers would disagree on; but in spite of these points of contention, *philosophy* as a spiritual practice can bring us closer to agreement and closer to enlightenment—for it allows us to think things through, and in this way it illuminates the spiritual truth of this world.

Spirituality, religion, and science

Finally, I want to consider two important background concerns of this book: (1) the relationship between spirituality and religion and (2) the relationship between spirituality and science. We have already discussed the former to some extent, but we need to say more about the latter. The conflict between spirituality and secularism is absolutely central to modern experience, and it is played out in the contest between science and religion. My own view is that both of these paradigms are incomplete, and for different reasons neither can provide us with an "answer" that is completely satisfying. Spirituality is distinct from both religion and science, and it offers us a third path, which brings our own life into focus.

Spirituality and religion have traditionally been thought together; for religion is supposed to circumscribe the authentic spiritual life, and it is held to be the precondition for it. Nevertheless, I have written this book with the conviction that spirituality and religion can be separated from each other, for while many define spirituality in terms of their religious beliefs, it is possible to be spiritual without being religious—and for that matter it is also possible to be religious without being spiritual—which implies that we can discuss spirituality without invoking faith. To generalize, religion is more concerned with doctrines and metaphysical claims, while spirituality is more tentative or even agnostic with regard to ultimate beliefs. Spirituality can lead to faith of one kind or another, but it may remain a kind of striving that lives with uncertainty concerning the absolute, and in this way it embodies "negative capability." The thinkers discussed in this book take spiritual issues seriously, and they value these things for their own sake. But none of this requires the affirmation *or* the rejection of religion, for religious experience, like spirituality, can also be viewed as the lived connection to a higher power, which means that every religious experience is also a spiritual experience which has passed through the framework of belief.

With science it is different: One of the goals of this book has been to cultivate a spiritual sensibility, as well as sensitivity to some of the most important spiritual themes and questions. But we need to bear in mind that solving a spiritual problem is *not* the same thing as solving a scientific problem. Perhaps we are not surprised when someone resolves a difficulty in science or a mathematical problem because we expect to make progress in these realms; but in the case of spiritual life, things are often much harder to discern. Spiritual questions are important, and they may even be crucial, but it is not clear that we can achieve a final resolution in spiritual life; for here there are no guarantees, and every resolution can be undone by further reflection and argument. Jung observes that there is a sense of "mystery" in the midst of life, and this is something that belongs to the very nature of ultimate reality. Interestingly enough, this is a point that is frequently affirmed in contemporary science: According to some writers on the new physics, for example, science must question its own traditional perspectives, and it must abandon its ordinary materialism as it begins to discern a new and more mysterious order which exists at the deepest level of reality itself. In the light of this mystery, *mechanism* is called into question along with the traditional concepts of space and time, cause and effect, and the separation of the observer from the world that he or she describes.[1]

And yet, *reductive* scientific materialism remains in the ascendant. This is science as an ideology—or what is sometimes referred to as *scientism*—and it is a restrictive worldview which curtails the possibilities of authentic thinking; for in allowing just one fixed model for thought, it impoverishes the world. As Nietzsche comments in *The Gay Science*, with a sense of disbelief, and even outrage:

> What? Do we really want to permit existence to be degraded for us like this—reduced to a mere exercise for a calculator and an indoor diversion for mathematicians? Above all, one should not wish to divest existence of its *rich ambiguity*: that is a dictate of good taste, gentlemen, the taste of reverence for everything that lies beyond your horizon. That the only justifiable interpretation of the world should be one in which *you* are justified because one can continue to work and do research scientifically in *your* sense (you really mean mechanistically?)—an interpretation that permits counting, calculating, weighing, seeing, and touching, and nothing more that is a crudity and naiveté, assuming that it is not a mental illness, an idiocy.
>
> Would it not be rather probable that, conversely, precisely the most superficial and external aspect of existence—what is most apparent, its skin and sensualization—would be grasped first—and might even be the only thing that allowed itself to be grasped? A "scientific" interpretation of the world, as you understand it, might therefore still be one of the most stupid of all possible interpretations of the world, meaning that it would be one of the poorest in meaning.[2]

In this section, called "Science as a Prejudice," Nietzsche is by no means rejecting everyday scientific materialism which is the basis of the scientific method. But he is opposed to *reductive* scientific materialism, because the scientific paradigm is simply not appropriate for grasping every aspect of reality. We need to remember that science is one dimension of the world that we belong to, but it is not the only dimension or even the most important dimension that we can encounter. And we must give ourselves permission to *think*, by refusing to follow a preordained method that constrains all our thinking in advance. This is why we need spirituality, philosophy, poetry, art, and myth of every kind, to acknowledge the "rich ambiguity," and the sacred *depth* of this world. Some things are necessary in order to live, but what we call "spirituality" makes life meaningful and therefore *worth living*.

The nine spiritual philosophers that I have discussed in this book are an eclectic group of thinkers, but we can respond to each one of them as an authentic "spiritual philosopher." Taken together they help to clarify the complexity of the spiritual realm as I have described it above. Schopenhauer, Nietzsche, Kandinsky, Benjamin, Jung, Hillman, Foucault, Derrida, and Irigaray allow us to make sense of the spiritual dimension of our lives; and with these spiritual philosophers, we can continue a conversation on the nature of spirituality and the value of spiritual life. Each of the spiritual philosophers focuses attention on spiritual issues and spiritual themes: not spiritual in the sense of being disconnected from the material world or being absorbed by otherworldly hopes, but spiritual in the sense of being more completely attuned to this world here and now; spiritual in the sense of being attentive to spiritual virtues and practices as I have described them in this book; and spiritual in the sense of feeling a sense of connection to a higher or a greater reality that goes beyond whatever is usually apparent. We can view the writings of these spiritual philosophers as a collective resistance to scientism *and* established religion or as a hidden genealogy of spiritual themes in the history of Western thought. But in either case, we follow their lead by recovering spiritual possibilities and the spiritual dimension of our lives.

Notes

Introduction

1. John Keats, *The Complete Poetical Works and Letters of John Keats* (Cambridge: Houghton Mifflin, 1899), 277.
2. Pierre Hadot, *Philosophy as a Way of Life*, trans. A. Davidson (Oxford: Blackwell, 1995), 265–6.
3. Plato, *Republic*, trans. Benjamin Jowett (New York: Vintage, 1991), 516c.
4. See Hadot, *Philosophy as a Way of Life,* 269–70.
5. Luce Irigaray, *Between East and West: From Singularity to Community*, trans. S. Pluhàček (New York: Columbia University Press, 2002), 74.
6. An exception might be Schopenhauer, who argues that this world is a place of suffering and a vale of tears. But even Schopenhauer seems to recognize the possibility of what I would call a "spiritual" experience—in his account of music, for example, and also in compassion.
7. For a discussion of Jung and Otto on this topic, see David Tacey, "The Role of the Numinous in the Reception of Jung" in Ann Casement and David Tacey (eds.), *The Idea of the Numinous: Contemporary Jungian and Psychoanalytic Perspectives* (London: Routledge, 2004), 213–28.
8. Jung, *Memories, Dreams, Reflections*, trans. R. Winston and C. Winston (New York: Random House, 1973), 356.
9. See also Linda Mercadante's general discussion of spirituality in *Beliefs without Borders: Inside the Minds of the Spiritual but Not Religious* (Oxford: Oxford University Press, 2014), 4–6.
10. See Derrida's essay "On Forgiveness" in M. Dooley and M. Hughes (trans.), *On Forgiveness and Cosmopolitanism* (London: Routledge, 2002).
11. In fact, one of Mercadante's most significant findings is that many of those who consider themselves to be "spiritual but not religious" also belong to spiritual communities of like-minded people. See Mercadante, especially 155–92.
12. William James, *The Varieties of Religious Experience* (New York: Vintage, 1990), 35.
13. See Slavoj Žižek, *On Belief* (New York: Routledge, 2001), especially 12–13.
14. See Richard White, "Starting with Compassion" in David McPherson (ed.), *Spirituality and the Good Life: Philosophical Approaches* (Cambridge: Cambridge University Press, 2017), 177–96.
15. Nietzsche, *Beyond Good and Evil*, trans. Walter Kaufmann (New York: Vintage, 1966), section 12.

Chapter 1

1. Schopenhauer, *The World as Will and Representation* vol. 1, trans. E.F.J. Payne (New York: Dover, 1969), 309; hereafter *WWR*.
2. Schopenhauer, *Parerga and Paralipomena* vol. 2, trans. E.F.J. Payne (Oxford: Oxford University Press, 1974), 397.
3. See, for example, Schopenhauer, *WWR* vol. 1: "On the contrary, Indian wisdom flows back to Europe, and will produce a fundamental change to our knowledge and thought" (357).
4. Schopenhauer, *WWR* vol. 2, 604.
5. For a discussion of the different ways in which nineteenth-century philosophers appropriated Asian philosophy, see J.J. Clarke, *Oriental Enlightenment: the Encounter between Asian and Western Thought* (London: Routledge, 1997).
6. Schopenhauer, *WWR* vol. 1, 275.
7. Schopenhauer, *WWR* vol. 2, 600.
8. Schopenhauer, *WWR* vol. 1, 392. For a more extended discussion of asceticism, see also *WWR* vol. 2, 607.
9. "Katha Upanishad" in trans. Eknath Easwaran, *The Upanishads* (California: Nilgiri Press, 1987), 96–7; hereafter *UP*.
10. "Chandogya Upanishad" in *UP*, 184–5.
11. For example, the image appears in the Chandogya Upanishad in *UP*, 187; also the Brihadaranyaka Upanishad in *UP*, 38.
12. "Brihadaranyaka Upanishad" in *UP*, 36.
13. Schopenhauer, *WWR* vol. 1, 388.
14. Schopenhauer, *WWR* vol. 1, 382.
15. Schopenhauer, *WWR* vol. 1, 264.
16. Schopenhauer, *WWR* vol. 1, 256.
17. Roger Scruton, *The Soul of the World* (Princeton: Princeton University Press, 2014), 167.
18. Scruton, *The Soul of the World*, 173.
19. Schopenhauer, *WWR* vol. 1, 256.
20. Schopenhauer, *WWR* vol. 1, 374.
21. Dalai Lama, *Ethics for the New Millennium* (New York: Riverhead Books, 1999), 124.
22. Schopenhauer, *On the Basis of Morality*, trans. E.F.J. Payne (Indianapolis: Hackett, 1998), 165; hereafter *OBM*.
23. Schopenhauer, *OBM*, 166.
24. See David Cartwright's "Introduction" to *OBM*, xxixff.
25. Schopenhauer, *OBM*, 210.
26. Quoted by Harry Oldmeadow in "Delivering the Last Blade of Grass: Aspects of the Bodhisattva Ideal in the Mahayana," *Asian Philosophy* vol. 7 no. 3, 1997, 184.

27 Schopenhauer, *OBM*, 178.
28 See Martha Nussbaum, "Compassion: The Basic Social Emotion," *Social Philosophy and Policy* vol. 13 no. 1, 1996, 27–58.
29 Aristotle, *Rhetoric* in *Basic Works of Aristotle* (New York: Random House, 1941), 1385b 12ff.
30 Schopenhauer, *Parerga* vol. 2, 373.
31 On this point, see John Atwell, *Schopenhauer: The Human Character* (Philadelphia: Temple University Press, 1990).
32 Schopenhauer, *OBM*, 187.
33 Dalai Lama, *Ethics for the New Millennium*, 124.
34 For *tonglen*, see Pema Chödrön, *The Places That Scare You: A Guide to Fearlessness in Difficult Times* (Boston: Shambhala, 2001), 55–60.
35 Schopenhauer, *WWR* vol. 1, 380.
36 Schopenhauer, *WWR* vol. 1, 382.
37 Schopenhauer, *WWR* vol. 1, 375.
38 See the story of "The Bodhisattva and the Hungry Tigress" in Edward Conze (ed.), *Buddhist Scriptures* (Harmondsworth: Penguin, 1959), 24–6.
39 On Buddhism and its reception by nineteenth-century philosophy, see Roger-Pol Droit, *The Cult of Nothingness: The Philosophers and the Buddha* (Charlotte: University of North Carolina Press, 2003); see also Clarke, *Oriental Enlightenment*.
40 On the varieties of engaged Buddhism, see Arnold Kotter (ed.), *Engaged Buddhist Reader* (Berkeley: Parallax Press, 1999).

Chapter 2

1 See Nietzsche, *The Gay Science*, trans. Walter Kaufmann (New York: Vintage, 1974), s. 125.
2 Compare this reading with Heidegger's important essay, "Nietzsche's Word: God Is Dead" in edited and translated by Julian Young and Kenneth Haynes, *Off the Beaten Track* (Cambridge: Cambridge University Press, 2002), 157–99.
3 See David Hume, *An Enquiry Concerning Human Understanding* (Oxford: Oxford University Press, 2008); Richard Dawkins, *The God Delusion* (New York: Mariner, 2008); Christopher Hitchens, *God Is Not Great: How Religion Poisons Everything* (New York: Hachette, 2014).
4 For Nietzsche's interpretation of Socrates, see Nietzsche, *The Birth of Tragedy*, trans. Walter Kaufmann (New York: Vintage, 1967), s. 13–15.
5 In his translation of *Thus Spoke Zarathustra*, R. Hollingdale translates *der schenkenden Tugend* as "the bestowing virtue." Stanton Coit, the translator of Hartmann's *Ethics*, uses "radiant virtue." I prefer Kaufmann's translation, "the

gift-giving virtue," because it emphasizes the connection to generosity and the gift. See Nietzsche, *Thus Spoke Zarathustra*, trans. R. Hollingdale (Harmondsworth: Penguin, 1971); Nicolai Hartmann, *Ethics* 3 volumes, trans. S. Coit (New York: Allen and Unwin, 1932).

6 Sovereignty is by no means a straightforward concept in Nietzsche's philosophy. Here, I use the term "sovereignty" in part to distinguish Nietzsche's ideal from the Kantian concept of "autonomy." On my reading, sovereignty is not self-control or complete openness to the world, but a process of self-overcoming that includes both of these moments. I have argued elsewhere that Nietzsche always has something like "sovereignty" as a goal from *The Birth of Tragedy* to *Ecce Homo*: see Richard White, *Nietzsche and the Problem of Sovereignty* (Urbana: University of Illinois Press, 1997). Christa Acampora points out that Nietzsche is critical of "the sovereign individual," and his thoughts about sovereignty may change at different points in his work. See Christa Acampora, "On Sovereignty and Overhumanity" in Christa Acampora (ed.), *Critical Essays on the Classics: Nietzsche's On the Genealogy of Morals* (Lanham: Rowman and Littlefield, 2006), 147–62. In book one of *Thus Spoke Zarathustra*, Nietzsche's account of the three metamorphoses of spirit—camel, lion and child—offers another version of sovereignty which is explicitly "spiritual" in nature.

7 Nietzsche, *Thus Spoke Zarathustra*, trans. Walter Kaufmann in *The Portable Nietzsche* (London: Chatto, 1971), "Zarathustra's Prologue," s. 4. All further references to *Thus Spoke Zarathustra* will refer to this edition, cited hereafter as *TSZ*.

8 Nietzsche, *TSZ* "Zarathustra's Prologue," s. 1.
9 Nietzsche, *TSZ* first part: "On the Gift-Giving Virtue," s. 1.
10 Nietzsche, *TSZ* first part: "On the Gift-Giving Virtue," s. 1.
11 Nietzsche, *TSZ* first part: "On the Gift-Giving Virtue," s. 1.
12 Nietzsche, *TSZ* first part: "On the Gift-Giving Virtue," s. 1.
13 Nietzsche, *TSZ* third part: "On the Three Evils," s. 2.
14 For example, see Nietzsche, *Beyond Good and Evil*, s. 211: "Genuine philosophers, however, are commanders and legislators … With a creative hand they reach for the future, and all that is and has been becomes a means for them, an instrument, a hammer."
15 Laurence Lampert, *Nietzsche's Teaching: An Interpretation of Thus Spoke Zarathustra* (New Haven: Yale University Press, 1986), 75.
16 Nietzsche, *TSZ* first part: "On the Gift-Giving Virtue," s. 2.
17 Nietzsche, *TSZ* first part: "On the Gift-Giving Virtue," s. 3.
18 Nietzsche, *TSZ* first part: "On the Gift-Giving Virtue," s. 3.
19 Stanley Rosen, *The Mask of Enlightenment: Nietzsche's Zarathustra* (Cambridge: Cambridge University Press, 1995), 129.
20 Nietzsche, *TSZ* first part: "On the Gift-Giving Virtue," s. 1.

21 Lampert, *Nietzsche's Teaching*, 79.
22 Nietzsche, *TSZ* first part: "On the Gift-Giving Virtue," s. 3.
23 Nietzsche, *TSZ* second part: "The Night Song."
24 See Gary Shapiro, *Alcyone: Nietzsche on Gifts, Noise and Women* (Albany: SUNY Press, 1991), 25. Also, Ralph Waldo Emerson, "Gifts" in S. Paul (ed.), *Essays* (New York: Everyman, 1978), 289–93.
25 Nietzsche, *TSZ* first part: "On the Gift-Giving Virtue," s. 3.
26 Nietzsche, *TSZ* second part: "On Self-Overcoming."
27 For more on the idea of overflow and superfluity in *Thus Spoke Zarathustra*, see Graham Parkes, *Composing the Soul: Reaches of Nietzsche's Psychology* (Chicago: University of Chicago Press, 1994), especially 138 and 152–5.
28 A virtue is a desirable disposition that makes a person "good" as opposed to bad. Nietzsche qualifies this with his perspectivism, according to which ascending and declining forms of life are enhanced by different virtues. On this view, generosity is an ethical virtue, but it is also a spiritual virtue. An ethical virtue inspires and enhances the individual self and makes us better. A spiritual virtue involves self-overcoming or ego-loss and is directed toward the enhancement of life, the truth, or any higher or greater reality than our own life. Of course, there is some overlap here, especially if we think of the ethical as a higher or greater reality, and hence as an aspect of the spiritual itself.
29 Nietzsche, *TSZ: Zarathustra's Prologue*, s. 5.
30 Nietzsche, *TSZ* fourth part: "The Drunken Song." My own translation.
31 Nietzsche, *TSZ: Zarathustra's Prologue*, s. 1.
32 Nicolai Hartmann, *Ethics, Volume II: Moral Values*, trans. Stanton Coit (New York: 1932), 335.
33 Hartmann, *Ethics* vol. II, 335.
34 Hartmann, *Ethics* vol. II, 334.
35 Hartmann, *Ethics* vol. II, 334–5.
36 Joseph Kupfer, "Generosity of Spirit," *Journal of Value Inquiry* vol. 32 no. 3, 1998, 366.
37 Kupfer, "Generosity of Spirit," 365.
38 Kupfer, "Generosity of Spirit," 366.
39 Kupfer, "Generosity of Spirit," 367.
40 John Coker, "On the Bestowing Virtue (*von der Schenkenden Tugend*) A Reading" *Journal of Nietzsche Studies*, no. 8, Autumn 1994, 5.
41 Nietzsche, *TSZ* first part: "On the Gift-Giving Virtue," s. 1.
42 Nietzsche, *TSZ* first part: "On the Gift-Giving Virtue," s. 1. I have followed Coker's decision to substitute "metaphor" for "parable" [*Gleichniss*] in both of these quotations. See Coker, "On the Bestowing Virtue," 15.
43 Coker, "On the Bestowing Virtue," 18.
44 Coker, "On the Bestowing Virtue," 22.

45 Nietzsche, *Beyond Good and Evil*, s. 295.
46 Nietzsche, *TSZ* second part: "On the Pitying."
47 Bernard Reginster, *The Affirmation of Life: Nietzsche on Overcoming Nihilism* (Cambridge: Harvard University Press, 2006), 185.
48 Nietzsche, *Beyond Good and Evil*, s. 293.
49 Bernard Reginster, *The Affirmation of Life,* 187.
50 Nietzsche, *The Will to Power*, trans. Walter Kaufmann and R. Hollingdale (New York: Random House, 1967), s. 367.
51 See Derrida, "On Forgiveness."
52 Nietzsche, *Ecce Homo*, trans. Walter Kaufmann (New York: Vintage, 1967), "Foreword."
53 The economy of the gift has become an important theme in recent continental philosophy. See Bataille on the concept of unproductive expenditure in Georges Bataille, *Visions of Excess: Selected Writings, 1927–1939*, trans. Allan Stoekl (Minneapolis: University of Minnesota Press, 1985); Heidegger on the gift of Being in Martin Heidegger, *Time and Being*, trans. J. Stambaugh (New York: Harper and Row, 1972); Mauss on the gift in Marcel Mauss, *The Gift*, trans. W.D. Hallis (London: Routledge, 1990); Derrida on the gift in Jacques Derrida, *Given Time: I Counterfeit Money*, trans. P. Kamuf (Chicago: University of Chicago Press, 1992); Jacques Derrida, *The Gift of Death*, trans. D. Willis (Chicago: University of Chicago Press, 1995). An interesting collection of essays on the gift is Alan Schrift (ed.), *The Logic of the Gift* (New York: Routledge, 1997).

Chapter 3

1 See Gordon Graham's discussion of secularization in *The Re-Enchantment of the World* (Oxford: Oxford University Press, 2007), 30–49.
2 Nietzsche, *Human, All Too Human*, trans. R. Hollingdale (Cambridge: Cambridge University Press, 1986), section 150, 81.
3 Matthew Arnold, *Essays in Criticism* (London: Dent, 1964), 235.
4 Kandinsky, "Whither the New Art?" in Kenneth Lindsay and Peter Vergo (eds.), *Complete Writings on Art* (Boston: G.K. Hall, 1982), 103.
5 John Golding, *Paths to the Absolute* (Princeton: Princeton University Press, 2000), 81.
6 Kandinsky, *Concerning the Spiritual in Art*, trans. M. Sadler (Boston: MFA Publications, 2006), 6–7.
7 Kandinsky, *Concerning the Spiritual in Art*, 106.
8 Donald Kuspit, "Reconsidering the Spiritual in Art" in *Blackbird: An Online Journal of Literature and the Arts* vol. 2 no. 1. Spring 2003: www.blackbird.vcu.edu/v2n1/gallery/kuspit_d/reconsidering_text.htm

9   Kandinsky, *Concerning the Spiritual in Art*, 14.
10 Kandinsky, *Concerning the Spiritual in Art*, 17.
11 Kandinsky, *Concerning the Spiritual in Art*, 19.
12 Kandinsky, "On the Question of Form" in W. Kandinsky and F. Marc (eds.), *The Blaue Reiter Almanac* (New York: Viking, 1974), 147.
13 Kandinsky, *Concerning the Spiritual in Art*, 7–8.
14 Michel Henry, *Seeing the Invisible: On Kandinsky*, trans. S. Davidson (London: Continuum, 2009), 16.
15 Kandinsky, "On the Question of Form," 173.
16 Kandinsky, *Concerning the Spiritual in Art*, 69.
17 See Plato, "Ion" in E. Hamilton and H. Cairns (eds.), *The Collected Works of Plato* (Princeton: Princeton University Press, 1978), 215–28.
18 Kandinsky, *Concerning the Spiritual in Art*, 41.
19 Kandinsky, *Concerning the Spiritual in Art*, 35.
20 See, for example, his argument in "On the Question of Form" that realism *and* abstraction represent the two most viable directions for the future of painting, in *The Blaue Reiter Almanac*, 147–87.
21 Kandinsky, "Reminiscences," in R. Herbert (ed.), *Modern Artists on Art*, 2nd edition (Mineola: Dover, 2000), 30–1.
22 Kandinsky, *Concerning the Spiritual in Art,* 56.
23 Kandinsky, *Concerning the Spiritual in Art,* 73.
24 Kandinsky, *Concerning the Spiritual in Art,* 51.
25 Peter Selz, "The Aesthetic Theories of Kandinsky and Their Relationship to the Origin of Non-Objective Painting" in H. Spencer (ed.), *Readings in Art History*, 3rd edition vol. 2 (New York: Scribner, 1982), 433.
26 Selz, "The Aesthetic Theories of Kandinsky," 433.
27 Kandinsky, *Concerning the Spiritual in Art,* 70.
28 Kandinsky, *Concerning the Spiritual in Art,* 107.
29 Kandinsky, *Concerning the Spiritual in Art,* 108.
30 Kandinsky, *Concerning the Spiritual in Art,* 10.
31 See Olaf Peters (ed.), *Degenerate Art: The Attack on Modern Art in Nazi Germany 1937* (New York: Prestel, 2014).
32 See the discussion by Rose-Carol Washton Long in "Expressionism, Abstractionism, and the Search for Utopia in Germany" in Maurice Tuchman et al. (eds.), *The Spiritual in Art: Abstract Painting 1890–1945* (New York: Abbeville, 1986), 201–18.
33 Kandinsky, "Reminiscences," 19–20.
34 Kandinsky, *Concerning the Spiritual in Art*, 99.
35 Kandinsky, *Concerning the Spiritual in Art,* 19–20.
36 See Kandinsky, *Concerning the Spiritual in Art,* 28–9. For a discussion of Kandinsky's relation to Theosophy, see Sixten Ringbom, "Transcending the Visible:

The Generation of the Abstract Pioneers" in Maurice Tuchman et al. (eds.), *The Spiritual in Art: Abstract Painting 1890–1945* (New York: Abbeville, 1986), 131–53. Also, Brian Etter, *From Classicism to Modernism: Western Musical Culture and the Metaphysics of Order* (Aldershot: Ashgate, 2001), especially chapter six, "The New Music and the Influence of Theosophy."

37 Kandinsky, *Concerning the Spiritual in Art,* 105.
38 Kandinsky, *Concerning the Spiritual in Art,* 106.
39 Kandinsky, "On Stage Composition," 191.
40 Kandinsky, "Reminiscences," 38.
41 For a very full discussion of the spiritual dimension of modern art, see Charlene Spretnak, The *Spiritual Dynamic in Modern Art: Art History Reconsidered, 1800 to the Present* (New York: Palgrave, 2014).
42 See Paul Tillich's discussion in "Contemporary Visual Arts and the Revelatory Character of Style" in John Dillenberger and Jane Dillenberger (eds.), *On Art and Architecture* (New York: Crossroad, 1987), 136.
43 Kandinsky, *Concerning the Spiritual in Art*, 98.
44 See Roger Lipsey, *The Spiritual in Twentieth Century Art* (New York: Dover, 2004), 211.
45 "Painting is a thundering collision of different worlds, intended to create a new world in, and from, the struggle with one another, a new world which is the work of art. Each work originates just as does the cosmos—through catastrophes which out of the chaotic din of instruments ultimately create a symphony, the music of the spheres. The creation of works of art is the creation of the world." Kandinsky, "Reminiscences," 31.
46 Kandinsky, "Reminiscences," 37.
47 See, for example, the discussion of this and other related themes in Arthur Danto, *After the End of Art* (Princeton: Princeton University Press, 1998).
48 Robert Wuthnow, *Creative Spirituality: The Way of the Artist* (Berkeley: University of California Press, 2001), 266.
49 Charles Pickstone, "A Return to the Spiritual: Wassily Kandinsky in the Twenty-First Century" in *Modern Painters*, 74.
50 See, for example, Donald Kuspit's comments throughout "Reconsidering the Spiritual in Art."

Chapter 4

1 Walter Benjamin, "The Work of Art in the Age of Mechanical Reproduction" in trans. Harry Zohn, *Illuminations* (New York: Random House, 1969), 217–52.
2 Benjamin, "The Work of Art," 221.

3   Benjamin, "The Work of Art," 242.
4   Walter Benjamin, "The Storyteller" in trans. Harry Zohn, *Illuminations* (New York: Random House, 1969), 83–109.
5   Benjamin, "The Storyteller," 87.
6   Benjamin, "The Storyteller," 84.
7   Benjamin, "The Storyteller," 91.
8   Benjamin, "The Storyteller," 86.
9   See Walter Benjamin, "Franz Kafka on the 10th Anniversary of His Death" in *Illuminations* (New York: Random House, 1969), 117.
10 Benjamin, "The Storyteller," 90.
11 See Montaigne, "Of Sadness" in trans. D. Frame, *The Complete Essays of Montaigne* (Stanford: Stanford University Press), 6.
12 Holy Bible: King James Version (Peabody, MA: Hendrickson Publishers, 2010), Luke 10: 29–37.
13 The story of Kisagotami is discussed by the Dalai Lama in *The Art of Happiness* (New York: Riverhead, 1999), 133–4.
14 Benjamin, "The Storyteller," 91.
15 Benjamin, "The Storyteller," 92–3.
16 Benjamin, "The Storyteller," 91.
17 Benjamin, "The Storyteller," 100.
18 Benjamin, "The Storyteller," 101.
19 Benjamin, "The Storyteller," 94.
20 Benjamin, "The Storyteller," 94.
21 Benjamin, "The Storyteller," 102.
22 Benjamin, "The Storyteller," 88.
23 Benjamin, "The Storyteller," 89.
24 Benjamin, "On Some Motifs in Baudelaire" in *Illuminations* (New York: Random House, 1969), 193.
25 Benjamin, "On Some Motifs in Baudelaire," 187.
26 Benjamin, "The Storyteller," 91.
27 Benjamin, "The Storyteller," 89.
28 Benjamin, "The Work of Art," 240.
29 For an excellent account of Benjamin's attitude toward the city and modernity in general, see Graeme Gilloch, *Myth and Metropolis* (Cambridge: Polity, 1997) especially 132–67.
30 See Jaron Lanier, *You Are Not a Gadget* (New York: Knopf, 2010), 28–9.
31 On reification, see Pericles Lewis, "Walter Benjamin in the Information Age? On the Limited Possibilities for a Defetishizing Critique of Culture" in trans. H. Gumbrecht et al., *Mapping Benjamin: The Work of Art in the Digital Age* (Stanford: Stanford University Press, 2003), 221–7.

32. See the discussion of Brand's claim in Tim Jordan, *Cyberpower: The Culture and Politics of the Internet* (London: Routledge, 1999), 193–4.
33. Kierkegaard, "The Present Age" in *The Two Ages*, trans. H. and E. Hong (Princeton: Princeton University Press, 1978), 91.
34. On the idea of community and the internet, see Hubert Dreyfus, *On the Internet* 2nd edition (London: Routledge, 2009), 136–41.
35. Benjamin, "The Storyteller," 83.
36. Benjamin, "The Storyteller," 83.
37. Benjamin, "The Storyteller," 108.
38. Benjamin, "The Work of Art," 228.
39. Dreyfus, *On the Internet*, 70–1.
40. Benjamin, "The Storyteller," 92. For more on the importance of the hand, in both storytelling and traditional production, see Esther Leslie, *Walter Benjamin* (London: Reaktion 2007), 167–71.
41. See Walter Benjamin, *Berlin Childhood around 1900*, trans. H. Eiland (Cambridge, MA: Harvard University Press, 2006).
42. See Benjamin's essay, "Unpacking My Library" in *Illuminations*, 59–67. Also, on the theme of storytelling and objects, see Eli Friedlander, *Walter Benjamin: a Philosophical Portrait* (Cambridge, MA: Harvard University Press, 2012), 180–9.
43. Benjamin, "The Storyteller," 108.
44. Benjamin, "The Storyteller," 109.
45. On the idea of philosophical strategy in Benjamin, see Rainer Rochlitz, *The Disenchantment of Art: The Philosophy of Walter Benjamin* (New York: Guilford Press, 1996), 117.

Chapter 5

1. Jung, *Memories, Dreams, Reflections*, edited by Aniela Jaffé and translated by Richard and Clara Winston (New York: Pantheon, 1973), ix; hereafter *MDR*.
2. Jung, *MDR*, 4–5.
3. Jung, *MDR*, 356.
4. Jung, "Approaching the Unconscious" in *Man and His Symbols* (New York: Dell, 1971), 84.
5. Jung, *Modern Man in Search of a Soul*, trans. W.S. Dell and Cary F. Baynes (San Diego: Harcourt, Brace, 1933), 122.
6. Jung, *Answer to Job*, trans. R.F.C. Hull (Princeton: Princeton University Press, 2010), 79; hereafter *AJ*.
7. Jung, "The Psychology of the Child Archetype" in trans. R.F.C. Hull, *The Archetypes and the Collective Unconscious* (Princeton: Princeton University Press, 1980), 160; hereafter *PCA*.

8   Jung, *PCA*, 176.
9   Jung, *AJ*, xiv.
10 On the metaphorical view of religion, see especially: John Shelby Spong, *Jesus for the Non-Religious* (New York: Harper, 1977); David Tacey, *Beyond Literal Belief: Religion as Metaphor* (Mulgrave: Garratt, 2015).
11 Jung, *AJ*, xii.
12 Jung, *AJ*, ix; for this and more background to *Answer to Job*, see Sonu Shamdasani's foreword to *AJ*, vii–x; also, Paul Bishop's excellent scholarly account, *Jung's Answer to Job: A Commentary* (New York: Brunner-Routledge, 2002).
13 Jung, *AJ*, 13.
14 See Emmanuel Levinas, "Transcendence and Evil" in trans. A. Lingis, *Collected Philosophical Papers* (Pittsburgh: Duquesne University Press, 1998), 175–86.
15 Jung, *AJ*, 33.
16 Jung, *AJ*, 18.
17 See Nietzsche, *On the Genealogy of Morals*, trans. Walter Kaufmann (New York: Vintage, 1989), Second Essay s. 23, 93.
18 Jung, *AJ*, 56.
19 Jung, *AJ*, 43.
20 Jung, *AJ*, 47.
21 Rudolf Otto, *The Idea of the Holy*, trans. John Harvey (Oxford: Oxford University Press, 1958).
22 Jung, *AJ*, 80.
23 Jung, *AJ*, 78–9.
24 Jung, *AJ*, 33.
25 Jung, *AJ*, 37.
26 See especially David Tacey, *Jung and the New Age* (Philadelphia: Brunner-Routledge, 2001).
27 Jung, *AJ*, 70.
28 Jung, *AJ*, 70.
29 Clodagh Weldon, "God on the Couch; Teaching Jung's Answer to Job" in Kelly Bulkeley and Clodagh Weldon (eds.), *Teaching Jung* (Oxford: Oxford University Press, 2011), 111–25.
30 Jung, *AJ*, 24.
31 Jung, *AJ*, 31.
32 Jung, *AJ*, 100.
33 Jung, *AJ*, 100.
34 Jung, *AJ*, 103.
35 See Bishop's discussion of the reception to *Answer to Job* in *Jung's Answer to Job*, 44–50.
36 Jung, *AJ*, 107.

37 Victor White, *Soul and Psyche: An Enquiry into the Relationship of Psychotherapy and Religion* (London: Collins/Harvill Press, 1960), 249.
38 Jung, *AJ*, 106.
39 Jung, *AJ*, 108.
40 Jung, *AJ*, 108.
41 Jung, "Relations between Ego and Unconscious" in David Tacey (ed.), *The Jung Reader* (New York: Routledge, 2012), 123; hereafter *REU*.
42 Jung, *Psychological Types* in *The Collected Works of Jung* vol. 6 (Princeton: Princeton University Press, 1976), 448.
43 Jung, *REU*, 126.
44 Jung, *REU*, 130.
45 Jung, *Psychology and Religion* in *The Collected Works of Jung* vol. 11 (Princeton: Princeton University Press, 1973), 16; hereafter *PR*.
46 Jung, *PR*, 12.
47 Jung, *AJ*, 108.
48 Jung, *AJ*, 108.

Chapter 6

1 See *The Republic of Plato*, trans. Allan Bloom (New York: Basic Books, 1991) Book VII 514a–517e.
2 Slavoj Žižek, *On Belief* (New York: Routledge, 2001), 12–13.
3 Nietzsche, *Beyond Good and Evil*, s. 12.
4 The first volume of Hillman's fascinating biography has recently been published. See Dick Russell, *The Life and Ideas of James Hillman* vol. 1 (New York: Helios Press, 2013).
5 Jung, "Approaching the Unconscious," 85.
6 James Hillman, *Re-Visioning Psychology* (New York: Harper, 1977), 67–8.
7 In a more extended discussion of his views on the soul, Hillman writes: "In another attempt upon the idea of soul I suggested that the word refers to that unknown component which makes meaning possible, turns events into experiences, is communicated in love, and has a religious concern. These four qualifications I had already put forth some years ago; I had begun to use the term freely, usually interchangeably with psyche (from Greek) and anima (from Latin). Now I am adding three necessary modifications. First, 'soul' refers to the *deepening* of events into experiences; second, the significance soul makes possible whether in love or religious concern, derives from its special *relation with death*. And third, by 'soul' I mean the imaginative possibility in our natures, the experiencing through reflective speculation, dream, image, and *fantasy*—that mode which recognizes all realities as primarily symbolic or metaphorical" (*Re-Visioning Psychology*, x).

8   Peter Tyler discusses some of these issues of interpretation in his book *The Pursuit of the Soul: Psychoanalysis, Soul-Making and the Christian Tradition* (London: Bloomsbury, 2016). The book includes a chapter on Hillman.
9   Hillman, "Peaks and Vales" in Jacob Needleman and Dennis Lewis (eds.), *On the Way to Self-Knowledge* (New York: Knopf, 1976), 115. The essay is also included in Hillman's *Senex and Puer: Uniform Edition of the Writings of James Hillman* vol. 3 (Thompson, CT: Spring Publications, 2005), 43–67.
10 Hillman, "Peaks and Vales," 115.
11 See, for example, Tyler's discussion in *The Pursuit of the Soul*, 130–2. Tyler points out that Rudolf Steiner had a very different interpretation of what happened at this Council.
12 I have used the King James Version of the Bible for all translations.
13 See Tyler, *The Pursuit of the Soul*, 50–3.
14 See Deepak Chopra, http://www.deepakchopra.com/blog/view/505/soul_and_spirit.
15 Hillman, "Peaks and Vales," 119.
16 St. Augustine, *Confessions*, trans. Maria Boulding (New York: Vintage, 1998), Book 9: 10: 24.
17 See Petrarch, "The Ascent of Mount Ventoux" in Amy Mandelker and Elizabeth Powers (eds.), *Pilgrim Souls: A Collection of Spiritual Autobiographies* (New York: Simon and Schuster, 1999), 400–7.
18 St. John of the Cross, "Stanzas Concerning an Ecstasy Experienced in High Contemplation" in trans. Kieran Kavanaugh and Otilio Rodriguez, *The Collected Works of St. John of the Cross* (Washington, DC: ICS Publications, 1991), 53.
19 Hillman, "Peaks and Vales," 120–1.
20 One of Hillman's students, Thomas Moore, has written a series of popular books on the care of the soul, and the sacred in everyday life. See, for example, Thomas Moore, *Care of the Soul: A Guide for Cultivating Depth and Sacredness in Everyday Life* (New York: Harper, 1992).
21 Hillman, "Peaks and Vales," 128.
22 See James Hillman, *A Blue Fire*, ed. Thomas Moore (New York: Harper, 1989), 126.
23 Hillman, "Peaks and Vales," 134.
24 John Keats, *Selected Letters*, ed. Robert Gittings (Oxford: Oxford University Press, 2009), 232–3.
25 Hillman, "Peaks and Vales," 137–8.
26 Hillman, *Archetypal Psychology* (Dallas: Spring Publications, 1985), 26.
27 See Philip Wheelwright, *Heraclitus* (Princeton: Princeton University Press, 1959), Fragment 42. It is also interesting how Hillman uses this passage: "Ever since Heraclitus brought soul and depth together in one formulation, the dimension of soul is depth (not breadth or height) and the dimension of our soul travel is downward." Hillman, *Re-Visioning Psychology*, xi.

28 This is of course a very condensed account. For a more extended discussion of the *anima mundi* in Jung and Hillman, see David Tacey's chapter, "The Return of Soul to the World: Jung and Hillman" in his excellent book *The Darkening Spirit: Jung, Spirituality, Religion* (New York: Routledge, 2013), 107–26.
29 For a full discussion of Jung's concept of individuation, see Edwin Edinger, *Ego and Archetype* (Baltimore: Penguin, 1974).
30 See, for example, the two-part essay by David Tacey: "James Hillman: The Unmaking of a Psychologist" *Journal of Analytical Psychology* vol. 59 no. 4, September 2014, 467–502.
31 These comments are on the original back cover of the paperback edition of the Needleman and Lewis anthology, *On the Way to Self-Knowledge*.
32 Tacey, "The Return of Soul to the World," 115.

Chapter 7

1 See, for example, Hadot, *Philosophy as a Way of Life*.
2 See Samuel Smiles, *Self-Help* (Oxford: Oxford University Press, 2008); Norman Vincent Peale, *The Power of Positive Thinking* (New York: Simon and Schuster, 2003).
3 See Don Miguel Ruiz, *The Four Agreements: A Practical Guide to Personal Freedom* (San Rafael: Amber-Allen, 1997); Eckhart Tolle, *The Power of Now: A Guide to Enlightenment* (Novato: New World Library, 2010); Deepak Chopra, *The Seven Spiritual Laws of Success: A Practical Guide to the Fulfillment of Your Dreams* (San Rafael: Amber Allen, 1994).
4 See Foucault, *The History of Sexuality, Vol. 1: An Introduction*, trans. R. Hurley (New York: Vintage, 1990), 21–3.
5 See, for example, Charles Taylor, "Foucault on Freedom and Truth" in David Hoy (ed.), *Foucault: A Critical Reader* (Oxford: Blackwell, 1986); Jürgen Habermas, *The Philosophical Discourse of Modernity* (Cambridge: Polity Press, 1992).
6 Foucault, *The Use of Pleasure*, trans. R. Hurley (New York: Vintage, 1986), 136.
7 Foucault, *The Use of Pleasure*, 10.
8 Plato, *The Last Days of Socrates*, trans. C. Rowe (London: Penguin, 2010), 48.
9 Foucault, *The Hermeneutics of the Subject*, trans. G. Burchell (New York: Picador, 2005), 9.
10 Foucault, *The Use of Pleasure*, 63.
11 Foucault, *The Use of Pleasure*, 29–30.
12 See Nietzsche, *On the Genealogy of Morals*, trans. Walter Kaufmann (New York: Vintage, 1969), 24–56.
13 See, for example, Elizabeth Anscombe, "Modern Moral Philosophy" in Roger Crisp and Michael Slote (eds.), *Virtue Ethics* (Oxford: Oxford University Press,

1997), 26–44; Alasdair MacIntyre, *After Virtue*, 2nd edition (Notre Dame: University of Notre Dame Press, 1984); Neil Levy, "Foucault as Virtue Ethicist," *Foucault Studies*, no. 1, December 2004, 20–31.
14 Foucault, *The Use of Pleasure*, 238.
15 Foucault, *The Use of Pleasure*, 74.
16 See also Foucault's discussion of Gregory of Nyssa's treatise "De Virginitate" and his interpretation of the parable of the drachma in Michel Foucault, "Technologies of the Self" in P.H. Hutton, H. Gutman, and L.H. Martin (eds.), *Technologies of the Self: A Seminar with Michel Foucault* (Amherst: University of Massachusetts Press, 1988), 21.
17 Foucault, *The History of Sexuality, Vol. 1: An Introduction*, 19.
18 Foucault, "The Ethics of Concern for Self as a Practice of Freedom" in *Ethics, Subjectivity and Truth* (New York: The New Press, 1997), 300–1.
19 Foucault, *The Use of Pleasure*, 26–8.
20 Foucault, "On the Genealogy of Ethics" in *Ethics, Subjectivity and Truth* (New York: The New Press, 1997), 258.
21 Cited by Paul Veyne, *Foucault: His Thought, His Character*, trans. J. Lloyd (Cambridge: Polity, 2010), 125–6.
22 Foucault, *The Hermeneutics of the Subject*, 12–13.
23 Foucault, "On the Genealogy of Ethics," 261.
24 Plotinus, *Enneads*, trans. A. Armstrong (Cambridge: Loeb, 1966), 13.
25 For further discussion of this, see Ed McGushin, "Foucault's Theory and Practice of Subjectivity" in Dianna Taylor (ed.), *Michel Foucault: Key Concepts* (Durham: Acumen, 2011), 127–42; Timothy O'Leary, *Foucault and the Art of Ethics* (London: Continuum, 2002).
26 Foucault, "What Is Enlightenment" in *Ethics, Subjectivity and Truth* (New York: The New Press, 1997), 312.
27 Foucault, *The Use of Pleasure*, 63.
28 Foucault, "The Ethics of Concern for Self as a Practice of Freedom," 288.
29 Kant, *Lectures on Ethics*, trans. L. Infield (Gloucester: Peter Smith, 1978), 142.
30 Kant, *Lectures on Ethics*, 118.
31 Kant, "An Answer to the Question: What Is Enlightenment?" in *Perpetual Peace and Other Essays*, trans. T. Humphrey (Indianapolis: Hackett, 1983), 41.
32 Foucault, "The Ethics of Concern for Self as a Practice of Freedom," 287.
33 On the complex relationship between Foucault and existentialism, see Brian Seitz, "Foucault and the Subject of Stoic Existence," *Human Studies* vol. 35, 2012, 539–54.
34 Foucault, "The Ethics of Concern for Self as a Practice of Freedom," 291.
35 See, for example, the discussion of this point in two review essays: Brendan Boyle, "Foucault among the Classicists, Again," *Foucault Studies*, no. 13, 2012, 138–56; Ruth Karras, "Active/Passive, Acts/Passions: Greek and Roman Sexualities," *American Historical Review* vol. 105 no. 4, 2000, 1250–65.

36 For further discussion of the nature of spirituality along these lines, see Philip Sheldrake, *Spirituality: A Very Short Introduction* (Oxford: Oxford University Press, 2012); Richard White, *The Heart of Wisdom: A Philosophy of Spiritual Life* (Lanham: Rowman and Littlefield, 2013); Roger Gottlieb, *Spirituality: What It Is and Why It Matters* (Oxford: Oxford University Press, 2013).

37 Foucault, "The Ethics of Concern for Self as a Practice of Freedom," 294.

38 See, for example, Hadot, *Philosophy as a Way of Life*.

39 Foucault, *The Use of Pleasure*, 8.

40 Foucault was doubtless influenced by Nietzsche's ideal of "experimentalism." For Nietzsche's ideal, see, for example, Hans Seigfried, "Nietzsche's Radical Experimentalism," *Man and World* vol. 22 no. 4, 1989, 485–50; also, on Nietzsche's "tragic experimentalism," see Robert Williams, *Tragedy, Recognition, and the Death of God: Studies in Hegel and Nietzsche* (Oxford: Oxford University Press, 2012), 264–72.

41 Foucault, "On the Genealogy of Ethics," 261.

Chapter 8

1 Epictetus, *The Handbook*, trans. N. White (Hackett: Indianapolis, 1983), section 3.

2 Freud, "Mourning and Melancholia" in *The Standard Edition of the Complete Psychological Works of Sigmund Freud* vol. XIV (London: Hogarth, 1978), 244.

3 Freud, "Mourning and Melancholia," 245.

4 Freud, "Mourning and Melancholia," 245. This summary of Freud owes much to Tammy Clewell, "Mourning beyond Melancholia: Freud's Psychoanalysis of Loss," *Journal of the American Psychoanalytic Association* vol. 52 no. 1, 2004, 43–67.

5 Freud, "Mourning and Melancholia," 246.

6 Freud, "Mourning and Melancholia," 249.

7 Freud, "The Ego and the Id" in *The Standard Edition of the Complete Psychological Works of Sigmund Freud* vol. XIX (London: Hogarth, 1978), 29.

8 This is to emphasize that the discussion which Freud begins in "Mourning and Melancholia" still continues in contemporary psychoanalytical debate. See, for example, Nicolas Abraham and Maria Torok, "Introjection–Incorporation: Mourning or Melancholia" in Serge Lebovici and Daniel Widlocher (eds.), *Psychoanalysis in France* (New York: International University Press, 1980), 3–16.

9 Derrida, *Memoires for Paul de Man*, revised edition, trans. Cecile Lindsay et al. (New York: Columbia University Press), 1989, 34.

10 Freud, "The Ego and the Id," 29.

11 Roland Barthes, *Camera Lucida: Reflections on Photography*, trans. Richard Howard (New York: Hill and Wang, 1981), 75.

12 Barthes, *Camera Lucida*, 27.
13 Barthes, *Camera Lucida*, 96.
14 Barthes, *Camera Lucida*, 96.
15 Barthes, *Camera Lucida*, 97.
16 Barthes, *Camera Lucida*, 109–10.
17 Barthes, *Camera Lucida*, 75.
18 For an excellent discussion of Freud and Barthes that emphasizes Barthes's desire to maintain his grief, rather than relinquishing it, see Kathleen Woodward, "Freud and Barthes: Theorizing Mourning, Sustaining Grief," *Discourse* vol. 13 no. 1, 1990–1, 93–110.
19 Barthes, *Camera Lucida*, 72.
20 Barthes, *Camera Lucida*, 72.
21 This interpretation of Barthes owes much to two very different readings of *Camera Lucida*: Jay Prosser, "Buddha Barthes: What Barthes Saw in Photography (That He Didn't in Literature)," in Geoffrey Batchen (ed.), *Photography Degree Zero: Reflections on Roland Barthes's Camera Lucida* (Cambridge, MA: MIT Press, 2009), 91–103; also in Batchen: Eduardo Cadava and Paola Cortes-Rocca, "Notes on Love and Photography," 105–39.
22 Derrida, *The Work of Mourning*, trans. Pascale-Anee Brault and Michael Naas (Chicago: University of Chicago Press, 2001), 44.
23 Dooley and Kavanagh argue convincingly for the centrality of mourning in Derrida's philosophical project. The first chapter of their book is entitled: "The Catastrophe of Memory: Identity and Mourning." See Mark Dooley and Liam Kavanagh, *The Philosophy of Derrida* (Montreal: McGill University Press, 2006).
24 Derrida, *Memoires for Paul de Man*, 34.
25 Derrida, *Memoires for Paul de Man*, 6.
26 See Jacques Derrida, "Fors: The Anglish Words of Nicolas Abraham and Maria Torok," trans. Barbara Johnson in Nicolas Abraham and Maria Torok, *The Wolfman's Magic Word: A Cryptonomy*, trans. Nicholas Rand (Minneapolis: University of Minnesota Press, 1986), xi–xlviii.

   For an in-depth discussion of Derrida's reading of Abraham and Torok, see Christopher Lane, "The Testament of the Other: Abraham and Torok's Failed Expiation of Ghosts" in *Diacritics* vol. 27 no. 4, 1997, 3–29.
27 Derrida, *The Work of Mourning*, 161.
28 Seneca, "To Marcia on Consolation," in trans. J. Basore, *Moral Essays* vol. 2 (London: Heinemann, 1935), 21.
29 Confucius, *Analects*, trans. D.C. Lau (Harmondsworth: Penguin, 1979), 147. For a comparison of Derrida and Confucius on mourning, see Amy Olberding, "Mourning, Memory and Identity: A Comparative Study of the Constitution

of the Self in Grief" *International Philosophical Quarterly* vol. 37 no. 1, 1997, 29–44.
30 Confucius, *Analects,* 155.
31 Jacques Derrida and Elisabeth Roudinesco, *For What Tomorrow ...: A Dialogue*, trans. Jeff Fort (Palo Alto: Stanford University Press, 2004), 78 (cited by Dooley and Kavanagh).
32 Derrida, *Memoires for Paul de Man,* 33.
33 See Joan Kirby, "'Remembrance of the Future': Derrida on Mourning," *Social Semiotics* vol. 16 no. 3, 2006, 461–72, for a discussion of Derrida's reading of Paul de Man. On page 468 of her article she describes Derrida's productive encounter with de Man's thought in more detail: "For instance, Derrida deploys de Man's work on Hegel's distinction between *Errinerung* and *Gedachtnis*, de Man's idea of rhetoricity, metonymy, the logic of sets and prosopopeia (the fiction of the voice from beyond the grave, which de Man argues is the constitutive trope of poetic discourse), his sense of memory as future-oriented and the concept of aporia, the impasse that provokes the thinking of new paths, as well as de Man's idea of the text as a promise."
34 Derrida, *The Work of Mourning,* 44.

Chapter 9

1   See Luce Irigaray, *The Way of Love*, trans. Heidi Bostic and Stephen Pluháček (London: Continuum, 2002), 1–12 (hereafter cited as *WOL*).
2   Irigaray, *WOL*, 2–3.
3   See Morny Joy, *Divine Love: Luce Irigaray, Women, Gender and Religion* (Manchester: Manchester University Press, 2014), 124–41. Significantly, this chapter is titled "Irigaray's Eastern Excursion."
4   Irigaray, *Sexes and Genealogies* (New York: Columbia University Press), 1993, 108.
5   Irigaray, *Conversations* (London: Continuum, 2008), 76.
6   Irigaray, *Conversations*, 2.
7   Plato, *Symposium*, 210a–12b. I have used the translation by Michael Joyce in *The Collected Dialogues of Plato*, ed. Edith Hamilton and Huntington Cairns (Princeton: Princeton University Press), 1978.
8   Plato, *Symposium*, 211d.
9   Irigaray, "Sorcerer Love: A Reading of Plato's Symposium, Diotima's Speech," trans. Eleanor Kuykendall, *Hypatia* vol. 3 no. 2, 1989, 32–44.
10 See, for example, Irving Singer, *The Nature of Love Vol. 1: Plato to Luther* (Chicago: University of Chicago Press: 1984), 82–7.
11 Irigaray, "Sorcerer Love," 38.

12 Irigaray, "Sorcerer Love," 40.
13 Plato, *Symposium*, 206b–7a.
14 Plato, *Symposium*, 206c.
15 Irigaray, "Sorcerer Love," 33.
16 Plato, *Symposium*, 211d.
17 Irigaray, *Conversations,* 80.
18 Irigaray, *Elemental Passions*, trans. Joanne Collie and Judith Still (New York: Routledge, 1992), 27.
19 Irigaray, *I Love to You: Sketch for a Felicity within History*, trans. Alison Martin (New York: Routledge, 1996), 138.
20 Irigaray, *Between East and West*, 87 (hereafter cited as *BEW*).
21 Irigaray, *I Love to You,* 104.
22 Irigaray, *BEW*, 9.
23 Irigaray, *BEW*, 119.
24 Irigaray, *An Ethics of Sexual Difference*, trans. Carolyn Burke and Gillian Gill (Ithaca: Cornell, 1993), 5.
25 See Buber, *I and Thou*, trans. Walter Kaufmann (New York: Simon and Schuster, 1970); Levinas, *Totality and Infinity; An Essay on Exteriority*, trans. Alphonso Lingis (Pittsburgh: Duquesne University Press), 1969.
26 Irigaray, *Elemental Passions*, 28.
27 Irigaray, *I Love to You,* 9.
28 Irigaray, *I Love to You,* 11.
29 Irigaray, *BEW*, 61–2.
30 Irigaray, *BEW*, 74–5.
31 Irigaray, *Teaching* (London: Continuum, 2008), 196.
32 Irigaray, *BEW*, 74.
33 Sokthan Yeng, "Irigaray's Alternative Buddhist Practices of the Self," *Journal of French and Francophone Philosophy* vol. XXII no. 1, 2014, 61–75.
34 Irigaray, *Conversations*, 104.
35 Nussbaum, "Compassion," 27–58.
36 Irigaray, *Teaching*, 232.
37 Irigaray, *Teaching*, 234.
38 Irigaray, *Teaching*, 236.
39 Irigaray, *Teaching*, 236.
40 Irigaray, *Teaching*, 234.
41 Irigaray, *Teaching*, 233.
42 See Irigaray's essay on Schopenhauer, "The Time of Life" in *BEW* 21–48.
43 Irigaray, *I Love to You,* 24.

Conclusion

1. See, for example, Roger Penrose, *Fashion, Faith, and Fantasy in the New Physics of the Universe* (Princeton: Princeton University Press), 2016; Brian Greene, *The Elegant Universe: Superstrings, Hidden Dimensions and the Quest for the Ultimate Theory*, 2nd edition (New York: W. W. Norton, 2009). Or for a pioneering work: Paul Davies, *God and the New Physics* (New York: Simon and Schuster, 1984).
2. Nietzsche, *The Gay Science,* section 373.

Bibliography

Abelsen, Peter. "Schopenhauer and Buddhism." *Philosophy East and West* 43.2 (1993): 255–78.

Abraham, Nicolas, and Maria Torok. "Introjection–Incorporation: Mourning or Melancholia." *Psychoanalysis in France*. Edited by Serge Lebovici and Daniel Widlocher. New York: International University Press, 1980. 3–16.

Acampora, Christa, "On Sovereignty and Overhumanity." *Critical Essays on the Classics: Nietzsche's on the Genealogy of Morals*. Edited by Christa Acompara. Lanham: Rowman and Littlefield, 2006. 147–62.

Anscombe, Elizabeth. "Modern Moral Philosophy." *Virtue Ethics*. Edited by Roger Crisp and Michael Slote. Oxford: Oxford University Press, 1997. 26–44.

Aristotle. *Nicomachean Ethics. Basic Works of Aristotle*. New York: Random House, 1941. 935–1127.

Aristotle, *Rhetoric. Basic Works of Aristotle*. New York: Random House, 1941. 1325–454.

Arnold, Matthew. *Essays in Criticism*. London: Dent, 1964.

Atwell, John. *Schopenhauer: The Human Character*. Philadelphia: Temple University Press, 1990.

Augustine, *Confessions*. Translated by Maria Boulding. New York: Vintage, 1998.

Barthes, Roland. *Camera Lucida: Reflections on Photography*. Translated by Richard Howard. New York: Hill and Wang, 1981.

Bataille, Georges. *Visions of Excess: Selected Writings, 1927–1939*. Translated by Allan Stoekl. Minneapolis: University of Minnesota Press, 1985.

Batchen, Geoffrey, ed. *Photography Degree Zero: Reflections on Roland Barthes's Camera Lucida*. Cambridge, MA: MIT Press, 2009.

Benjamin, Walter. "Franz Kafka on the 10th Anniversary of his Death." *Illuminations*. Translated by Harry Zohn. New York: Random House, 1969. 111–40.

Benjamin, Walter. "The Storyteller." *Illuminations*. Translated by Harry Zohn. New York: Random House, 1969. 83–109.

Benjamin, Walter. "Unpacking My Library." *Illuminations*. Translated by Harry Zohn. New York: Random House, 1969. 59–68.

Benjamin, Walter. "The Work of Art in the Age of Mechanical Reproduction." *Illuminations*. Translated by Harry Zohn. New York: Random House, 1969. 217–52.

Benjamin, Walter. *Berlin Childhood around 1900*. Translated by Howard Eiland. Cambridge: Harvard University Press, 2006.

Bhagavad Gita. Translated by Eknath Easwaran. California: Nilgiri Press, 1985.

Bishop, Paul. *Jung's Answer to Job: A Commentary*. New York: Brunner-Routledge, 2002.

Boyle, Brendan. "Foucault among the Classicists, Again." *Foucault Studies*, no. 13 (2012): 138–56.

Buber, Martin. *I and Thou*. Translated by Walter Kaufmann. New York: Simon and Schuster, 1970.

Bulkeley, Kelly, and Clodagh Weldon, eds. *Teaching Jung*. Oxford: Oxford University Press, 2011.

Cadava, Eduardo, and Paola Cortes-Rocca. "Notes on Love and Photography." *Photography Degree Zero: Reflections on Roland Barthes's Camera Lucida*. Edited by Geoffrey Batchen. Cambridge, MA: MIT Press, 2009. 105–39.

Cartwright, David. "Introduction." Schopenhauer, *On the Basis of Morality*. Translated by E.F.J. Payne. Indianapolis: Hackett, 1998.

Casement, Ann, and David Tacey, eds. *The Idea of the Numinous: Contemporary Jungian and Psychoanalytic Perspectives*. London: Routledge, 2004.

Chödrön, Pema. *The Places That Scare You: A Guide to Fearlessness in Difficult Times*. Boston: Shambhala, 2001.

Chopra, Deepak. http://www.deepakchopra.com/blog/view/505/soul_and_spirit.

Chopra, Deepak. *The Seven Spiritual Laws of Success: A Practical Guide to the Fulfillment of Your Dreams*. San Rafael: Amber Allen, 1994.

Clarke, J.J. *Oriental Enlightenment: The Encounter between Asian and Western Thought*. London: Routledge, 1997.

Clewell, Tammy. "Mourning beyond Melancholia: Freud's Psychoanalysis of Loss." *Journal of the American Psychoanalytic Association* 52.1 (2004): 43–67.

Coker, John. "On the Bestowing Virtue (*von der Schenkenden Tugend*) A Reading." *Journal of Nietzsche Studies*, no. 8, Autumn (1994): 5–31.

Confucius. *Analects*. Translated by D.C. Lau. Harmondsworth: Penguin, 1979.

Conze, Edward, ed. *Buddhist Scriptures*. Harmondsworth: Penguin, 1959.

Dalai Lama. *The Art of Happiness*. New York: Riverhead, 1999.

Dalai Lama. *Ethics for the New Millennium*. New York: Riverhead Books, 1999.

Danto, Arthur. *After the End of Art*. Princeton: Princeton University Press, 1998.

Davies, Paul. *God and the New Physics*. New York: Simon and Schuster, 1984.

Dawkins, Richard. *The God Delusion*. New York: Mariner, 2008.

Delattre, Pierre. *Tales of a Dalai Lama*. Sandpoint: Lost Horse Press, 2011.

Derrida, Jacques. "Fors: The Anglish Words of Nicolas Abraham and Maria Torok." Translated by Barbara Johnson. *The Wolfman's Magic Word: A Cryptonomy*. Nicolas Abraham and Maria Torok. Translated by Nicholas Rand. Minneapolis: University of Minnesota Press, 1986. xi–xlviii.

Derrida, Jacques. *Memoires for Paul de Man*. Revised edition. Translated by Cecile Lindsay et al. New York: Columbia University Press, 1989.

Derrida, Jacques. *Given Time: I. Counterfeit Money*. Translated by Peggy Kamuf. Chicago: University of Chicago Press, 1992.

Derrida, Jacques. *The Gift of Death*. Translated by D. Willis. Chicago: University of Chicago Press, 1995.

Derrida, Jacques. *The Work of Mourning*. Translated by Pascale-Anne Brault and Michael Naas. Chicago: University of Chicago Press, 2001.

Derrida, Jacques. "On Forgiveness." *On Forgiveness and Cosmopolitanism*. Translated by M. Dooley and M. Hughes. London: Routledge, 2002.

Derrida, Jacques, and Elisabeth Roudinesco. *For What Tomorrow …: A Dialogue*. Translated by Jeff Fort. Palo Alto: Stanford University Press, 2004.

Dooley, Mark, and Liam Kavanagh. *The Philosophy of Derrida*. Montreal: McGill University Press, 2006.

Dreyfus, Hubert. *On the Internet*, 2nd edition. London: Routledge, 2009.

Droit, Roger-Pol. *The Cult of Nothingness: The Philosophers and the Buddha*. Charlotte: University of North Carolina Press, 2003.

Edinger, Edwin. *Ego and Archetype*. Baltimore: Penguin, 1974.

Emerson, Ralph Waldo, "Gifts." *Essays*. Edited by S. Paul. New York: Everyman, 1978. 289–93.

Etter, Brian. *From Classicism to Modernism: Western Musical Culture and the Metaphysics of Order*. Aldershot: Ashgate, 2001.

Foucault, Michel. *The Use of Pleasure*. Translated by R. Hurley. New York: Vintage, 1986.

Foucault, Michel. "Technologies of the Self." *Technologies of the Self: A Seminar with Michel Foucault*. Edited by P.H. Hutton, H. Gutman, and L.H. Martin. Amherst: University of Massachusetts Press, 1988. 16–49.

Foucault, Michel. *The History of Sexuality, Vol. 1: An Introduction*. Translated by R. Hurley. New York: Vintage, 1990.

Foucault, Michel. "On the Genealogy of Ethics." *Ethics, Subjectivity and Truth*. New York: The New Press, 1997. 253–80.

Foucault, Michel. "The Ethics of Concern for Self as a Practice of Freedom." *Ethics, Subjectivity and Truth*. New York: The New Press, 1997. 281–301.

Foucault, Michel. *The Hermeneutics of the Subject*. Translated by G. Burchell. New York: Picador. 2005.

Freud, Sigmund. "The Ego and the Id." *The Standard Edition of the Complete Psychological Works of Sigmund Freud*, vol. XIX. London: Hogarth, 1978. 12–66.

Freud, Sigmund. "Mourning and Melancholia." *The Standard Edition of the Complete Psychological Works of Sigmund Freud*, v. XIV. London: Hogarth, 1978. 237–58.

Freud, Sigmund. "On Transience." *The Standard Edition of the Complete Psychological Works of Sigmund Freud*, v. XIV. London: Hogarth, 1978. 305–7.

Friedlander, Eli. *Walter Benjamin: A Philosophical Portrait*. Cambridge, MA: Harvard University Press, 2012.

Gilloch, Graeme. *Myth and Metropolis*. Cambridge: Polity, 1997.

Golding, John. *Paths to the Absolute*. Princeton: Princeton University Press, 2000.

Gottlieb, Roger. *Spirituality: What It Is and Why It Matters*. Oxford: Oxford University Press, 2013.

Gowans, Christopher. *Philosophy of the Buddha*. New York: Routledge, 2003.

Graham, Gordon. *The Re-Enchantment of the World*. Oxford: Oxford University Press, 2007.

Greene, Brian. *The Elegant Universe: Superstrings, Hidden Dimensions and the Quest for the Ultimate Theory*. 2nd edition. New York: W. W. Norton, 2009.

Habermas, Jürgen. *The Philosophical Discourse of Modernity*. Cambridge: Polity Press, 1992.

Hadot, Pierre. *Philosophy as a Way of Life*. Translated by A. Davidson. Oxford: Blackwell, 1995.

Harris, Sam. *Waking Up: A Guide to Spirituality without Religion*. New York: Simon and Schuster, 2014.

Hartmann, Nicolai. *Ethics, Volume II: Moral Values*. Translated by Stanton Coit. New York: Allen and Unwin, 1932.

Heidegger, Martin. *Time and Being*. Translated by Joan Stambaugh. New York: Harper and Row, 1972.

Heidegger, Martin. "Nietzsche's Word: God Is Dead." *Off the Beaten Track*. Translated and edited by Julian Young and Kenneth Baynes. Cambridge: Cambridge University Press, 2002.

Henry, Michel. *Seeing the Invisible: On Kandinsky*. Translated by S. Davidson. London: Continuum, 2009.

Hillman, James. "Peaks and Vales." *On the Way to Self-Knowledge*. Edited by Jacob Needleman and Dennis Lewis. New York: Knopf, 1976. 114–47.

Hillman, James. *Senex and Puer: Uniform Edition of the Writings of James Hillman, Volume 3*. Thompson, CT: Spring Publications, 2005.

Hillman, James. *Re-Visioning Psychology*. New York: Harper, 1977.

Hillman, James. *The Dream and the Underworld*. New York: William Morrow, 1979.

Hillman, James. *A Blue Fire*. Edited by Thomas Moore. New York: Harper, 1989.

Hillman, James. *The Soul's Code*. New York: Grand Central, 1997.

Hitchens, Christopher. *God Is Not Great: How Religion Poisons Everything*. New York: Hachette, 2014.

Holy Bible: King James Version. Peabody, MA: Hendrickson Publishers, 2010.

Hume, David. *An Enquiry Concerning Human Understanding*. Oxford: Oxford University Press, 2008.

Hunt, Lester. *Nietzsche and the Origin of Virtue*. New York: Routledge, 1991.

Irigaray, Luce. "Sorcerer Love: A Reading of Plato's Symposium, Diotima's Speech." Translated by Eleanor Kuykendall. *Hypatia* 3.2 (1989): 32–44.

Irigaray, Luce. *Elemental Passions*. Translated by Joanne Collie and Judith Still. New York: Routledge, 1992.

Irigaray, Luce. *An Ethics of Sexual Difference*. Translated by Carolyn Burke and Gillian Gill. Ithaca: Cornell, 1993.

Irigaray, Luce. *Sexes and Genealogies*. Translated by Gillian Gill. New York: Columbia University Press, 1993.

Irigaray, Luce. *I Love to You: Sketch of a Possible Felicity in History*. Translated by Alison Martin. London: Routledge, 1996.

Irigaray, Luce. *Between East and West: From Singularity to Community*. Translated by Stephen Pluháček. New York: Columbia University Press, 2002.

Irigaray, Luce. *The Way of Love*. Translated by Heidi Bostic and Stephen Pluháček. London: Continuum, 2002.

Irigaray, Luce. *Conversations*. London: Continuum, 2008.

Irigaray, Luce. *Teaching*. London: Continuum, 2008.

James, William. *The Varieties of Religious Experience*. New York: Vintage, 1990.

John of the Cross, St. *The Collected Works of St. John of the Cross*. Translated by Kieran Kavanaugh and Otilio Rodriguez. Washington DC: ICS Publications, 1991.

Jordan, Tim. *Cyberpower: The Culture and Politics of the Internet*. London: Routledge, 1999.

Joy, Morny. *Divine Love: Luce Irigaray, Women, Gender and Religion*. Manchester: Manchester University Press, 2014.

Jung, Carl. *Modern Man in Search of a Soul*. Translated by W.S. Dell and Cary F. Baynes. Harcourt Brace: San Diego, 1933.

Jung, Carl. *Man and His Symbols*. New York: Dell, 1971.

Jung, Carl. *Memories, Dreams, Reflections*. Edited by Aniela Jaffé and translated by Richard and Clara Winston. New York: Pantheon, 1973.

Jung, Carl. *Psychology and Religion. The Collected Works of Jung*, vol. 11. Princeton: Princeton University Press, 1973.

Jung, Carl. *Psychological Types. The Collected Works of Jung*, vol. 6. Princeton: Princeton University Press, 1976.

Jung, Carl. "The Psychology of the Child Archetype." *The Archetypes and the Collective Unconscious*. Translated by R.F.C. Hull. Princeton: Princeton University Press, 1980.

Jung, Carl. *Answer to Job*. Translated by R.F.C. Hull. Princeton: Princeton University Press, 2010.

Jung, Carl. "Relations between Ego and Unconscious." *The Jung Reader*. Edited by David Tacey. New York: Routledge, 2012. 93–134.

Kandinsky, Wassily. *Complete Writings on Art*. Edited by K. Lindsay and P. Vergo. Boston: G.K. Hall, 1982.

Kandinsky, Wassily. "Reminiscences." *Modern Artists on Art*. 2nd edition. Edited by R. Herbert. Mineola: Dover, 2000. 19–39.

Kandinsky, Wassily. *Concerning the Spiritual in Art*. Translated by M. Sadler. Boston: MFA Publications, 2006.

Kandinsky, Wassily. and Franz Marc, eds. *The Blaue Reiter Almanac*. Translated by H. Falkenstein. New York: Viking, 1974.

Kant, Immanuel. "An Answer to the Question: What Is Enlightenment?" Translated by Ted Humphrey. *Perpetual Peace and Other Essays*. Indianapolis: Hackett, 1983.

Kant, Immanuel. *Lectures on Ethics*. Translated by Louis Infield. Gloucester: Peter Smith, 1978.

Karras, Ruth. "Active/Passive, Acts/Passions: Greek and Roman Sexualities." *American Historical Review* 105.4 (2000): 1250–65.

Keats, John. *The Complete Poetical Works and Letters of John Keats*. Cambridge: Houghton, Mifflin, 1899.

Keats, John. *Selected Letters*. Edited by Robert Gittings. Oxford: Oxford University Press, 2009.
Kierkegaard, Søren. "The Present Age." *Two Ages*. Translated by Howard Hong and Edna Hong. Princeton: Princeton University Press, 1978.
Kirby, Joan. "'Remembrance of the Future': Derrida on Mourning." *Social Semiotics* 16.3 (2006): 461–72.
Kotter, Arnold, ed. *Engaged Buddhist Reader*. Berkeley: Parallax Press, 1999.
Kupfer, Joseph. "Generosity of Spirit." *Journal of Value Inquiry* 32.3 (1998): 357–68.
Kuspit, Donald. "Reconsidering the Spiritual in Art." *Blackbird: An Online Journal of Literature and the Arts* 2.1. Spring 2003. www.blackbird.vcu.edu/v2n1/gallery/kuspit_d/reconsidering_text.htm.
Lampert, Laurence. *Nietzsche's Teaching: An Interpretation of Thus Spoke Zarathustra*. New Haven: Yale University Press, 1986.
Lane, Christopher. "The Testament of the Other: Abraham and Torok's Failed Expiation of Ghosts." *Diacritics* 27.4 (1997): 3–29.
Lanier, Jaron. *You Are Not a Gadget*. New York: Knopf, 2010.
Leslie, Esther. *Walter Benjamin*. London: Reaktion, 2007.
Levinas, Emmanuel. *Totality and Infinity: An Essay on Exteriority*. Translated by Alphonso Lingis. Pittsburgh: Duquesne University Press, 1969.
Levinas, Emmanuel. "Transcendence and Evil." *Collected Philosophical Papers*. Translated by Alphonso Lingis. Pittsburgh: Duquesne University Press, 1998. 175–86.
Levy, Neil. "Foucault as Virtue Ethicist." *Foucault Studies* 1 (2004): 20–31.
Lewis, Pericles. "Walter Benjamin in the Information Age? On the Limited Possibilities for a Defetishing Critique of Culture." *Mapping Benjamin: The Work of Art in the Digital Age*. Edited by H. Gumbrecht et al. Stanford: Stanford University Press, 2003. 221–7.
Lipsey, Roger. *The Spiritual in Twentieth Century Art*. Mineola: Dover, 2004.
Long, Rose-Carol Washton. "Expressionism, Abstractionism, and the Search for Utopia in Germany." *The Spiritual in Art: Abstract Painting 1890–1945*. Edited by Maurice Tuchman et al. New York: Abbeville, 1986. 201–18.
MacIntyre, Alasdair. *After Virtue*. 2nd edition. Notre Dame: University of Notre Dame Press, 1984.
Mandelker, Amy, and Elizabeth Powers, eds. *Pilgrim Souls: A Collection of Spiritual Autobiographies*. New York: Simon and Schuster, 1999.
Mauss, Marcel. *The Gift*. Translated by W.D. Hallis. London: Routledge, 1990.
McGushin, Edward. "Foucault's Theory and Practice of Subjectivity." *Michel Foucault: Key Concepts*. Edited by Dianna Taylor. Durham: Acumen, 2011: 127–42.
Mercadante, Linda. *Beliefs without Borders: Inside the Minds of the Spiritual but Not Religious*. Oxford: Oxford University Press, 2014.
Montaigne, Michel de. *The Complete Essays of Montaigne*. Stanford: Stanford University Press, 1958.
Moore, Thomas. *Care of the Soul: A Guide for Cultivating Depth and Sacredness in Everyday Life*. New York: Harper, 1992.

Needleman, Jacob, and Dennis Lewis, eds. *On the Way to Self-Knowledge*. New York: Knopf, 1976.
Nietzsche. *The Birth of Tragedy*. Translated by Walter Kaufmann. New York: Random House, 1967.
Nietzsche. *The Will to Power*. Translated by Walter Kaufmann and R. Hollingdale. New York: Random House, 1967.
Nietzsche. *Ecce Homo*. Translated by Walter Kaufmann. New York: Random House, 1969.
Nietzsche. *Thus Spoke Zarathustra*. Translated by R. Hollingdale. Harmondsworth: Penguin, 1971.
Nietzsche. *Thus Spoke Zarathustra*. Translated by Walter Kaufmann. *The Portable Nietzsche*. London: Chatto, 1971.
Nietzsche. *The Gay Science*. Translated by Walter Kaufmann. New York: Random House, 1974.
Nietzsche. *Human, All Too Human*. Translated by R. Hollingdale. Cambridge: Cambridge University Press. 1986.
Nietzsche. *On the Genealogy of Morals*. Translated by Walter Kaufmann. New York: Vintage, 1989.
Nietzsche, Friedrich. *Beyond Good and Evil*. Translated by Walter Kaufmann. New York: Random House, 1966.
Nussbaum, Martha. "Compassion: The Basic Social Emotion." *Social Philosophy and Policy* 13 (1996): 27–58.
O'Leary, Timothy. *Foucault and the Art of Ethics*. London: Continuum, 2002.
Olberding, Amy. "Mourning, Memory and Identity: A Comparative Study of the Constitution of the Self in Grief." *International Philosophical Quarterly* 37.1 (1997): 29–44.
Oldmeadow, Harry. "Delivering the Last Blade of Grass: Aspects of the Bodhisattva Ideal in the Mahayana." *Asian Philosophy* 7.3 (1997):1 81–94.
Otto, Rudolf. *The Idea of the Holy*. Translated by John Harvey. Oxford: Oxford University Press, 1958.
Parkes, Graham. *Composing the Soul: Reaches of Nietzsche's Psychology*. Chicago: University of Chicago Press, 1994.
Peale, Norman Vincent. *The Power of Positive Thinking*. New York: Simon and Schuster, 2003.
Penrose, Roger. *Fashion, Faith, and Fantasy in the New Physics of the Universe*. Princeton: Princeton University Press, 2016.
Peters, Olaf, ed. *Degenerate Art: The Attack on Modern Art in Nazi Germany 1937*. New York: Prestel, 2014.
Pickstone, Charles. "A Return to the Spiritual: Wassily Kandinsky in the Twenty-First Century." *Modern Painters* June (2006): 72–5.
Plato. *Ion*. Translated by Lane Cooper. *The Collected Dialogues of Plato*. Edited by Edith Hamilton and Huntington Cairns. Princeton: Princeton University Press, 1978. 215–28.

Plato. *Symposium*. Translated by Michael Joyce. *The Collected Dialogues of Plato*. Edited by Edith Hamilton and Huntington Cairns. Princeton: Princeton University Press, 1978. 526–74.

Plato. *The Republic*. Translated by Benjamin Jowett. New York: Basic Books, 1991.

Plato. *The Republic of Plato*. Translated by Allan Bloom. New York: Basic Books, 1991.

Plato. *The Last Days of Socrates*. Translated by C. Rowe. London: Penguin, 2010.

Plotinus. *Enneads*. Translated by A. Armstrong. Loeb: Cambridge, 1966.

Prosser, Jay. "Buddha Barthes: What Barthes Saw in Photography (That He Didn't in Literature)." *Photography Degree Zero: Reflections on Roland Barthes's Camera Lucida*. Edited by Geoffrey Batchen. Cambridge, MA: MIT Press, 2009. 91–103.

Reginster, Bernard. *The Affirmation of Life: Nietzsche on Overcoming Nihilism*. Cambridge MA: Harvard University Press, 2006.

Ringbom, Sixten. "Transcending the Visible: The Generation of the Abstract Pioneers." *The Spiritual in Art: Abstract Painting 1890–1985*. Edited by Maurice Tuchman. Los Angeles: LACMA, 1986. 131–53.

Rochlitz, Rainer. *The Disenchantment of Art: The Philosophy of Walter Benjamin*. New York: Guildford Press, 1996.

Rosen, Stanley. *The Mask of Enlightenment: Nietzsche's Zarathustra*. Cambridge: Cambridge University Press, 1995.

Ruiz, Don Miguel. *The Four Agreements: A Practical Guide to Personal Freedom*. San Raphael: Amber-Allen, 1997.

Russell, Dick. *The Life and Ideas of James Hillman*, vol. 1. New York: Helios Press, 2013.

Schopenhauer. *The World as Will and Representation*, vols. 1 and 2. Translated by E.F.J. Payne. New York: Dover, 1969.

Schopenhauer. *Parerga and Paralipomena*, vol. 2. Translated by E.F.J. Payne. Oxford: Oxford University Press, 1974.

Schopenhauer, Arthur. *On the Basis of Morality*. Translated by E.F.J. Payne. Indianapolis: Hackett, 1998.

Schrift, Alan, ed. *The Logic of the Gift*. New York: Routledge, 1997.

Scruton, Roger. *The Soul of the World*. Princeton: Princeton University Press, 2014.

Seigfried, Hans. "Nietzsche's Radical Experimentalism." *Man and World* 22.4 (1989): 485–501.

Seitz, Brian. "Foucault and the Subject of Stoic Existence." *Human Studies* 35 (2012): 539–54.

Selz, Peter. "The Aesthetic Theories of Kandinsky and Their Relationship to the Origin of Non-Objective Painting." *Readings in Art History*, 3rd Edition, vol. 2. Edited by H. Spencer. New York: Scribner, 1982. 421–40.

Seneca. "To Marcia on Consolation." *Moral Essays*, vol. 2. Translated by J. Basore. London: Heinemann, 1935. 2–97.

Shamdasani, Sonu. "Foreword." *Answer to Job*. Translated by R.F.C. Hull. Princeton: Princeton University Press, 2010.

Shapiro, Gary. *Alcyone: Nietzsche on Gifts, Noise and Women*. Albany: SUNY Press, 1991.

Sheldrake, Philip. *Spirituality: A Very Short Introduction*. Oxford: Oxford University Press, 2013.

Singer, Irving. *The Nature of Love vol. 1: Plato to Luther*. Chicago: University of Chicago Press, 1984.

Smiles, Samuel. *Self-Help*. Oxford: Oxford University Press, 2008.

Spong, John Shelby. *Jesus for the Non-Religious*. New York: Harper, 1977.

Spretnak, Charlene. *The Spiritual Dynamic in Modern Art: Art History Reconsidered, 1800 to the Present*. New York: Palgrave, 2014.

Tacey, David. *Jung and the New Age*. Philadelphia: Brunner-Routledge, 2001.

Tacey, David. "The Role of the Numinous in the Reception of Jung." *The Idea of the Numinous: Contemporary Jungian and Psychoanalytic Perspectives*. Edited by Ann Casement and David Tacey. London: Routledge, 2004. 213–28.

Tacey, David. *The Spirituality Revolution: The Emergence of Contemporary Spirituality*. Routledge: London, 2004.

Tacey, David, ed. *The Jung Reader*. New York: Routledge, 2012.

Tacey, David. *The Darkening Spirit: Jung, Spirituality, Religion*. New York: Routledge, 2013.

Tacey, David. "James Hillman: The Unmaking of a Psychologist." *Journal of Analytical Psychology* 59.4 (2014): 467–502.

Tacey, David. *Beyond Literal Belief: Religion as Metaphor*. Mulgrave: Garratt, 2015.

Taylor, Charles. "Foucault on Freedom and Truth." *Foucault: A Critical Reader*. Edited by David Hoy. Oxford: Blackwell, 1986 69–102.

Tillich, Paul. "Contemporary Visual Arts and the Revelatory Character of Style." *On Art and Architecture*. Edited by John Dillenberger and Jane Dillenberger. New York: Crossroad, 1987.

Tolle, Eckhart. *The Power of Now: A Guide to Enlightenment*. New World Library: Novato, 2010.

Tolstoy, Leo. *The Death of Ivan Ilych and Other Stories*. Translated by Aylmer Maude. New York: New American Library, 1960.

Tuchman, Maurice, ed. *The Spiritual in Art: Abstract Painting 1890–1945*. New York: Abbeville, 1986.

Tyler, Peter. *The Pursuit of the Soul: Psychoanalysis, Soul-Making and the Christian Tradition*. London: Bloomsbury, 2016.

The Upanishads. Translated by Eknath Easwaran. California: Nilgiri Press, 1987.

Veyne, Paul. *Foucault: His Thought, His Character*. Translated by J. Lloyd. Cambridge: Polity, 2010.

Weldon, Clodagh. "God on the Couch; Teaching Jung's Answer to Job." *Teaching Jung*. Edited by Kelly Bulkeley and Clodagh Weldon. Oxford: Oxford University Press, 2011: 111–25.

Wheelwright, Philip. *Heraclitus*. Princeton: Princeton University Press, 1959.

White, Richard. *Nietzsche and the Problem of Sovereignty*. Urbana: University of Illinois, 1997.

White, Richard. *The Heart of Wisdom: A Philosophy of Spiritual Life*. Lanham: Rowman and Littlefield, 2013.

White, Richard. "Starting with Compassion." *Spirituality and the Good Life; Philosophical Approaches*. Edited by David McPherson. Cambridge: Cambridge University Press, 2017. 177–96.

White, Victor. *Soul and Psyche: An Enquiry into the Relationship of Psychotherapy and Religion*. London: Collins/Harvill Press, 1960.

Williams, Robert. *Tragedy, Recognition, and the Death of God: Studies in Hegel and Nietzsche*. Oxford: Oxford University Press, 2012.

Woodward, Kathleen. "Freud and Barthes: Theorizing Mourning, Sustaining Grief." *Discourse* 13.1 (1990–1): 93–110.

Wuthnow, Robert. *Creative Spirituality: The Way of the Artist*. Berkeley: University of California Press, 2001.

Yeng, Sokthan. "Irigaray's Alternative Buddhist Practices of the Self." *Journal of French and Francophone Philosophy* XXII.1 (2014): 61–75.

Žižek, Slavoj. *On Belief*. New York: Routledge, 2001.

Index

Abraham, Nicolas 149
Alcibiades 51, 167
Aquinas, Thomas 4
archetype 92, 94, 101–3, 107, 123
Aristotle 12, 31, 38, 44, 46
Arnold, Matthew 55
art 7, 12–14, 26, 55–72, 74–5, 83, 105, 115, 123, 129, 134–5, 182
artist 48, 55–6, 58–64, 67, 70–1, 105, 123, 134
asceticism 20, 23–5, 32–3, 99, 179
Atman 21–2, 110
Atwell, John 31
Augustine 99, 111, 119
Aurelius, Marcus 141, 145

Barthes, Roland 14, 146, 150–4, 156–7, 160–1
Baudelaire, Charles 73, 81–2, 84, 128, 134, 136
Benjamin, Walter 11, 12–13, 73–90, 182, 186
Bhagavad Gita 19, 21, 24–5, 94. *See also* Vedanta
Blavatsky, Madame 36
Blue Rider group 57, 59, 69
body 175–6, 179–80, 183. *See also* embodiment
Brahman and Brahmanism 21–5, 30, 110. *See also* Vedanta
Brand, Stewart 84
breathing 6, 117, 164–6, 170, 175–7, 180
Buber, Martin 174
Buddha and Buddhism 4, 12, 17–19, 25, 27–31, 33–4, 78, 88, 110, 112, 121, 125, 136, 143

capitalism 10, 112, 117
care of the self 14, 127–44
Cave story 3, 5, 74,110–11, 118–19, 178
childhood 65–6, 73, 87
Chopra, Deepak 118, 127

Christianity 12, 17–19, 30, 78, 94–104, 110, 116–18, 130, 132
city 73, 76, 81, 83, 87
Coker, John 46, 49
community 9, 74, 81–2, 85, 87–9, 112, 130, 157, 160, 175, 177
compassion 12, 17–18, 25, 27–35, 52–3
Confucius and Confucianism 4, 88, 158
consumerism 5, 10–11, 27, 109, 126, 181, 183
couple 173. *See also* partners

Dalai Lama 10, 28, 31, 34, 112, 119–20
Dante 119
Daoism 4, 10, 18, 110
Dawkins, Richard 37
Day, Dorothy 112
death 3, 14, 18, 63, 78, 80, 105–6, 126, 130, 140, 143, 145–62, 167. *See also* mourning
death of God 5, 12, 37–8, 45
Degenerate Art (1937 exhibit) 65
Delattre, Pierre 120
de Man, Paul 149, 154, 159, 204 n.33
Derrida, Jacques 1, 5, 8, 14, 53, 145–62, 183, 186
Descartes, René 4
Diogenes 142
Diotima 15, 166–70, 175
disenchantment 5, 82, 114, 183. *See also* enchantment
Dreyfus, Hubert 86–8
Droit, Roger-Pol 34

embodiment 74, 81, 86–7, 116, 122. *See also* body
Emerson, Ralph Waldo 43
enchantment 14, 95, 115, 123, 126. *See also* disenchantment
Epictetus 141, 145
Epicurus and Epicureanism 3, 127, 142–3, 145

Erfahrung (experience) 82, 85, 88
Erlebnis (experience) 81–2, 85
eternal recurrence 12, 37–9, 45
ethics 8, 12, 18, 27–8, 30, 38, 44, 49, 53, 64, 128–43, 153, 160, 174, 191 n.28
existentialism 139

Facebook 85
film 56, 71, 73, 83, 85–6
forgiveness 8, 10, 48, 53–4, 97, 100, 112, 146, 182
Foucault, Michel 5, 14, 127–44, 154, 182–3, 186
freedom 3–4, 21, 24, 50, 128–9, 133, 136, 139–40, 143–4, 146, 172
Freud, Sigmund 13, 14, 101, 108, 146–50, 153–8, 160–1
fundamentalism 2, 181

Gandhi, Mohandas 7, 112
generosity 1, 8–12, 37–54, 126, 181–3, 191 n.28
gift 88, 146, 192 n.53. *See also* generosity; gift-giving virtue
gift-giving virtue (Nietzsche) 12, 38–54. *See also* generosity
God 4–5, 9, 13, 18, 37–8, 102–4, 107, 109–10, 117, 119, 122–4, 181. *See also* Yahweh
Golding, John 56
Good Samaritan story 78

Hadot, Pierre 3–4, 127, 141–2
Hartmann, Nicolai 46–8
Hebel, Johann 76–7
Hegel, Georg 19, 70, 154
Heidegger, Martin 174, 189 n.2
Henry, Michel 59–60
Herodotus 77–8
Hillman, James 1, 13, 109–26, 182–3, 186, 198 n.7
Hinduism 110, 173. *See also* Vedanta
Hitchens, Christopher 37
Holy Spirit 95, 99–100, 104, 107
Hume, David 37–8

imagination 14, 79, 114–15, 120–1, 123, 125, 126, 198 n.7
Imbeni, Renzo 174
incarnation 13, 94–5, 97–104, 107–8, 175

individuation 13, 17, 25, 30, 32–3, 93, 100, 104–8, 125
information 13, 40, 73–4, 76–8, 81–90, 122, 178
internet 74, 76, 83–9
intuition 2, 62
Irigaray, Luce 1, 6, 11, 14–15, 163–80, 183
Islam 18

James, William 9–10
Jesus 13, 88, 97–102, 117
Job 93–8
John of the Cross 119
Joy, Morny 164
Judaism 17
Jung, Carl 1, 5–7, 13, 91–108, 109, 111, 113–14, 122, 124, 182–3, 185–6

Kafka, Franz 73, 77, 90
Kandinsky, Wassily 1, 12, 55–72, 182–3, 186
Kant, Immanuel 63, 102, 104, 128, 138–9, 142, 154
Keats, John 2, 122–3
Kierkegaard, Søren 84
King, Martin Luther 112
Kirby, Joan 204 n.33
Kisagotami 78
Klee, Paul 56, 65
Kupfer, Joseph 46, 48
Kuspit, Donald 57–8

Lampert, Laurence 41, 43
Lanier, Jaron 84
Lascaux 55, 75
Leskov, Nikolai 76–7, 85, 89–90
Levinas, Emmanuel 96, 138, 154, 174
Lipsey, Roger 70
listening 86, 164–5, 170, 175, 177–9
love 1, 7–8, 11, 14, 68–9, 95, 98–9, 112, 116, 122, 132–3, 153, 160–1, 163–80, 182–3, 198 n.7
Lucretius 145

Mahasattva 33
Marc, Franz 57, 65
Marx, Karl 75, 112
Mary 95, 99, 101–2
materialism 1, 12, 51, 56–9, 61, 67–8, 102, 113, 126, 181, 183, 185

meditation 3, 8, 22, 24, 31, 55–6, 70, 130, 132–3, 136, 143, 165
melancholia and melancholy 121, 125, 148–9
Mercadante, Linda 187 n.9, 187 n.11
monotheism 124
mourning 1, 9, 14, 78, 145–61, 181–3
music 19, 26–7, 61, 64, 68–9, 71–2, 158
myth 13, 33, 37–8, 91–5, 113–15, 121, 126, 186

nature 3, 6–8, 13, 18, 20, 38, 41, 61, 69, 79, 95, 101–2, 114, 123–4, 132, 145, 163–4, 166, 168
negative capability 2, 184
New Age 10, 112, 117–18, 121, 125, 127
Nhat Hanh, Thich 10, 34
Nietzsche, Friedrich 1, 4–5, 7, 11–14, 34, 37–55, 97, 113, 124, 126, 131, 134, 139, 143–4, 182–3, 185–6
non-Western thought 1, 4, 10–11, 17, 108, 120, 158, 175, 177, 179–80. *See also* Buddha and Buddhism; Confucius and Confucianism; Daoism; Hinduism; Vedanta
novel 79–81, 84, 89
numinous 6–7, 13, 91–2
Nussbaum, Martha 31, 177

Otto, Rudolf 6, 98
overman 12, 38–45, 51

parables 33, 37, 40, 77–8, 80, 88–9
parrhesia 142
partners 132, 164, 169, 173–4, 179. *See also* couple
Paul, St. 99, 116–17
Peale, Norman Vincent 127
perfection 97–9, 130, 183
Petrarch 119
Philosophy. *See* spirituality, and philosophy
photography 14, 82, 150–2, 161
Picasso, Pablo 69
Pickstone, Charles 71
pity 52–3
Plato 3, 5, 15, 51, 61, 74, 110–11, 118–19, 137, 165–7, 169–70, 172, 174, 179. *See also* Cave story
Plotinus 135–6

pneuma 115–17
polytheism 114, 124–5
prayer 8, 143
Psammenitus 78
psyche 93, 106–7, 115–18, 121, 124–5, 146, 198 n.7
psychology 102, 106, 108, 114–16, 118, 121, 123–5
Pythagoras 3, 127
reason 2, 11, 18, 28–9, 33, 38, 93–4, 103, 106, 115, 130, 158
Reginster, Bernard 52

religion 4–12, 19, 37, 45, 56, 64, 68–70, 74, 91–108, 109–10, 112–14, 136, 144, 179, 182, 184
Rosen, Stanley 42
Roudinesco, Elizabeth 159
Ruiz, Don Miguel 127
Ruskin, John 55

sacred 5–7, 9, 12, 23, 37–8, 41, 45, 54–5, 60, 69, 75, 91–108, 109, 113–14, 122–3, 125–6, 169, 186, 199 n.20
Sartre, Jean-Paul 139
Schoenberg, Arthur 61, 68
Schopenhauer 1, 4–5, 11–12, 17–35, 51, 61, 179–80, 182–3, 186
science 4–5, 10, 57, 66, 92, 108, 114–15, 126, 183–6, 206 n.1
Scriabin, Alexander 61, 68
Scruton, Roger 26
secular and secularism 5, 10, 55, 76, 94, 102, 110, 129
self-help movement 14, 127
selfishness 18, 39–40, 45–6, 54, 183
Selz, Peter 63
Seneca 145, 158, 161
sex 14, 99, 101, 117, 128–33, 175. *See also* sexual difference
sexual difference 14, 164–5, 173–5
Shapiro, Gary 43, 49
Smiles, Samuel 127
Socrates 2–8, 38, 51–2, 88, 127, 130, 133, 141–2, 166–70
soul 3, 8–10, 13, 27, 39–40, 51–2, 56–7, 59–64, 67, 70, 73, 86–7, 90, 93–4, 106, 109–27, 130, 132, 135, 141, 152, 159, 166, 168–9, 175, 183, 198 n.7

sovereignty 39, 42–3, 46, 49–54, 136, 138, 143, 190 n.6
spirit 13, 46, 48–9, 58–60, 66–7, 92, 109, 115–18, 125, 155, 170, 182, 198 n.7. *See also* Holy Spirit
spiritual but not religious 1, 9, 38, 110, 187 n.9, 187 n.11
spiritualism 6, 57, 66, 146
spirituality 5–11, 141–4, 181–4, 202 n.36
    and art 7, 12–14, 26, 55–72, 74–5, 83, 105, 115, 123, 129, 134–5, 182
    and ethics 8, 18, 30, 44, 49, 53, 128, 141–3, 160, 174, 191 n.28
    and nature 3, 6–8, 13, 18, 20, 38, 41, 61, 69, 95, 101–2, 114, 123–4, 132, 145, 163–6, 168, 182–3
    and philosophy 2–5, 8, 10–12, 17, 127–8, 133, 135–6, 141–4, 146, 159, 161, 163, 180, 182–3
    and politics 111–12
    and religion 4–12, 19, 37, 45, 56, 64, 68–70, 74, 91–110, 112–14, 136, 144, 179, 182, 184
    and science 4, 5, 10, 57, 66, 92, 108, 114–15, 126, 183–6, 206 n.1
    and self-overcoming 6, 8, 13, 18, 35, 37, 50, 109–10, 118, 127, 176, 182–3, 190 n.6
spiritual points of focus 8, 19, 182. *See also* art; nature; religion; sacred; soul; spirit
spiritual practices 2, 8–10, 12, 128, 130, 132–3, 143, 146, 160–1, 170, 175, 182. *See also* care of the self; love; meditation; mourning; prayer; spirituality, and philosophy; wonder
spiritual virtues 8–9, 112, 182, 186, 191 n.28. *See also* compassion; generosity; forgiveness; wisdom
Stoicism 3, 12, 18, 110, 127, 132, 136, 138, 140, 142–3, 145–6, 158. *See also* Aurelius, Marcus; Epictetus; Seneca

storytelling 74–90
suffering 13, 17, 20–1, 23–5, 28–32, 34, 45, 52, 55, 69, 78, 96, 98, 106, 109–11, 114, 116, 118, 121–4
symbol 92, 94, 101–2, 114

Tacey, David 99, 126, 187 n.7
teacher 4, 43, 49, 52, 78, 86, 88–9, 123, 169, 178–9
teaching 115, 164, 178–80
theosophy 55, 57, 66
thinking 170, 177–8, 185–6
Tolle, Eckhart 127
Tolstoy, Leo 106–7
Torok, Maria 149
trauma 121–2
Tyler, Peter 117, 199 n.8

understanding 74, 76, 81–4, 86–7, 107
Upanishads 19, 21–5, 27. *See also* Vedanta

Valéry, Paul 79
Vedanta 4, 17, 19–25, 179–80

"Walter" 128, 140
Weldon, Clodagh 100, 197 n.29
White, Fr. Victor 102–3
Wilde, Oscar 55, 134
will 17–18, 20–5, 27–8, 32–4, 179
will to power 38, 41
wisdom 2–4, 10, 13–14, 17, 19, 21–4, 30, 35, 39–40, 45, 53, 73–90, 93–4, 100, 106–7, 110, 112, 117, 119, 163–5, 167–9, 176–7, 180
wonder 8, 10, 66, 92, 113, 123, 125, 166, 172
Wuthnow, Robert 71

Yahweh 96–8, 100

Zarathustra 12, 37–54
Žižek, Slavoj 10, 112–13, 118, 125